Desktop Publisher's Dictionary

Other books by the author

Desktop Publisher's Bibliography
Fruit of a Fleeting Joy
Genesis of the Bicycle in the United States, 1865–1895

Desktop Publisher's Dictionary

by

Larry S. Bonura

Wordware Publishing, Inc.
Plano, Texas

Library of Congress Cataloging in Publication Data

Bonura, Larry S. (1950–)
Desktop Publisher's Dictionary
Bibliography p.
1. Dictionaries— Computers. 2. Computers— Desktop publishing.

ISBN: 1-55622-406-1

1506 Capital Avenue
Plano, TX 75074

Printed in the United States of America

1 2 3 4 5 6 7 8 9

8811

All inquiries for volume purchases of this book should be addressed to: Wordware
Publishing, Inc., at the above address. Telephone inquiries may be made by calling:
(214) 423-0090

Dedication

To my family:

Nana, Papa, Pa, Granny, Bea, Leo, Peg, Al,
Dan, Shirley, Tony, Tina, Stuart,
Marilyn, and Sean,

For your support, encouragement, and love,

Thank you.

Table of Contents

Acknowledgment

I would like to thank the following people for their help: Tony Bonura for introducing me to computers and for sharing his enthusiasm and knowledge, Leigh Ellert of Wordtek for his technical review, Martha McCuller and Dennis Howard of Wordware Publishing for editing the final manuscript, Russ Stultz of Wordware Publishing for saying yes, Art Fischman of CONVEX Computer Corporation for his technical review, Jana Koch of Wordware Publishing for her production coordination, Alan McCuller of Wordware Publishing for designing the cover, Ruth and Charles Moncrief of Hemisphere Systems, Inc., for sharing their scanner and helping with the illustrations, Bob Hopkins of CONVEX Computer Corporation for his technical review, Bernice Henry of Wordware Publishing for her promotional work, Tonia Bonura for entering data, and a special thanks to Marilyn Ward of Word Workers for researching and technical editing. Even though every effort has been made to make this dictionary as complete and accurate as possible, errors may occur. The author accepts full responsibility for all such errors.

Preface

The *Desktop Publisher's Dictionary* contains 4,163 of the most frequently used terms, words, acronyms, and abbreviations involved in desktop publishing. It contains most of the terms that often confuse a beginner. All definitions are given in clear, easy-to-understand language. In many cases, definitions are supported by 148 illustrations.

This dictionary is especially informative because it contains words and definitions that, until now, have been used in totally separate occupations and industries. Terms are drawn from the many fields that comprise desktop publishing, including: binding and finishing, journalism, layout and design, graphic arts, typography, telecommunications, microcomputers, desktop publishing, and printing.

This book is intended for several kinds of readers. It is a basic reference book for the person who knows little or nothing about desktop publishing but wants to learn. It is hoped that business people, professionals, students, teachers, and others will find it a useful source and reference book.

The keynote of this book is clarity—without sacrifice of authority and precision. All definitions are simple and stand as independent units of explanation. Technical terms are kept out of the definitions as much as possible. In a few cases where a special terminology is required, the expressions used are carefully defined, and related terms or concepts are indicated by cross-references.

I have been active in the field of journalism and production for more than 20 years. The methods of writing, laying out, and producing publications have changed often in those years, from hot type to cold type, from optical character recognition to scanners, from duplicating machines to lasers. Because of my long association with writing and publishing, and with the advent of desktop publishing, I sensed the need for a current and comprehensive, one-stop dictionary of desktop publishing that would present all terms in a simple, understandable manner.

The selection of words for a dictionary inevitably involves a personal choice, and one has to balance a desire to be comprehensive against the need to be concise. The task of preparing this dictionary involved the collection, correlation, and analysis of thousands of words, phrases, and acronyms used in connection with desktop publishing. If you come across a term you think should be in this book, please drop me a line in care of Wordware Publishing and I'll try to include it in a future edition.

It is my hope that the *Desktop Publisher's Dictionary* will help you have a better understanding of the various industries, skills, and processes, as well as bring them into perspective to help make you a better desktop publisher.

Larry S. Bonura
Richardson, Texas

How to Use This Dictionary

Explanatory Notes

Main Entries
A boldface word set flush left is a main entry.

Order of Main Entries
The main entries follow one another in alphabetical order word-by-word, with hyphens and spaces used as spaces. For example:

- **type style**
- **type wheel**
- **typeface**

Arabic numerals are alphabetized as if spelled out.

When more than one definition exists for a term, the different meanings are arranged numerically. This method does not, however, imply a preferred order of meaning.

Guide Words
A pair of guide words is printed at the top of each page. The entries that fall alphabetically between the guide words are found on that page.

Page numbers are also designed to guide the user to a location. Each alphabet letter precedes the page number for that letter section. For example, A-1 is page 1 of the A's, M-5 is page 5 of the M's.

Verbs
Definitions of verbs precede those of nouns.

Nouns
Singular forms of words are given. Nouns follow verbs in definitions.

Capitalization
Most entries in this dictionary begin with a lowercase letter. If an entry is capitalized, the word is usually capitalized.

Dates

A date enclosed in parentheses is found after many words in this dictionary. This is the date of the earliest recorded usage, as far as could be determined, of the word's use in this sense. Dates with publications or organizations indicate when the publication was first issued or when that organization was started.

Cross-References

All cross-references in this dictionary are directional. They direct the user to look elsewhere for further information. A *compare* indicates that the referred term is either dissimilar or similar to the one to which it is appended. The *see* tells the user that the referenced word is the preferred entry. And a *see also* cross-reference tells the user that more information can be found under another entry. A bold word within a definition indicates the word is a defined term also.

Appendixes

The seven appendixes in the back of the dictionary contain two pica-inch-point conversion charts, a listing of ASCII codes, proofreader's marks, and a bibliography. The trademark notices for products mentioned in the dictionary are listed in Appendix 6. The last appendix contains information about how the book was produced.

Dictionary of Terms

Be not the slave of words.
— Thomas Carlyle

A

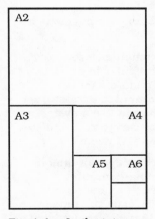

Fig. A-1   In the international standard range of paper sizes, each size is half the area of the next size above it, e.g., A5 is half the area of A4 and twice the area of A6, but the proportions are the same for all sizes.

A4   An international paper size, measuring 21.0 cm (8.3 in) x 29.7 cm (11.7 in). *See also* **A series**.

A-page   A page inserted between existing pages in a **document** to show **revisions** or updates. Also called *overflow page*.

A series   Series of stock paper sizes, widely used in Europe, based on a rectangular sheet one square meter in area. Throughout the series, stock sizes have the same proportion of short-to-long-side, namely, one to the square root of two. *See also* **A4**; **B5**; **B series**.

AA   *See* **author's alteration**.

A and I   *See* **abstracting and indexing**.

AAP   *See* **Association of American Publishers**.

AAUP   *See* **Association of American University Presses**.

ABA   *See* **American Bookseller's Association**.

ABC *See* **Audit Bureau of Circulations**.

ABI form *See* **Advance Book Information form**.

abort To terminate a process, function, or procedure in a controlled manner because it is impossible or undesirable for the activity to be completed.

ABPA *See* **American Book Producers Association**.

abstract A shortened representation— in outline or summary form— of the contents of a document. It often prefaces a document, telling what the document is about and what conclusions have been reached.

abstracting and indexing Refers to services provided by some **service bureaus**.

AC *See* **alternating current; author's correction**.

ACADE *See* **Association for Computer Art and Design Education**.

accent (1885) A **diacritical** mark used to indicate a specific sound value, stress, or pitch.

acceptance, payment on *See* **payment on acceptance**.

access (1966) (1) In computer terminology, the ability to find a particular location in a body of stored data: To store data in or remove data from a **computer data-storage device**. (2) Authorization to use a system or program, usually via a password. *See also* **random access; sequential access**.

access time (1950) The length of time required to gain access to a **computer data-storage device** such as **memory, tapes,** and **disks**. Specifically the time interval between when an **instruction** initiates a call for data and when the delivery of data is completed. Access time for rotating magnetic storage media equals **latency** plus **transfer time**.

accordion fold To make a series of parallel folds in which the paper is pleated by making each fold in the opposite direction.

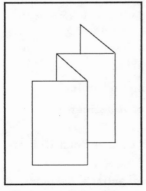

Fig. A-2   Accordion fold.

Also called *concertina fold. See also* **accordion pleat**.

accordion pleat One of a series of narrow, evenly-spaced parallel pleats set into a material. *See also* **accordion fold**.

accuracy aids Preprogrammed techniques in interactive graphics to help the designer achieve positioning accuracy on the screen. They include constraints, screen grids, distance roundoff, and point placement by numeric coordinates.

acetate overlay Transparent plastic sheet placed over a **mechanical** on which colors can be indicated or directions to the platemaker given.

acknowledgment (1) The author's expressed appreciation to those individuals or organizations who contributed to the book. Usually a part of the book's **front matter**. (2) The transmission, by a receiver, of acknowledge characters as an affirmative response to a sender.

acoustic coupler (1965) A cheap, relatively slow **modem** that does not need to be directly wired to the telephone system— the telephone handset fits into cups. The coupler contains sound transducers that convert electronic impulses into sounds so that they can be transmitted down through the phone system.

acquisition editor A person in a publishing house who specializes in acquiring new **manuscripts** rather than **editing** manuscripts.

acquisition librarian The librarian who orders new library books.

acronym (1940) A word formed from the initial letter or letters of each of the major parts of a compound term. For example, laser (*L*ight *A*mplification by *S*timulated *E*mission of *R*adiation) or DOS (*D*isk *O*perating *S*ystem). Also called *monogram*.

activating a window Locating a **mouse** arrow inside the borders of a **window** in a graphic user interface.

active white space White space that separates and differentiates between text elements. Compare **passive white space**.

actual data transfer rate The average number of **bits**, **characters**, or **blocks** per unit of time transferred from a data source to a data destination.

actual size A command in the **PageMaker** page menu that displays a page approximately the size in which that page will be printed, depending on the screen's characteristics. Same as **normal view** in **Ventura**.

acute accent (1560) A **diacritical** mark (´) that indicates a sound value. For example, the é in moiré.

adaptable fraction *See* **built-up fraction**.

adapter (1) Generally, a mechanism for attaching parts; for example, parts that have different diameters. (2) Sometimes used to refer to a **printed circuit board** that plugs into a computer and controls an input/output device, such as a **display** or a **printer**, and allows **compatibility** between different equipment.

adapter card *See* **adapter**.

addendum (1684) Supplementary information added to the end of a book, often written by another author.

add-on (1946) The ability to increase a computer system's storage capacity, to modify its architecture, or to upgrade its performance by adding components or devices.

addition button In **Ventura**, an indicator that allows a user to add a frame, tag, or text attribute, depending on which function is currently enabled.

address (1) In computer terminology, the specific memory location of a piece of data. (2) The location of a **peripheral device**.

address bus Conductors used for transmitting **address** signals from a source to a destination. *See also* **data bus**.

addressable point (1950) Any screen position that can be expressed in **device**

coordinates. The smallest addressable point in a **raster display** is the **pixel**. Also called *addressable position.*

addressable position *See* **addressable point**.

addressable vertical point In computer graphics, the number of positions, within a specified **raster**, at which a full-length horizontal line can be placed. Also called *display column.*

adhesive binding (1950) Style of unsewn binding in which the backs of **gathered** sections are cut off and the **leaves** are held together at the binding edge by glue or synthetic adhesive and (in a **case binding**) a suitable lining. Also called *perfect binding.*

adjust A word processing line-end feature that automatically adjusts the line endings of text to comply— within the **line-ending zone**— with the original margin setting. Also called *wraparound.*

Adobe Systems, Inc. (1982) Developers of **PostScript**, a page image description language for text and graphics systems.

adoption A book accepted for use as a textbook in schools and universities.

advance Fee or front money paid to an author for selling a **manuscript** or **reprint rights** to a publisher. This money is paid before a book's publication as an advance installment against future **royalties**.

Advance Book Information form A brief summary of a book on special forms filed by a publisher with R.R. Bowker, who uses the information to list books in its directories, i.e., *Books in Print.* This form, abbreviated *ABI*, should accompany an **advance copy** when sent out for review.

advance copy Copy of a book sent to a select audience prior to publication. Usually these books are for reviewers. Also called *review copy.*

advertisement A paid announcement of goods for sale in newspapers or magazines or other media.

Advertising Age (1930) A weekly **offset** tabloid that covers the advertising and marketing trades.

aerate To introduce air between sheets of paper, either by riffling them manually or by employing a device to facilitate feeding in the printing press or to establish uniform thickness during bookbinding. Aerating is also accomplished mechanically in some copying machines.

afterword (1890) The author's parting remarks to the reader. An afterword may contain the author's biography. Many are written and added at any time after the initial publication. Part of a book's **back matter**. Compare **foreword**.

against the grain Feeding paper to a printing process in a direction across the **grain** of the paper fibers. So also is folding paper in that direction for **binding**. Also called *cross-grain folding, cross-grain binding*.

agate Type size of 5.5 points.

agate line (1880s) Vertical unit of measurement used in calculating advertising space: 14 agate lines equal one column inch.

agent An author's representative who normally handles submissions and contract negotiations for a set percentage.

AIGA *See* **American Institute of Graphic Arts**.

aiming symbol A movable **cursor** on a display screen, indicating where a **pick** device, such as a **light pen**, is pointing. *See also* **screen cursor**.

air Excess space in line or photographic art or in text matter. Too much air indicates poor planning and **layout**.

aka *See* **also known as**.

ALA *See* **American Library Association**.

aliasing Undesirable visual effects—particularly jagged lines and edges (**jaggies**) and **moiré patterns**—in raster images caused by improper sampling techniques. *See also* **antialiasing; dejagging**.

This text is aligned to the right; therefore, the right margin is flush.

This text is aligned to the left; therefore, the left margin is flush.

This text is aligned right and left; therefore, the left and right margins are flush.

Fig. A-3   Examples of text alignment.

align To line up. To place letters or words on the same horizontal or vertical line.

aligning figure A numeral that aligns with the capitals of the typeface to which it belongs. For example: 1 2 3 4 5 6 7 8 9 0. Also called *lining figure, modern figure*. Compare **hanging figure**. *See also* **Arabic numeral**.

alignment (1) Arrangement of type within a line so that the base of each character (excluding descenders) rests on the same imaginary line, i.e., *base aligning*. This positioning of each letter on the **baseline** makes the text line itself appear straight. (2) The positioning of lines of text on a page or in a **column** so that the ends of the lines appear even on the page:

- aligned left (flush left— aligned along the left margin, ragged right— not aligned, but stopping in a zone near the margin)
- centered
- aligned right (flush right, ragged left)
- justified (flush on both left and right)

The positioning may be the beginning or ending of a line. Also called *range*.

alive matter Type after it has been set, before it is ready for distribution. Also called *live matter*. Compare **dead matter**.

alive type *See* **alive matter**.

all published An uncompleted set. For example, if an article or book that is to appear in several volumes is suspended, the fact is stated that it is "all published."

all rights All legal claims to any artistic or literary endeavors. To sign these rights away means that the author forfeits the right to use his or her material in its present form elsewhere. *See also* **rights**.

all rights reserved A printed notice— required for copyright protection in certain Latin American countries under the Buenos Aires Convention— in a publication that any use of the book or article will not be permitted without the consent of the **copyright** owner. These **rights** include dramatic, television, broadcasting, motion picture, serial, re-publication, etc.

alley *See* **gutter**.

allowance (1) A partial payment made by a publisher on advertising costs shared with the retailer. Also called *cooperative advertising*. (2) A payment by the publisher on the cost of freight.

alphabet (14c) An ordered set of all the letters used in a language, including **diacritical** marks where necessary, but not including **punctuation marks**.

alphabet length The horizontal measurement, in **points**, of the lowercase alphabet, set in type, of a particular **typeface** and **size**. The ideal measure for a line of printed text matter is considered to be 1.5 alphabet lengths, or 39 characters. The number 341 divided by the alphabet length in points gives **characters per pica**.

alphabetize To arrange in the order of the letters of the alphabet.

alphameric *See* **alphanumeric**.

alphanumeric (ca. 1950) A general term for alphabetic letters (a–z or A–Z), numerical digits (0–9), and special characters, punctuation marks, or symbols (-, /, *, &, $, etc.). Also called *alphameric*.

alphanumeric keyboard A keyboard used to enter letters, numbers, punctuation, and special characters into a computer.

also known as A term referring to another name used for self-promotion or advertising a business. Abbreviated *aka*. Compare **doing business as**.

alteration Any change in copy after it has been typeset. *See also* **author's alteration**; **printer's error**.

alternate spelling Two equally correct and accepted ways to spell the same word: *ax* and *axe*.

alternating current (1839) An electric current that reverses its direction at regular, recurring intervals. Abbreviated *AC*.

alternative title A **subtitle** introduced by "or" or its equivalent.

ALU *See* **arithmetic and logic unit**.

amberlith Orange-colored **acetate overlay** used to make a **window** on the **page board** for the printing of **halftones**. The coating is designed to be "peeled off" in unwanted areas.

American Book Prices Current (1895) A publication listing the annual sales of books and **manuscripts** at auctions.

American Book Producers Association A national association of producers of finished manuscripts, art and layouts, production, ready film, and camera-ready copy. Abbreviated *ABPA*.

American Bookseller A monthly trade journal that covers publishers' activities as well as the major concerns of booksellers.

American Bookseller's Association (1900) A trade association for operators of retail bookstores. Abbreviated *ABA*.

American Institute of Graphic Arts (1914) A professional organization founded to raise the standard and the extension and development toward perfection of the graphic arts in the United States. Abbreviated *AIGA*.

American Library Association (1876) A professional association of librarians and others interested in the educational, social, and cultural responsibilities of libraries. Abbreviated *ALA*.

American Newspaper Publishers Association (1887) An association of daily and non-daily newspapers in the Western Hemisphere that advances the concept of a strong, free press and ensures that the press has the economic strength to serve the public. Abbreviated *ANPA*.

American point system (1886) The system adopted by the United States Type Founders' Association, according to which the various sizes of type characters bear a fixed and simple relation one to another. It is based upon the **pica** body, which is

5
6
8
10
12
18
24
36
48
56
72

Fig. A-4 American point system, developed in 1886.

divided into twelfths, or **points**. *See also* Appendix 1; **Cicero**; **Didot**.

AP *See* **Associated Press**.

American Printer (1883) A monthly magazine that covers the printing and publishing market.

American Records Management Association (1975) An association of administrators, managers, and educators that seeks to promote a scientific interest in records and information management. Abbreviated *ARMA*.

American Society of Indexers (1968) A nonprofit, educational and charitable organization for free-lance and salaried indexers, abstractors, librarians, editors, publishers, and organizations employing indexers. Abbreviated *ASI*.

American Society for Information Science (1968) A professional association of information specialists, scientists, librarians, and administrators in the use, organization, storage, retrieval, evaluation, and dissemination of recorded specialized information. Abbreviated *ASIS*.

American Standard Code for Information Interchange (1966) A standard code, abbreviated *ASCII* (pronounced "askey"), for the storage and transmission of computer data. This standardized, 7-bit character set, is used by nearly all manufacturers of computers, printers, and software. ASCII code assigns numbers in the range of 0 to 127 to a wide variety of symbols, including the 26 uppercase letters of the alphabet, the 26 lowercase letters, the 10 numerals, and punctuation symbols such as the period, comma, and exclamation point. ASCII files, often called *print files*, include all the characters of the text itself (including tabs and carriage returns), but not the extended (high-order, or 8-bit) codes used to indicate character and paragraph formats. Text in this format is stored in exactly the same order as shown on a printed page, with no additional characters added or deleted. *See* *also* Appendix 3; **binary digit**; **byte**; **carriage return**; **line feed**; **memory, external**; **memory, internal**; **parity bit**; **text-only file**.

American Standard Code for Information Interchange file A file consisting of characters that conform to the **American Standard Code for Information Interchange**.

American Standard Code for Information Interchange keyboard A keyboard including keys for all of the characters of the ASCII character set. Usually includes three cases for each alpha character: **uppercase**, **lowercase**, and **Ctrl**.

ampersand (1828) Name of the type character "&" used in lieu of "and." Derived from the Latin *et*, the symbol is called a *short and*.

analog (1946) Representation of information in physical terms. For example, the sweep of the hands around the face of a clock physically represents the concept of the passing of time.

analog computer (1948) A computer that operates by directly measurable quantities, such as voltages or angles. Compare **digital computer**.

anchor To keep a frame together with the text that references that frame.

anecdote (1721) A brief story used to illustrate a particular point.

angle (1) An aspect or emphasis played up by a writer. (2) The rows of dots in a **halftone** are usually set at an angle to create a more pleasing visual effect than the grid that would result from placement at 0 degrees. The least obtrusive and most commonly used angle is 45 degrees.

angle bracket (ca. 1956) One of the pair of marks (< >) used to enclose matter. *See also* **bracket**.

Anglo-American point system The system of type sizing used in most English-speaking countries where type is measured vertically by **points** and the width of type is measured by **em spaces**. Compare **Cicero**; **Didot**. *See also* **American point system**; Appendix 1; **en**; **pica**.

annex A **supplement** or **appendix** bound as part of a technical publication. While an annex is related to the main body of the subject matter of which it is a part, its content is such that it can be more conveniently used by the reader as a separate entity within the publication. Compare **attachment**.

annotate *v.* To furnish explanatory notes that may or may not complement the subject matter of the text. *n.* A note accompanying an entry in a **bibliography** or catalog that describes or evaluates the work cited.

annual A publication issued regularly once a year.

anon. *See* **anonymous**.

anonymous (1601) Authorship unknown or unavowed. Abbreviated *anon. See also* **apocryphal**.

ANPA *See* **American Newspaper Publishers Association**.

anthology (1640) A collection of writings by one or more authors published as a single work. Anthologies are usually on one theme, literary type, period, nation, or the like.

antialiasing Software technique to reduce unwanted visual effects, such as those of jagged lines in **raster images** and false colors. *See also* **aliasing**; **dejagging**; **dithering**.

antiquarian bookseller (1771) One who specializes in buying and selling old or rare books.

antique (1) An uncoated printed paper with a **matte** or rough surface, especially suitable for printing type and line engravings by **letterpress**. This **wove paper** of low-finish character has no visible laid lines or chain marks and is designed to imitate the finish of handmade paper. (2) The original name for what is now called **Egyptian** typefaces.

anti-set-off A drying powder sprayed onto newly printed sheets as they leave the machine, to prevent the ink on one sheet from **offsetting** on the next sheet above it as they are stacked at the delivery end of the printing press.

apocryphal (1590) Of unknown authorship or doubtful authenticity. *See also* **anonymous**.

appendix (1542) Supplementary information added to a book's **back matter**. Usually contains matter—such as a list of resources or tables—that is relevant but not essential to the body of the book and that could be awkward or distracting if it were presented in the main text. Compare **supplement**.

Apple DOS The **disk operating system** for the Apple computer.

applications program A computer program designed to aid in the solution of a specific user-oriented task, such as **word processing**, **desktop publishing**, or **graphics**. Compare **systems program**.

APPM *See* **Association of Publications Production Managers**.

apprentice A printer, one step below a **journeyman**, who is learning his or her trade on the job.

apron On a **foldout** page, additional white space left along the **binding margin**. Also called *protective margin*.

Arabic figure *See* **Arabic numeral**.

Arabic numeral (ca. 1847) Ten figures (zero and numerals 1 through 9) so called because they originated in Arabia. In many type fonts they are available in two forms:

- aligning, or lining (1 2 3 4 5 6 7 8 9 0)—invariably used in tabular matter
- old style, abbreviated *O.S.* (1 2 3 4 5 6 7 8 9 0), characterized by **ascenders** and **descenders**.

Compare **Roman numeral**.

archive (ca. 1934) *v.* To duplicate files on a separate disk or on a backup tape for safekeeping. *n.* The data files so stored. *See also* **BACKUP**; **RESTORE**.

argument An item of information following a **command**. It may, for example, modify the command or identify a file to be effected.

arithmetic and logic unit A part of a computer that performs arithmetic (adding, subtracting, etc.) and logic (and, or, not) operations. Abbreviated *ALU*. *See also* **central processing unit**.

ARMA *See* **American Records Management Association**.

array A number of mathematical elements arranged in rows and columns. Also called *matrix.*

arrow key *See* **directional arrow**; **scroll arrow**.

arrowhead An indicator shaped like an arrowhead and used at the end of a line to direct attention to an object or a point of reference in conjunction with a **callout** number, letter, or other symbol. *See also* **exploded view**; **lead line**.

art *See* **artwork**.

art director In the traditional publishing process, one who sets the direction of the **design** and **artwork** for a publication.

art file number Key file number placed within the image area of each piece of original artwork. Also called *file number, illustration file number.*

art paper Glossy, **coated paper** intended to carry **halftone** reproduction by **letterpress printing**.

art parchment *See* **diploma paper**.

artist (1581) In the traditional publishing process, a person who creates **artwork**.

artwork (1877) A generic phrase that refers to any original **photograph**, **illustration**, **chart**, **graph**, or **ornament**— anything other than straight text— prepared for reproduction. There are two types: **line art** and **halftone**. Also called *continuous-tone art,*

Fig. A-5   An arrowhead.

halftone art, illustration, mechanical, or *visual.*

as told to A book produced by a writer in collaboration with a nonwriter, the latter often a celebrity. The writer is credited as coauthor, e.g., *My Story* by Sophia Loren as told to Alan Levy. Compare **ghost writer**.

ascender (1867) That part of the **lowercase** letter that rises above the body of the letter, such as the upper part of the letters *b, d, f, h, k, l,* and *t*. Technically, only three letters of the alphabet have ascenders: *b, d,* and *h*. Compare **descender**. *See also* **ascender line; x-height**.

Ascenders

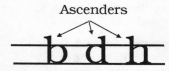

Fig. A-6   Examples of as-cenders.

ascender line In typography, the hypothetical horizontal line that connects the tops of **ascenders**. *See also* **cap line**.

ASCII *See* **American Standard Code for Information Interchange**.

ASI *See* **American Society of Indexers**.

ASIS *See* **American Society for Information Science**.

aspect ratio (1907) The ratio of the frame width to the frame height. The aspect ratio of a standard television frame is 4:3.

assembled view In technical publications, a **line drawing**, **halftone**, or **photograph** of an object drawn or photographed to show the object assembled as one piece. *See also* **exploded view; frontispiece**.

assembler A program used to convert a file containing **instructions** recognizable by programmers into **machine language** recognizable by the processor in use.

assembly language (1964) A mnemonic code representing the basic instructions understood by a particular computer's **assembler** program.

ASSIGN A **PC/MS-DOS** command that reassigns the specified disk drive designator (A:, B:, C:, etc.).

assignment (1) Generally, a writing or editing task. (2) More specifically, a definite commission given a writer by an editor to do a specific piece of writing. Compare **speculation**.

assignment list (1986) In **Ventura**, the list of **files**, **tags**, or **attributes** that can be transferred to the selected **frame**, **paragraph**, or selected **text**. Shown in the **sidebar** on the left side of the screen.

Associated Press (1848) An international news gathering agency that sells stories to its members. Abbreviated *AP*.

Association for Computer Art and Design Education A nonprofit organization that promotes the use of computer graphics products in art and design. Abbreviated *ACADE*.

Association of American Publishers (1970) A trade association of publishers of general, educational, trade, reference, religious, scientific, technical, and medical books. Abbreviated *AAP*.

Association of American University Presses (1937) A trade association for scholarly publishing divisions of colleges and universities in the United States and Canada. Abbreviated *AAUP*.

Association of Publications Production Managers (1939) Association of production managers whose objective is to exchange and study experiences, problems, and new developments in production and manufacture of periodicals. Abbreviated *APPM*.

asterisk (14c) (1) Symbol (*) used to key text or tabular matter to a **footnote**. It is the first in a series of **reference marks**. (2) Used to indicate missing letters or words and for **global** file manipulations.

asymmetrical layout An off-center arrangement. Compare **symmetrical layout**.

asynchronous A communications format that is independent of instructions (or **synchronous**) from another computer with which it is communicating.

asynchronous communications adapter A device attached to a computer that enables it to effect asynchronous data communications over standard telephone facilities.

asynchronous communication port *See* **COM1, COM2, COM3, COM4**.

attachment An **appendix** or **supplement** to a technical manual that is bound by itself. Compare **annex**.

ATTRIB A **PC/MS-DOS** command that sets (turns "on") or resets (turns "off") the "read only" and "archive" file attributes.

attribute (1) Generally, any style used to enhance the **readability** of text. (2) The weight and slope of a **typestyle**. Typical attributes include **boldface**, underline, and *italic*. (3) **Font** changes assigned to selected text are also considered attributes; examples include **point** size, color, and **kern**.

auction Competitive bidding for a book manuscript or proposal following simultaneous submissions to several publishers. Usually publishers are given a minimum bid and a date by which to respond.

auction gallery An auction house that catalogs and sells private libraries, rare books, autographs, and manuscripts.

Audit Bureau of Circulations (1914) Association that provides audited circulation data on advertisers, advertising agencies, and publishers of daily and weekly newspapers, consumer magazines, and business publications in the United States and Canada. Abbreviated *ABC*.

author (14c) In the traditional publishing process, a person who writes.

author-publisher A writer who is his own publisher. *See also* **cooperative publishing**; **privately printed**; **self-publishing**; **subsidy press**.

author-title index In a **bibliography**, an **index** that enters each book by title as well as by the author's name, either in two alphabets, or combined in one alphabet.

authoring system Software program that automatically performs the programming

---

Boldface

SMALL CAPS

Italic

Underline

Fig. A-7   Examples of text attributes.

tasks involved with creating, storing, organizing, and presenting **online documentation**.

author's alteration Any change in copy, made by an author, after the copy has been **typeset**. Specifically, this is a change from the manuscript copy introduced in a typeset **galley** or **proof**, distinguished from a correction made to eliminate a **printer's error**. Abbreviated *AA*. *See also* **royalty**.

author's correction A correction made by an author. Abbreviated *AC*.

author's notes A record of any special development techniques used by a **documentation** author to enable the writer who will be updating the documentation to follow the same development techniques. These notes are made by the original author immediately after the **draft** version.

author's proof A **proof** that is taken from set type, arranged in **galley** form, and printed as a strip and sent to the author for the purpose of having it returned marked "OK" or "OK with corrections." *See also* **proofreader; proofreader's marks**.

author's rights *See* **rights**.

autoanswer A **modem** that can automatically answer incoming telephone calls from computers and route the data into a computer.

autodialer A **modem** that can automatically dial outgoing telephone calls.

AUTOEXEC.BAT A **PC/MS-DOS batch file** used to perform a desired set of start-up **disk operating system** procedures without having to type the commands each time the system is started.

automatic pagination An applications program function that automatically prints page numbers, headers, and footers at the bottom, top, left, and right side of each page. It also breaks text into pages.

autograph party A gathering, usually at a bookstore, where an author signs customers' copies of his or her book.

Fig. A-8   A floppy disk
may be an auxiliary
storage device.

automatic repeat key A key that continues to operate as long as it is depressed. Also called *live key*, *repeat-action key*.

aux A **PC/MS-DOS** standard device, it is the first serial communication port known to **DOS**, usually COM1.

auxiliary equipment *See* **offline equipment**.

auxiliary storage A form of computer memory storage that is physically external to the main computer memory— such as **magnetic tape**, **floppy disks**, and **magnetic drums**. Also called *secondary storage*. *See also* **external memory**.

available command Command you can choose from a menu. Available commands appear in regular, not **ghost** letters. Compare **unavailable command**.

available point In computer graphics, an **addressable point** at which characteristics such as color, intensity, or on/off condition, may be changed. Also called *available position*.

available position *See* **available point**.

avant garde The expression— by an individual or a literary group— of experimental or unorthodox forms, ideas, and theories, usually addressed to a small audience.

axis constraint An **accuracy aid** in an interactive system that locks a newly entered axis onto an existing axis already defined. A **gravity field** around the existing axis "attracts" the new one.

azerty keyboard A European keyboard layout, common in France and Germany. Compare **qwerty keyboard**, **Dvorak keyboard**.

Notes and New Words

B

b *See* **binary digit; byte.**

B series An international paper size, cut in sizes between successive **A series** sizes. *See also* **B5.**

B&W *See* **black and white photograph.**

B5 An international paper size, measuring 18.2 cm (7.2 in) x 25.7 cm (10.1 in). *See also* **A4; A series; B series.**

back cover Back outside surface of a **hardbound** or **softcover** book. *See also* **cover paper; second cover; self-cover; third cover.**

back flap The back inner fold of a **dust jacket.** It often has a continuation of copy from the **front flap,** as well as a photo and a brief biography of the author.

back margin Inside **margin** of a page. Also called *gutter margin.*

back matter Portion of a book or other publication that follows the main body of the text. Also called *end matter.* Compare **front matter.** *See also* **addendum; afterword;**

appendix; bibliography; colophon; end matter; glossary; index.

back of the book Last section of a magazine, usually made up of materials that appear after the main editorial section.

back order A book order waiting to be filled when a new supply of books becomes available.

back slant Inclination of a **typeface**, usually a **display** face, in which the characters slant backward. Compare **italic**, **script**.

back strip See **backstrip**.

back-to-back Printing on both sides of a sheet.

back up See **backup**.

backbone See **spine**.

background (1) Running of system so that the **console** is left free for other uses. (2) Portion of an image that is behind the principal object being illustrated or photographed. (3) Information relayed or interview given to members of the press for background purposes only, not for publication.

background print A printing job that does not interrupt normal use or operation of the program or equipment.

backing In **case binding**, applying the **backstrip**.

backlining Paper cemented to the **backbone** of a book that binds the **signatures** and allows space between the backbone and the cover.

backlist Previously published books that are still in print and available from a publisher. Compare **frontlist**. See also **list**.

backlog A reserve of unprocessed material.

backslant See **back slant**.

backspace (1911) *v.* To move the **cursor** back a predetermined amount. *n.* A keyboard key labeled "Backspace," with a single, left-pointing arrow. It erases entered characters, one at a time.

Fig. B-1   A backspace key.

backstrip In **case binding**, a paper strip glued to a piece of binding cloth to form the **spine** in a **hardbound** book.

BACKUP A **PC/MS-DOS** command that copies files from a fixed disk to flexible disks to produce "insurance," or duplicate copies of working files and programs. *See also* **BAK**.

backup *v.* (1) To copy one or more files to diskettes or tapes for safekeeping, in case something happens to the original. (2) To print the second, or reverse, side of a sheet or page already printed on one side, ideally so that the lines on one side match the position of those on the other. *See also* **crop mark**. *n.* A file copy set aside for safekeeping in case something happens to the original. Also called *backup copy, backup diskette, backup file.*

backup copy *See* **backup**.

backup disk *See* **backup**.

backup file *See* **backup**.

bad break (1) The dividing of a word at the end of a line at an incorrect place within the word. (2) The dividing of text between pages in a way that leaves a **widow** or **orphan**. (3) In **page makeup**, any of various unsightly or misleading arrangements of type occurring at the bottom or top of a **page** or **column**, a **subhead** falling on the last line of a page or column, starting a page with a **hyphenated** word, etc. *See also* **nonbreaking space**.

bad copy Any **manuscript** that is illegible, improperly edited, or otherwise unsatisfactory to the typesetter.

BAK An extension assigned by many word processing programs to the penultimate version of a text file. If the working copy of a file is damaged, the BAK file can be used to salvage a near-current version of the document. *See also* **BACKUP; backup**.

balance Arrangement of heavier and lighter elements of text and artwork in a manner pleasing to the eye. *See also* **layout**.

balanced columns The ability to take the text in two adjacent **columns** and make it balance out, so that the last line of one column is about at the same level as the last line in the other.

balloon (1) Rough circle or envelope used in cartoon strips and sometimes in advertising illustrations to encircle dialogue spoken by the characters. (2) Any circle that encloses copy, such as index numbers or letters placed beside the bill of material on an engineering drawing or keyed to material on the face of a drawing. Also called *bubble*.

bang Slang for exclamation point. Also called *screamer*. *See also* **interrobang**.

bank (1) Thin tough writing paper. Compare **bond paper**. (2) A stand to hold type and spacing material. *See also* **case, type**. (3) A row of keys on a **keyboard**.

bank head A **subhead** under a **main head**, as distinct from a **crosshead** or **subhead** in text matter.

banner (1) A **headline** in large type running across a newspaper page. (2) Often used more loosely for the title heading on a journal or newspaper.

bar chart (1923) Charts that indicate quantities by varying lengths of horizontal bars that usually represent quantity. Time, distance, or some other value is shown on the other dimension of the chart. A bar chart may also have a vertical baseline that divides the bars, with negative results to the left and favorable results to the right. Also called *bar graph, horizontal bar chart. See also* **column chart; curve chart; pie chart; surface chart**.

bar graph *See* **bar chart**.

base A number equal to the number of units in a given digit's place that—for a given system of writing numbers—is required to give the numeral 1 in the next higher place. *See also* **numbering system**.

base alignment In **photocomposition** or computer typesetting, the automatic **alignment** of different type sizes on a **baseline**.

base line *See* **baseline**.

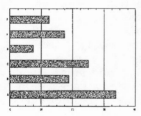

Fig. B-2   A bar chart.

baseline (1750) In typography, an imaginary horizontal line that connects the bottoms of **lowercase** characters that do not have **descenders**. *See also* **base alignment**; **x-height**.

base stock Foundation **stock** from which various papers are made.

BASIC *See* **Beginner's All-Purpose Symbolic Instruction Code**.

basic (1941) Colloquial term for an original work, such as a technical manual, a planning document, or a commercial brochure in which changes and revisions are made.

Basic Input/Output System The primitive programming, abbreviated *BIOS*, that controls the basic operation of a computer's input/output system, which is the operation of standard devices such as **console, I/O ports**, etc. In microcomputers, BIOS usually resides in **read-only memory** and partly on the boot device (disk).

basic reproduction page Page containing **camera-ready copy**.

basic size Predetermined size assigned to a class of paper. The basic size of **bond** and writing papers is 17 in x 22 in.

basic weight *See* **basis weight**.

basis weight (1) Weight, in pounds, of 500 sheets of paper in a certain size. (2) When the letter *M* is used in the weight designation, the weight of 1,000 such sheets. *See also* **grammage**.

bastard title *See* **half-title page**.

BAT *See* **BATCH**.

BATCH A **PC/MS-DOS** text file whose extension is BAT. When entered while at the command level, DOS carries out the commands in the file.

batch A collection of similar work that could be entered into a computer at one operation.

batch file **Software** that accumulates a **batch** of **instructions** then runs them all at once, later. This type of program does not permit the **operator** to carry on a dialogue with the computer. Compare **interactive program**.

batch-processing program *See* **batch file**.

battered type Type that has been damaged or broken or is otherwise defective.

baud (1931) A measure of data transmission speed that refers to the rate of change in the carrier. Specifically, it is the maximum rate of modulation for a message exchange in a given system. Usually, one change equals 1 **bit** of information.

baud rate The transmission rate that is in effect during data transmission. *See also* **baud**.

BBS *See* **bulletin board system**.

beard In **hot-type**, the beveled space below the face of a type.

beat The area— geographical or by subject matter— to which a writer is assigned or has a special competence.

beating the Shift A **keyboard** action in which a fast or erratic typist may cause a misprint of a character following or preceding a Shift.

bed The part of a **flatbed press** on which the **chase** of composed type is secured for printing. *See also* **platen**.

Beginner's All-Purpose Symbolic Instruction Code (1967) A **high-level language** for microcomputers. Abbreviated *BASIC*.

beginning-of-line commands A typesetting term that tells the typesetting machine how the information to follow should be set.

beginning-of-tape marker A marker— such as a transparent section of tape or a photo-reflective strip— that indicates the beginning of the recording area on a **magnetic tape**. Abbreviated *BOT marker*. Compare **end-of-tape marker**.

belt press An expensive and sophisticated printing press that prints and binds a book in one pass. Also called *Cameron belt press*.

Benday process (1903) A method of laying a **screen** on line plates by the use of gelatin films to give the printed image an appearance of tone. Named for the inventor, Benjamin Day (1838-1916). *See also* **halftone; halftone screen; mechanical screen**.

bent lead line *See* **dogleg**.

best-seller (1889) A nationally popular book. Best-seller lists are compiled weekly by the *New York Times, Publishers Weekly, Time*, and others.

beta test The part of a **field test** performed outside the company or unit that produced the **documentation**. It is the portion of field testing in which actual users report on how difficult or easy it is to use the documentation. Also called *external field test*. Compare **controlled field test**.

bevel The sloping edge of an **electrotype** or **stereotype** by which the plate is attached to the base with catches while being printed.

beveled rule In **hot-metal composition**, a rule on which the printing surface is on one side rather than the center, so that perfect joints can be made.

bf Proofreader's abbreviation for **boldface**.

Bible paper Light, thin, strong, opaque paper used for Bibles, dictionaries, sales manuals, and other purposes. Also called *India paper*.

bibliography A list of works referred to in a text or consulted by the author in its production and placed at the end of a chapter or in the **back matter** of a publication.

bidirectional printing (1928) Lines of text or graphics printed both left to right and right to left, thus using the carriage-return interval and increasing throughput.

biennially Once every two years.

bi-level scan A 1-**bit-per-pixel** scan saved as a **bit-mapped image**.

bimetallic plates Lithographic plates with a top surface of copper, which readily accepts printing ink, on a base of stainless steel or chromium, which does not.

bimonthly Once every two months.

binary digit (1948) (1) In computer terminology, the smallest unit of information making up the digital representation of a **text character** or **graphics character**. Abbreviated *bit.* Generally, **strings** of bits are broken into larger units called **words**. (2) Also represents a numerical value, depending on its position. *See also* **binary notation**; **byte**; **computer**; **machine language**; **number systems**.

binary file (1948) A file made up of **binary digits**, which is more space efficient than the 7-bit **ASCII** code.

binary notation (1948) A **numbering system** that uses only the digits 0 and 1. Because the binary system is easily represented as a series of discrete electronic states, it is the ideal form for encoding information within a digital computer. Any decimal number between 0 and 255 can be expressed by an 8-bit **binary digit**. *See also* **base**; **bit**; **decimal**; **hexadecimal**.

binary number *See* **binary digit**.

binder (1) A cover for sheets. (2) One who does bindery work.

binder's boards A stiff, high-grade composition material used in **bookbinding**, usually inside the cloth.

binder's die *See* **die-stamping**.

bindery (1810) A shop where books are assembled.

binding (13c) (1) A covering for the pages of a book. (2) The process by which such a covering is attached, including **case binding**, **perfect binding**, and **mechanical binding**. *See also* **comb binding**; **saddle-stitched binding**; **side-stitched rivet binding**; **side-wired binding**; **signature**; **Smythe sewn**; **spiral binding**; **square backed**; **velo binding**.

binding cloth *See* **cover materials**.

Fig. B-3   Plastic binding, also called comb binding.

binding edge Edge of a sheet or page that is nearest the **saddle** of the book.

binding margin The additional space added to the side of the page that will be drilled or punched prior to insertion into a binder.

binding, mechanical *See* **mechanical binding**.

bionote A sentence or brief paragraph about the writer located at the bottom of the first page or last page on which an article appears in a publication. *See also* **contributor's page**.

BIOS *See* **Basic Input/Output System**.

bisynchronous A computer communications format that relies on interaction (**synchronization**) with another computer with which it is communicating. Compare **asynchronous**.

bit *See* **binary digit**.

bit map (1) A graphics image or text formed by a pattern of dots. These **low-resolution graphics**, produced by **paint** programs, usually have a lower number of **dots per inch** than **high-resolution graphics**. (2) An area in the computer's storage reserved for **graphics**. The bit map holds the picture that is continuously transmitted to the display screen. The **resolution** of the printed output will be the same as the resolution shown on the screen.

bit-mapped graphics Images constructed with a **matrix** of **bits** of dots. Compare **curve-linear graphics**. *See also* **bit map**; **raster graphics**.

bit-mapping A system for creating computer graphics in which individual **bits** within the computer's video memory represent the individual **pixels** on the video display.

bit per pixel A measure of **gray scale** in which the more bits per pixel, the more gray levels a scanner can save. A 4-bit-per-pixel scan saves 16 levels of gray; a 6-bit-per-pixel scan yields 64 levels; and an 8-bit-per-pixel scan produces a 256-level image.

bit rate The speed at which **bits** are transmitted, usually expressed as **baud**. *See also* **bits per second**.

bit stream Referring to the binary signal without regard to groupings by character, usually when talking about **serial** data transfer.

bits per second Refers to communications speed. Being replaced by **baud**. Abbreviated *bps*.

biweekly Once every two weeks.

black and white photograph A photograph that is black and white and all shades of gray in between.

black box (1945) Refers to the operating unit or *brains* of a computer. It has input and output but no explanation of how the output is generated.

black letter The **Old English** or **text** type style. *See also* **Fraktur**; **type style**; **typeface nomenclature**.

black patch Black masking patch that is pasted or mortised into position in the exact size of a photograph on reproduction line copy. Also called *blackout, window*.

blackface *See* **boldface**.

blackite A black and white photograph.

blackout *See* **black patch**.

blade-coated paper Paper that is **coated** with a **china clay** coating by a thin steel blade at very high speed, high enough to make the process economic even though it is an additional operation after the paper has left the papermaking machine.

blanc fixe (1866) White material used with **china clay** as a filler for **coating** and creating **enameled finish** book papers.

blank (1) An unprinted page that is part of a **signature**. (2) Heavy paper used for advertising display purposes such as posters and window displays. *See also* **ply**. (3) An unformatted **diskette**.

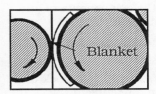

Fig. B-4   A blanket off-sets ink onto paper.

blanket In **offset lithography**, the rubber covering of the **blanket cylinder**, which receives the ink impression from the plate cylinder and offsets it onto the paper.

blanket cylinder The cylinder of an offset press that carries the rubber **blanket**.

blanking In computer graphics, the suppression of the display of one or more display elements or groups.

bleach-out *See* **drop-out**.

bleed (1937) In printing, an **image** that continues off the page when the edge of the paper has been trimmed away.

bleeding edge Blocks of words on the cover of a document that are lined up with colored splotches along the outer edges of pages so that required sections can be found easily. Compare **thumb index**.

blind folio Page number counted but not printed. *See also* **folio**.

blind keyboard In photocomposition, a tape-producing keyboard that has no visual display and produces no **hard copy**.

blind reference In **indexing**, a cross-reference that sends the reader to a nonexistent **entry**.

blind stamping Pressing a design into a book cover with tools or dies, without the use of ink or gold leaf. Also called *blind tooling, blocking*.

blind tooling *See* **blind stamping**.

blinking In computer graphics, an intentional regular change in the intensity of a display element, group, or space.

block (1) A hardwood or metal base for letterpress plates. (2) A woodcut. (3) In the playscript writing style, the spacing of material so that it forms discrete physical blocks. (4) In the structured writing style, an outlined paragraph of information on a page. (5) A standard chunk of **memory**, typically consisting of 512 **bytes**, used as a unit by the computer. *See also* **text block**.

block diagram (1944) Drawing in which blocks or rectangles are used to show the relationship between the components of an item or a piece of equipment.

block letter (1908) **Gothic**, or **sans serif**, typeface. *See also* **type style**.

block move A process in which a block of text is relocated within a document. *See also* **column move; move**.

block quotation *See* **extract**.

blocking (1) Decorating with foil through the hot foil stamping process. Also called *dry printing*. (2) Mounting a letterpress plate. (3) *See* **blind stamping**.

blocking out Eliminating characters, portions of art, or any part of an image on **reproduction copy** or negatives by pasting over them, whiting them out with paint, or **masking** them.

blow up To enlarge a photograph, artwork, or type for any purpose. Compare **reduce**. *See also* **blowup**.

blowback Act or result of making an enlarged print or copy, particularly from microfilm. The term is derived from *blow up* and *back* and means reproduction back to a larger size.

blowup A photograph, chart, figure, etc., that undergoes enlargement. *See also* **blow up**.

blue line *See* **blueline**.

blue, nonreproducing pencil (1893) A colored pencil or pen whose marks will not photograph, making it ideal for marking **camera-ready copy**.

blue-pencil (1888) To correct or indicate a **rewrite** of **copy**. *See also* **blueline**.

blue streak Streak of blue ink imposed along the margin on the front page of some daily newspapers to indicate a specific edition when more than one daily edition is published.

blueline (1) Copy used as proofs of a printer's negatives that are the author's final check before printing. It has blue lines with a white background and is used as a preliminary proof for checking purposes. Also called *blues, blueprint, brownline, vandyke.* *See also* **prepress proof; press proof.** (2) Traditionally, a guide line drawn with a blue pencil or printed in light blue ink on the **boards** and used for manually pasting up a page **layout.**

blueprint (1886) (1) Print in which white lines are produced on a blue background and used for production, construction, and architectural drawings. (2) Blue contact photoprints used as a preliminary proof for checking purposes. Also called *blueline, blues.* *See also* **proof.**

blurb (1907) A short, appreciative description of a book or article used as a promotional phrase, announcement, or advertisement, particularly copy on a book **jacket.**

board (1) Any heavy, stiff material, such as that used for mounting art or making displays. (2) The heavier paper on which **galleys** are pasted up. *See also* **mechanical.** (3) The stiff material to which the cover of a book is attached in bookbinding. (4) *See* **layout board.**

body (1) The main part of the **character.** (2) Body text default value for most **desktop publishing** programs. (3) The part of a piece of **hot metal type** that serves as a base for the raised printing surface. (4) The size of type from the bottom of the **descender** to the top of the **ascender,** excluding **leading.** (5) Block of **text,** as well as the main part of a book or other publication, exclusive of **front** and **back matter.** *See also* **body size; body width; font; measurement; sort; type size.**

body copy The main part of the text of a publication. Also called *body text.* Compare **heading; caption.**

body matter *See* **body type.**

body size Depth of the body of a piece of type measured in points. This dimension, measured in points, corresponds to the height of the printed letter and is the same for all characters in the **font**. See also **body**; **body width**.

body text See **body type**.

body type Type used for straight matter composition and regular paragraph type. Popular sizes range from 8 to 12 points, 9 and 10 points being common. Also called *body copy, body matter, body text, reading type, text type*. Compare **display** type. See also **type specimen**.

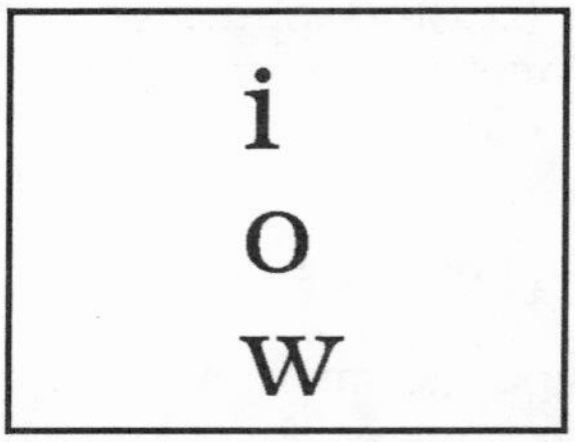

body width The dimension corresponding to the width of the printed letter, which varies from character to character. See also **body**; **body size**.

boilerplate (1893) (1) Centrally prepared material supplied especially to small newspapers for use as **filler**. (2) Construction of a document using parts of many other documents or a list of paragraphs. (3) Standardized text or format that is often used again in other documents. See also **template**.

bold *v.* To make **boldface**. *n.* The heavy version of a particular typeface.

boldface (1889) Typeface that is heavier and darker than the body type. Compare **lightface**. Abbreviated *bf.* Also called *blackface.* See also **display type**; **type style**; **typeface**.

bolts The edges of a folded section of paper before it is trimmed.

bond paper (1877) A strong and durable paper used for ruling, printing, typewriting, and pen writing. Compare **bank**.

book (1) In typography, a **typeface** of medium weight intended for continuous text. (2) A nonperiodical publication containing 49 or more pages. Compare **booklet**.

book auction Selling the **rights**— paperback, movies, etc.— of a hardback book to the highest bidder.

book cloth Cotton cloth, sized, glazed, or impregnated with synthetic resins, used for book **covers** and available in a large variety

i

o

w

Fig. B-5   The body width of the *i* is thinner than that of the *o*, which is thinner than the *w*.

of weights, **finishes**, colors, and patterns. *See also* **cover materials; cover stock**.

book developer *See* **book packager**.

book endpaper *See* **endleaf**.

book face Any typeface suitable for the text of a book.

book fair An event where publishers rent tables or booths to display and sell their wares.

book jacket *See* **jacket**.

book lining *See* **endleaf**.

book makeup Act of **collating**, arranging, and numbering pages of **reproduction copy** of a book. It is the last function that prepares the book for printing.

Book Manufacturers Institute (1933) An association of manufacturers of books and suppliers of book materials.

book packager An individual or company contracting with a **publisher** to draw all elements of a book together, from the initial concept, to writing and marketing strategies, and beyond. Also called *book developer, book producer.*

book paper Paper made principally for the manufacture of books, pamphlets, and magazines. Compare **cover stock; newsprint; writing paper**.

book producer *See* **book packager**.

Book Review Digest (1905) A monthly periodical presenting excerpts from book reviews.

bookbinding The process of binding a book. *See also* **binding, mechanical**.

booklet (1859) Small **book** consisting of as much as, but not more than 24 pages, yet having a sufficient number of pages not to be classified as a **pamphlet**.

bookmarking A software technique that stores the location in the **online documentation** at which the user signs off. When the user next accesses the bookmarked online document, he or she can return to that location to continue reading the document.

boot *See* **bootstrap**.

bootstrap A technique or device that brings itself into a desired state through its own action. For example, a routine in which the first few instructions are sufficient to make the rest of the routine be brought into the computer from an **input device**. Also called *boot up, bootstrap*.

boot up *See* **boot**.

border Decorative line or design used to surround artwork or a page.

BOT marker *See* **beginning-of-tape marker**.

bottom margin The **margin** at the bottom of a page. Also called *foot margin, tail margin*.

bottom out In page **layout**, to indicate that a page of text closes near the bottom limitations of the page.

bounce Effect of "bouncing" characters produced by type, usually display type, set with a photographic typesetter.

bound galley *See* **uncorrected proof**.

boundary rectangle *See* **bounding box**.

bounding box A rectangle that can be adjusted in size to enclose a symbol, text, or group of display elements. The bounding box separates the elements from the rest of the displayed image so that it can be moved or scaled. Also called *boundary rectangle, bounding rectangle*.

bounding rectangle *See* **bounding box**.

bourgeois Old type size, now equal to about 9 points.

Bowker, R.R. *See* **R.R. Bowker**.

bowl The curved part of rounded letters such as *B, R, b, p*.

box *v.* To rule off text on all four sides to draw attention to a certain paragraph or feature. Also called *boxed in. n.* A printed rec-

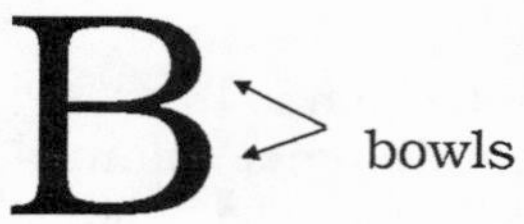

Fig. B-6   Two bowls on the letter B.

tangle enclosing typeset matter or an illustration.

box text Text that is **boxed**.

boxed in *See* **box**.

boxhead Column heading in a **table**. All
matter appearing directly under each heading is pertinent to that heading.

boxing The use of bounding boxes to select
particular graphic entities on the screen.
Once **boxed**, an entity can be moved,
scaled, or otherwise manipulated.

bps *See* **bits per second**.

brace Character ({ or }) used to group type
matter or to enclose, connect, and show
relationships of text or illustrative matter.

bracket (1580) (1) Character ([or]) used
to enclose words, figures, etc., from the text.
(2) Pair of marks used to set off matter extraneous or incidental to the context. (3)
Used to mark additional wording not in the
original text or optional omissions. Also
called *square brackets*.

bracketed serif A serif that is joined to the
stroke with a curved line.

branch A decision point, or branch, in the
flow of a program, process, or structure.

Branch Report on Electronic Publishing
(1985) A bimonthly newsletter on **electronic
publishing**.

brand name A name given by a manufacturer or merchant to an article or service to
distinguish it as produced or sold by him
and that may be used and protected as a
trademark. Also called *trade name*.

brayer A handled inking roller used in
proofing metal type.

BREAK A **PC/MS-DOS** command that
checks for a **Ctrl-Break** from the keyboard
during program operation.

break (1) An interruption in the flow of text
from one paragraph, line, column, or page
to the next. (2) An action that causes the

currently executing program to stop executing. *See also* **Break key; Ctrl-Break.**

break for color To indicate or separate the parts of a **mechanical** to be printed in different colors.

Break key A **keyboard** key that causes the currently executing program to stop executing. *See also* **Ctrl-Break.**

break up In **letterpress printing**, to separate a **form** that is no longer needed into its component parts— **hot metal type, furniture, engravings,** etc.— and to dispose of each appropriately.

breakeven point The number of copies of a book that must be sold to recover its costs.

breakpoint A forced interruption within a computer program at a predetermined location or event, usually used in program development.

brevier Old type size, now equal to about 8 points.

brightness One of the three perceived color dimensions, the attribute that indicates the degree of whiteness or blackness. *See also* **brightness ratio; hue; saturation.**

brightness ratio A measure of contrast. The ratio between the brightest and darkest parts of a printed paper sheet.

brilliant Old type size of 3.5 points, now seldom used.

bristol board (1809) A fine grade of cardboard.

broad fold Having the grain running along the short dimension, said of paper. Compare **long fold.**

broadsheet *See* **broadside.**

broadside (1575) (1) A large, specially folded advertising sheet, usually a self-mailer. (2) A page designed to be read normally when the book is turned 90 degrees. Also called *broadsheet, horizontal page, landscape page.*

broadside cut An **illustration** or **table** laid on its side to fit the page, the left side being at the bottom of the page.

broadside page *See* **broadside**.

broadside table Large tables that are broader than they are long and set **broadside** in some publications. *See also* **continued table; doubled table; parallel table**.

brochure (1748) A folded **pamphlet** or small **booklet**.

brownline A photoprint made from a negative and used as a **proof** to check the position of the elements before the printing plate is made. Also called a *brownprint, vandyke. See also* **blueline**.

brownprint *See* **brownline**.

brush In computer **painting**, a tool that draws a line or a pattern, much as a paintbrush does, on the display surface.

brush-coated paper **Coated paper** that is run through a special brush-coating machine.

bubble (1) In technical illustrations, any circle that encloses copy, such as **index numbers** or letters placed beside the bill of material on an engineering drawing and **keyed** to material on the face of the drawing. Also called *balloon*. (2) Air beneath loosely mounted copy.

buckles In binding, wrinkles near the head and back of the folded **signatures** where the paper is folded at right angles. Also called *gussets*.

buckram (15c) A heavy **book cloth** much used for library bindings or for binding large, heavy books.

buffer (1) A section of a computer's memory in which data, often in large amounts, can be temporarily stored prior to processing or transferred to an **auxiliary storage device**. (2) A device that supplies extra **random access memory**, separate from that directly connected to the **central processing unit** of the computer, that can be used to store in-

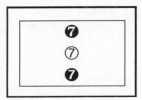

Fig. B-7   Index numbers as bubbles.

formation prior to transmission or processing. *See also* **print buffer**.

BUFFERS A **PC/MS-DOS** command that allocates a number of disk buffers— between 1 and 99— in memory. These are activated from the **CONFIG.SYS** file, which is automatically read at turn on.

bug (1945) In computer technology, something that causes a system to malfunction, such as a mechanical defect or a programming error. *See also* **debug**; **glitch**.

built-up fraction Fraction made up from two or more characters. For example, 3/16 would be made from a 3 followed by a / followed by a 16. Also called *adaptable fraction.* Compare **case fraction**; **piece fraction**.

bulk (1) The thickness of **paper** in number of **pages per inch**. (2) The thickness of the **pages** of the book, not counting the **cover**. (3) To make a book appear longer (thicker) than the amount of text would otherwise require, by using thick, light paper.

bulk eraser *See* **degausser**.

bulk storage *See* **mass storage**.

bulking dummy A **layout** that resembles the finished book in every respect except that the pages and cover are blank. *See also* **dummy**.

bulletin (1765) One in a series of factual reports issued irregularly.

bulletin board system A computer term referring to an electronic communication program allowing the sending and storing of information between or among computers. Also called *electronic bulletin board.* Abbreviated *BBS. See also* **telecommunications**.

bullet A small black dot (•) used to set off items in an indented list to make them easier to read. Also called *meatball.*

bundle Two **reams** of paper, or 1,000 sheets.

bundling (1) Compressing book signatures to make them lie flat in **bookbinding**. (2)

Tying **signatures** of a book together during the **binding** process.

burin (1662) A steel cutting tool used in **engraving**. Its blade is ground obliquely to a sharp point. Also called *graver*.

burning plates The making of printing plates from negatives.

burnish A **paste-up** term meaning to rub the **boards** with a tool to smooth and firmly affix the **galleys** to them.

bus One or more conductors used to transmit signals or power from one or more sources to one or more destinations. *See also* **address bus**; **data bus**.

business-size envelope The standard size envelope used in sending business correspondence. Also called *#10 envelope*.

button (1) Both a **logical** and a **physical input device**, used for selecting from a set of alternative choices. Typical button devices include:
- programmed keyboard keys
- function keys
- keys on tablet cursors (hand cursors)
- keys on a mouse

(2) In some **interactive programs**, an on-screen area activated by a **mouse**.

butt slugs To join two short **Linotype** slugs with no space between them, making one long line of type or spacing material.

byte (1962) The unit of measure used for computer memory and data storage in 8-bit microcomputers. One byte contains eight bits and can store one character (letter, number, punctuation mark, or other symbol). *See also* **American Standard Code for Information Interchange**; **binary digit**; **binary notation**.

Byte (1975) Monthly magazine for business and technical professionals who are users and buyers of microcomputers and related products.

Notes and New Words

C

C (1) A **high-level language** that combines **statements** with low-level machine control to produce efficient, easy-to-use **software** for **microcomputers**. *See also* **BASIC; FOR-TRAN; machine language**. (2) Abbreviation for **copyright**.

C1S *See* **coated one side**.

C2S *See* **coated two side**.

c&lc *See* **caps and lowercase**.

c&sc *see* **caps and small caps**.

cable An electrical wire or bundle of wires used to connect two parts of a computer. It carries electrical power or electrical signals.

cable connector Male and female plugs used for connecting **cables** between a **computer** and **peripheral equipment**.

cache In a **central processing unit**, a high-speed buffer storage area that is continually updated to contain recently accessed contents of main storage. Its purpose is to reduce **access time**.

CAD *See* **computer-aided design**.

calender (1688) *v*. To run paper through a calender (metal rollers) to achieve varying degrees of finish. *n*. Part of a papermaking machine that gives the **finish** to paper.

calendered finish Paper with a smooth surface. Also called *machine finish*. Compare **supercalendered finish**.

California job case The most popular type storage case, in which handset type is stored and from which it is set. *See also* **case**.

caliper (1588) (1) The thickness of a sheet of **paper** or **board**, measured in **mils** for paper and **points** for board. (2) The instrument that measures that thickness.

call A program **instruction** that either fetches or sends one or more **control codes** or characters to a device or memory location within the computer.

calligraphy (1613) Elegant handwriting, or the art of producing such handwriting. Also called *engrossing*.

callout Text that has been "called out," or removed, from an **illustration** so that it can act as a label, describing some part of the illustration. The assigned number is found in an accompanying **legend** or **illustrated parts breakdown** where other information concerning the particular part or item may be obtained. *See also* **exploded view; key; lead line; pull-out quote**.

camera-ready art Any piece of **artwork** ready for pasting up for **camera-ready copy**. *See also* **mechanical**.

camera-ready copy **Artwork**, type **proofs**, typewritten material, etc., ready to be photographed for printing without further alteration. It should be free of smudges and of unclear, broken, or faint type. Also called *reproduction copy*. *See also* **mechanical**.

Cameron belt press *See* **belt press**.

cancel *v*. To cut out blank pages of a signature that do not have print on them. *n*. (1) A **keyboard** operation that deletes the line cur-

Fig. C-1   A California job case, used to hold handset type.

rently being typed. (2) A new **leaf** or **signature** replacing a defective one or one containing errors. (3) A book is said to have a *cancel title* if the original **title page** has been cut out and new one pasted in.

canned software Programs prepared by computer manufacturers or another supplier and provided to a user in ready-to-use forms. Compare **custom software**.

cap (1) *See* **capital letter** (2) A 14-in x 17-in sheet of paper.

cap height The height of a **capital letter** in a font of type.

cap line In typography, the hypothetical line that connects the tops of **capital letters**. *See also* **ascender line**.

capacity The number of items of data that a **storage device** is capable of containing. Frequently defined in terms of computer **bytes, characters, words**.

capital letter (1611) In typography, capitals are normally aligned with the tops of **lowercase ascenders**. Text set in all capitals reduces the average reading speed by about 14%. Also called *caps* or *uppercase*.

caps *See* **capital letter**.

caps and lowercase Capital letters used for initial characters, followed by **lowercase** characters. Abbreviated *c&lc*.

caps and small caps Capital letters used for initials, followed by **small caps** instead of **lowercase**: THIS IS SET IN CAPS AND SMALL CAPS. Abbreviated *c&sc*.

caption (1670) Originally, a title or **headline** over an illustration; now a description of the content matter of a photograph. Also called *cutline*.

captive shop A printing shop that belongs to a publication and is used to print that publication. Compare **job shop**.

captured keystroke A computer term meaning that information, once **entered**, is retained by the computer and, therefore, does not need retyping.

car card A large card **advertisement** used in subway cars and buses.

carbon tissue A light-sensitive, gelatin-covered paper **stock** used in **gravure printing**.

carbonless paper A type of paper that permits impressions from copy to copy without the use of carbons, made possible when special coatings on the back of one sheet and the face of the following sheet are brought together under pressure. Also called *impact paper, NCR paper*.

card *See* **printed circuit board**.

cardinal number (12c) A number used in counting to indicate how many elements there are in an assemblage. Compare **ordinal number**.

carding (1) Inserting strips of heavy paper or extra **leads** between lines to lengthen a page or column. Also called *faking*. (2) *See* **feather**.

caret (1681) (1) A **diacritical** mark (^) that indicates a sound value. For example, the ô in *hôtel*. (2) A triangular symbol (^) used on a screen as a **cursor** to show where text should be inserted. (3) In editing, a **proofreader's mark** showing where to insert a correction or additional material written immediately above the line in **manuscripts** or at the side on **proofs**.

caricature (1712) Good-humored or bitterly satirical representation of a person or thing that shows a deliberate exaggeration and distortion of features or mannerisms.

carriage return (1) The operation that prepares for the next character to be printed or displayed at the specified first position on the next line. (2) A control code that returns the print position to the left margin. Abbreviated *CR*. Also called *hard carriage return, return*. *See also* **bidirectional printing**; **print head**; **soft carriage return**.

carrier holes The holes in **continuous-form** paper used by **tractor feeders** to transport paper through the printer.

carry forward To transfer text to the next column or page.

carry-over title Second or any succeeding line of a sentence, paragraph, or nonsentence list item. The carry-over line may be either **flush left** or a **hanging indention**.

cartridge A plug-in module containing **software** permanently stored in **read-only memory**. A cartridge is convenient, easy to use, soundless, and cannot be erased.

cartridge tape A small, self-contained volume of **magnetic tape** used for **data storage**. Also called *cassette*.

case (1) Capitalized (**uppercase**) or uncapitalized (**lowercase**) form of letter. (2) A **cover** or **binding**, made by a casemaking machine or by hand and usually printed, stamped, or labeled before it is glued to a book. The process of applying such a ready-made cover is called *casing in*. (3) A shallow tray divided into compartments to hold individual pieces of type. Uppercase letters are stored in the upper drawer, or case, and lowercase letters in the lower drawer, or case. The California job case, however, has only one storage drawer for all characters, sorts, rules, and the like.

case binding Binding in which sewn **signatures** with **endpapers** glued on are fastened to a cover with gauze (**super**) and glue. In case binding, sewn signatures plus endpapers are enclosed in a rigid cover. Also called *cased book, hard cover*. *See also* **sidestitched binding**; **Smythe sewing**; **spine**; **unbound signature**. Compare **paperback**.

case bound *See* **hard cover**.

case fraction A fraction that is available as a single character. Compare **built-up fraction**; **piece fraction**.

case significant Making a distinction between **uppercase** and **lowercase** letters.

case stand A framework used to hold **type cases**. Also called *bank*.

case study An extended example throughout a document that uses a reader's known environment to explore new material.

case, type *See* **case**.

casebound *See* **hard cover**.

cased book *See* **case binding**.

casing in *See* **case**.

cassette A small, self-contained volume of **magnetic tape** used for **data storage**. Also called *cartridge tape*.

cast In **linecasting machines**, to force molten metal into a type mold against matrices. Type may be cast as single characters or as complete lines.

cast-coated paper A **coated paper** that has coating dried in contact with a highly polished heated chromium cylinder to produce an almost mirrorlike finish.

castoff *v.* To estimate the length of a **manuscript** when **typeset**. *n.* The result of making a castoff.

casting off *See* **castoff**.

casting up *See* **castoff**.

casual users Users who use a piece of software infrequently and resent being required to read extensive pieces of documentation.

catalog sheet A low-key book promotional page including contents, author, and ordering information, often used as a **flier**.

Cataloging in Publication (1) Pre-designated reference numbers provided by the Library of Congress and included in the **front matter** of a book as well as on the **spines**. (2) A process that aids librarians in ordering and cataloging a book. Abbreviated *CIP*.

catchline Wording at the head of a **proof**, included for ease of identification but not necessarily to be retained in the printed page.

cathode-ray tube (1905) (1) An electronic tube with a screen upon which information may be displayed. This is the **display screen** contained in the video monitor; it is similar to a television screen. A beam of electrons is controlled to form alphanumeric characters or symbols on a screen. (2) In phototypesetting, an electronic tube used to transmit letter images, in the forms of dots or lines, onto film, photopaper, microfilm, or offset plates. Abbreviated *CRT*. *See also* **CRT composition; display; screen; video display terminal; video terminal**.

cathode-ray tube display (1905) A device that presents data in visual form by means of controlled electron beams. The data display produced by the **cathode-ray tube**.

caveman Slang, referring to an antiquated computer or any obsolete data processing equipment.

CBA *See* **Christian Booksellers Association**.

CD *See* **CHDIR**.

cedilla (1599) The **diacritical** mark that indicates a sound value. For example: The ç in *Françoise*.

cellulose A fibrous substance obtained from cotton, linen, hemp, and wood to make **paper**.

center (14c) *v.* A **keyboard** function to place the information being typed in the center of the line. *n.* Lines of type set centered on the line **measure**. *See also* **flush left; flush right**.

center head Caption or **title** that appears in the center of a page or column, for example, a chapter title or **subhead**.

center spread (1952) (1) Generally, the pair of facing pages in the center of a magazine, book, or other publication. (2) In books, the center spread is the center fold, where one printing plate may be used for both facing pages. There are as many center spreads as there are signatures. Also called *double-page spread*.

centered dot (1) *See* **bullet**. (2) Used in mathematical composition as a multiplication sign.

centered type *See* **center**.

centerfold (1952) *See* **center spread**.

• This is a bullet.
• This is a bullet.
4 • 3 = 12

Fig. C-2   A centered dot is used in bullet lists and as a multiplication sign.

central processing unit (ca. 1969) The portion of a computer where program instructions are processed and their execution coordinated. Abbreviated *CPU*. Also called *central processor, microprocessor, mainframe*. *See also* **arithmetic and logic unit**; **input/output port**.

CGA *See* **color graphics adapter**.

chains A sequence of location pointers that connect, or *chain together*, the parts of a disk file.

change bar A line or symbol put in the **margin** of a page alongside updated material in order to call the reader's attention to the fact that something has been changed on the page since the last release of the documentation.

channel (1) A path for electrical transmission between two or more points. Also called *path, link, line, facility, circuit.* (2) A transmission path that connects **auxiliary devices** to a computer.

channel capacity In data communications, the maximum **baud rate** that may be accommodated by a **channel**. Also called *bits per second.*

chapbook (1798) A small book or pamphlet of popular tales, ballads, poems, or tracts.

chapel An organization of union workmen in a printing shop. *See also* **closed shop**; **open shop**.

chapter (1) In **Ventura**, any single document that is edited at one time. Chapters can be printed in sequence to form longer documents. A combination of text and picture files, formatted with a **style sheet**. A chapter file consists of pointers to each of these files, along with instructions on how to combine them together on the computer screen or on the printer. (2) A division of a book or other writing.

chapter head Title or number of the opening page of each **chapter**.

character (14c) A letter, number, punctuation mark, space, or special graphic used for the production of text. On a computer, characters may be represented visually on the video display or in electronic form within the computer's memory, according to special encoding systems such as the **ASCII** code.

character assembly *See* **typesetting**.

character code A code designating a unique numerical representation for a **character set**.

character count The length of a piece of copy is usually expressed in terms of the number of **characters** that it contains. *See also* **copyfitting**.

character display device. *See* **readout device**.

character density A measure of the horizontal spacing of characters.

character generation The projection or formation of typographic images on the face of a **cathode-ray tube**, usually in association with a high-speed computerized photocomposition system.

character generator In computer graphics, a functional unit that converts the coded representation of a graphic character into the shape of the character for display.

character key (1) A control used to process text one character at a time. (2) A key on the **keyboard**.

character outline The graphic pattern established by the stroke edges of a character.

character pitch In a line of text, the number of **characters per pica**. *See* **elite**; **pica**.

character printer *See* **serial printer**.

character set (1) The set of characters—alphabetic, numeric, punctuation marks, graphic characters, etc.—that a computer is capable of displaying on its video screen or printing to hard copy. (2) The characters that can be displayed on the screen. (3) For a printer, the characters that it can print.

character string A group of characters that are treated as a set of letters or numbers, rather than as a command.

characters per inch The measurement of the packing density of a magnetic tape, drum, disk, or any device on which that information is recorded. Abbreviated *cpi*.

characters per pica System of **copyfitting** that uses the average number of characters per **pica** as a means of determining the length of the copy when set in type. Abbreviated *cpp*. *See also* **alphabet length**.

characters per second A measurement referring to the output speeds of phototypesetting equipment. Abbreviated *cps*.

chart (1571) Graphical representation showing values and quantities by means of bars, curves, columns, and symbols. *See also* **bar chart**; **column chart**; **curve chart**; **pie chart**; **surface chart**.

chart, organization *See* **organization chart**.

chase (1612) *v.* To ornament metal by embossing or engraving. *n.* An iron or steel frame in which type **forms** are locked for **letterpress** printing presses.

CHCP A **PC/MS-DOS** command that changes the **character set** to a specified national language **code page**. *See also* **NLSFUNC**.

CHDIR A **PC/MS-DOS** command that changes the directory in use. Short form is **CD**.

check box In a **dialog box**, the area touched and clicked on to turn an option on or off.

check-out chart Chart form of presentation resembling a **Christmas tree**, a name by which it is sometimes known. It is used in technical publications as a kind of troubleshooting chart to check the operating accuracy of a system in logically sequenced steps.

checking copy Page from a publication containing an **advertisement**, sent to the advertiser as proof that the ad was run properly.

chemical pulp Pulp for papermaking made from **cellulose**-containing substances by chemical means. Compare **mechanical wood pulp**. *See also* **sulfate process**; **sulfite process**.

children's books *See* **juvenile books**.

china clay (1840) Filler used with **blanc fixe** for coating book papers during the paper manufacturing process.

chip (1) A **microprocessor**. (2) The unpackaged wafer of silicon material incorporating a microelectronic circuit. *See also* **integrated circuit**.

chipboard (1919) A cheaper grade of binder's material.

CHDSK A **PC/MS-DOS** command that checks disks for file integrity, file fragmentation, and to show space occupied by **files** and space remaining for use.

Christian Booksellers Association A trade association of religious bookstores and suppliers. Abbreviated *CBA*.

Christmas tree *See* **check-out chart**.

chroma (1889) The degree of intensity from black to white.

chromalin Four-color **proof** made from **color separations** to check color before printing.

chunk In structured writing, a sentence.

chunk makeup Makeup, in either metal or direct-image composition, whereby portions of the page are made up by the **compositor** and **proofed**, to be fully made up later by other workers.

Cicero Typographic unit of measurement—predominant in Europe—approximately the same as the **pica**: 1 Cicero = 4.511 mm = 12 **Didot** points = 12.835 **points**. *See also* **measurement system**.

CIP *See* **Cataloging in Publication**.

circle chart *See* **pie chart**.

1 Cicero =
4.511 mm =
12 Didot points =
12.835 points

Fig. C-3 The Cicero is the predominant unit of typographic measurement in Europe.

circuit *See* **channel**.

circular (1789) Advertising matter in the form of letters and **handbills**.

circumflex (1609) A **diacritical** mark that indicates a sound value. For example, the ô in *aussitôt*.

classified advertisement Advertisements classified under descriptive headings, composed of words only and sold by the line. Compare **display advertisement**.

clay-coated paper A **coated paper** with a thin layer of clay for better definition of printed material, used for high-quality art books.

clean copy A **manuscript** or **galley** free from corrections, cross-outs, wrinkles, smudges, deletions, and other unnecessary marks. Compare **dirty copy**.

clear (1) A **keyboard** function that removes the contents from the **display screen**. (2) In computer technology, to erase stored data and to restore circuits to their beginning state.

clear for 10 An **instruction** for the **compositor** not to set numbers 1 through 9 **flush left** but to leave enough space so that the numbers will **align** over the 0 in 10.

click To press and immediately release the **mouse** button.

click on Positioning the **cursor** on a location, character, or **button** and clicking a **mouse** button.

clip art Non-copyrighted **camera-ready art** that can be cut from a book and pasted in another publication or that can be electronically copied from a **graphics file** and inserted in a **text file**.

clipboard A temporary, invisible holding place for text, pictures, and graphics. Any text block or picture placed on the clipboard using a cut or copy operation can be placed anywhere else in the chapter.

Fig. C-4   The map symbols are part of clip art provided by GEM Draw Plus

clipping (1) A news item of interest that is cut by a **clipping service** for a customer. (2) *See* **scissoring**.

clipping bureau *See* **clipping service**.

clipping service A firm that, for a fee, watches almost all national publications and a wide selection of local ones and clips items of interest to its clients. Also called *clipping bureau.*

clips Samples, usually from newspapers or magazines, of an author's published works.

clipsheet (1926) A sheet of newspaper material issued by an organization for **clipping** and reprinting. Also called *press book.*

clobber (1) To wipe out a file. (2) To write new data over the top of good data in a file or otherwise damaging a file so that it becomes useless.

clone Any microcomputer that imitates the **operating system** and basic architecture of the IBM-PC, IBM-XT, or IBM-AT.

close (1) To go back to the previous folder or the root directory of a disk. (2) To exit a program. (3) To stop work on the current publication.

close bracket A punctuation mark ( ]) used to end a bracketed expression.

close parenthesis A punctuation mark ( )) that ends a parenthetical expression.

close punctuation A pattern of punctuation that makes liberal use of punctuation marks, often including one wherever the grammatical structure of the sentence will allow it. Compare **open punctuation**.

close quote *v.* To end a quotation with ending quotation marks ("). *n.* The punctuation mark (") that ends a quotation.

close up A **proofreader's mark** that indicates to bring typographical elements closer together by removing space.

closed architecture A computer, such as the Apple Macintosh, whose design makes it difficult to upgrade the system, increase computing power, or add accessories. Compare **open architecture**.

closed shop (1904) A shop in which only union workers are employed. Compare **open shop**.

cloth A material used for **binding**, or casing, of books.

closure (1) In online tutorials, the completion of a discrete lesson. (2) In a paragraph, the complete revelation of a single thought.

clothbound A book protected by a rigid cover, usually **cloth** wrapped around **boards**. Also called *hardback*. *See also* **paperbound**.

CLS A **PC/MS-DOS** command that clears the screen.

coarse fatting pattern In **scanners**, a **halftone** pattern that gives the broadest range of gray shades. *See also* **fatting pattern**.

coated finish High-gloss **finish** in papers used for fine color work or halftone reproductions.

coated offset paper *See* **offset paper**.

coated one side A **coated paper**—on one side only—used for applications requiring high-quality printing and one side of which may be adhesive-backed or pasted. Abbreviated *CIS*.

coated paper Paper to which a surface coating of clay or other opaque material has been applied to provide a smooth printing surface. *See also* **blade-coated paper; brush-coated papers; cast-coated paper; coated one side; coated two sides; machine-coated paper; matte finish**.

coated two side A **coated paper**—coated on both sides—used for applications requiring quality printing. Abbreviated *C2S*. *See also* **coated paper**.

cockle finish Rough, wrinkled, irregular **finish** in paper.

code A combination of letters, numbers, and symbols, entered through a keyboard, used as **instructions** for a typesetting system.

code page In **PC/MS-DOS**, a table containing characters and symbols that correspond to specific countries. *See also* **CHCP**.

coffee table book An oversized book, heavily illustrated, that is suitable for display on a coffee table.

cognitive mapping The ability to solve problems or develop theories by recognizing patterns in things.

coherence (1578) The smooth linkage of ideas in a text achieved through repeated words and phrases or transitional words and phrases.

cold boot The act of applying power to a computer and loading an **operating system** into it. *See also* **warm boot**.

cold composition *See* **cold type**.

cold copy *See* **cold type**.

cold type (1949) Composition by machines such as typewriters, laser printers, and phototypesetting machines or in any manner in which no molten metal is used to form the image. It specifically refers to composition produced directly on paper by a typewriter mechanism. The term was derived as the opposite of **hot type**. Also called *cold composition, cold copy*. *See also* **cast; direct-image composition; offset lithography; rub-on type; typesetting; typewriter composition**.

collage (1919) An illustration made by pasting photographs, line cuts, types, etc., in combination.

collate (1612) (1) In general, to merge documents into a sequence. (2) To print in numerical order with the first page on top of the stack that comes out of the printer. (3) In bookmaking, to arrange folded signatures of a book in proper sequence for binding. *See also* **signature**.

collaterals Accompanying or auxiliary pieces, especially in advertising.

collating mark Markings made on the outside of the fold of each **signature** by a short **rule** positioned on the press. When the signatures are collated, these marks align diagonally. A miss means an omitted signature; two side by side mean a duplication.

College Media Advisers (1954) Professional association serving directors, advisers, and chairpersons of boards of college student media.

collotype (1883) A **lithographic** method of printing from a plane surface of hardened gelatin treated so that a greasy ink adheres to the parts of the plate bearing the image and from there is transferred to paper. Used principally for the reproduction of pictorial copy.

colophon (1621) (1) A Greek term meaning *finishing touch.* (2) Brief technical description placed at the end of a book, giving information on the typeface and design, the paper used, production facts, and printing techniques, or other physical aspects of the work. (3) An emblem or device identifying a printer or publisher. It may appear on the **cover**, **title page**, **spine**, or **jacket** of a book. *See also* **back matter**.

The Colophon A large-format publication for users of Adobe Illustrator and Adobe's downloadable typefaces. Contains technical how-to tips with whimsical treatment of typography-related issues.

color *v.* (1) To enliven writing. (2) To exaggerate and falsify. *n.* A **hue** that is not black, white, or gray.

color correction Change made in reproduction work to correct the rendition of a color by **masking**, dot etching, re-etching, or **scanning**.

color display adapter *See* **color graphics adapter**; **enhanced graphics adapter**; **video graphics adapter**.

color form The **form** making the second color in a printing job.

color graphics A system that uses color to create graphs or draw pictures.

Fig. C-5   Colophon for Word Workers.

color graphics adapter (1981) The original color display adapter, abbreviated *CGA*, for the IBM PC. It was able to display text and low- to medium-resolution **bit-mapped graphics** on a color display. The CGA standard has been widely cloned but is now obsolete, having been replaced by the much higher resolution **enhanced graphics adapter** and, most recently, the **video graphics adapter** standards.

color graphics card A computer **printed circuit board** that makes it possible to use a color or graphics monitor. *See also* **monochrome**.

color graphics printer An output device that creates original color prints on plain paper directly from computer graphic systems.

color keys A group of four **acetate overlays**, each of which has one of the four basic colors of a photograph printed on it, that allows checking the quality of **four-color separation**.

Color News (1985) A quarterly magazine devoted to studies of color and its affect on society.

color printing Usually any printing color, other than black, on white paper. For instance, a work with three different colored inks is referred to as *three-color printing*. *See also* **process color printing**.

color separation Breaking down color artwork into separate negatives— one for each to be printed. **Desktop publishing** programs allow users to create masters for color separations by preparing different pages with the elements to be printed in one color on each page. *See also* **four-color separations**; **overlay**.

columbian Old type size, now equal to about 16 points.

column (15c) (1) A vertical arrangement of characters or other expressions. (2) A vertical section of printed matter, usually running from the top of the page to the bottom, as in a newspaper. Compare **row**.

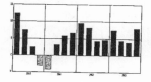

Fig. C-6   A column chart compares quantities over time.

column break An interruption in the flow of text from one column to the next. Compare **line break**; **page break**. *See also* **bad break**.

column chart Shows the comparison between quantities over a period of time, with quantities expressed in a series of vertical columns and time indicated in the horizontal axis. Column charts are **bar charts** with vertical bars. Also called *vertical column chart. See also* **curve chart**; **pie chart**; **surface chart**.

column guide A dotted vertical nonprinting line that marks left and right edges of a **column**. Used as an aid in **layout**.

column head In **tables**, single words or concise phrases that categorize the data listed in the vertical columns below them. *See also* **decked heads**.

column inch Space one column wide and one inch high, used to establish rates for display advertising.

column move A process in which a vertical column of data is moved from one part of a document to another, or from one document to another. *See also* **block move**; **move**.

column rule Vertical line separating one **column** of type from another.

columnar arrangement Division of a page into two or more **columns** of display or text matter.

columnist (1920) One who writes a column for a newspaper, magazine, newsletter, or other publication.

columns, balanced *See* **balanced columns**.

COM A **PC/MS-DOS filename extension** indicating that the file contains machine **instructions** and can be executed.

COM1, COM2, COM3, COM4 The addresses of the **serial communications ports** in an IBM PC or compatible. All versions of **PC/MS-DOS** recognize COM1 and COM2. Other versions may also recognize COM3 and COM4. Abbreviation for **com-**

munications. Also called *asynchronous communication port.*

comb binding Form of mechanical binding with a plastic center strip from which curving prongs extend. The prongs are inserted in holes punched in the paper. The name is derived from the resulting comb effect. Also called *GBC* binding, *plastic binding.*

combination (1) A printing plate combining halftone matter with line engraving, as when lettering appears on a photographic illustration. (2) Combining more than one job into a flat in offset lithographic stripping.

COMDEX Preview and COMDEX Show Daily (1983) A semiannual report published before the computer trade show and the conference with interviews and show-related industry news.

COMM In typesetting, a format that can be used in telecommunications. It converts a document into a 7-bit ASCII intermediate document, which can then be communicated through a modem.

comma fault (ca. 1934) The use of a comma between coordinate main clauses that are not joined by a conjunction. *See also* run on.

command Although *command* sometimes refers to instructions within a computer program, it more often refers to instructions that are typed directly on the keyboard of the computer and executed immediately.

command button A large rectangular area in a dialog box that contains a command such as "OK" or "cancel."

command file A file containing the program or instructions required to carry out a command. *See also* BAT; COM; EXE.

command interpreter A program that accepts commands from the keyboard and causes the commands to be executed.

command line A line consisting of one or more commands, each followed by its arguments, if any.

commercial art (1935) **Artwork** of any kind prepared for predetermined commercial purposes such as advertising and general promotion. Compare **fine arts**.

Committee of Small Magazines, Editors, and Publishers (1969) An international association of independent publishers and small presses to increase promotion and distribution of member publications. Abbreviated *COSMEP*.

communications The transmission of **data** between **computers**. Also called **telecommunications**.

communications channel The physical means of connecting one location or device to another to transmit or receive data.

communications port Outlet on a computer to which is attached a hardware device, such as a **mouse, modem,** or **printer**. *See also* **port**.

COMP A **PC/MS-DOS** command that compares designated files.

comp *See* **compose; compositor; comprehensive**.

compaction Packing of **data** to make room in storage.

company magazine *See* **house organ**.

compatible (1) A quality possessed by a computer system that enables it to handle both data and programs devised for some other type of computer system. If an element in a system is fully compatible with the functional (**software**) and physical (**hardware**) characteristics of a system, it can be incorporated into the system without modification. (2) Any third-party microcomputer meeting the operational standards of the IBM PC, IBM XT, or IBM AT computers.

compatibility *See* **compatible**.

compiler A computer program used to convert a **program** written in a high-level programming language, such as FORTRAN or Pascal, into machine-recognizable **code**.

compose To set type—whether by **hot-metal composition**, **photocomposition**, or **typewriter composition**. Abbreviated *comp*.

composing machine Device used to produce single types and lines of type on one slug, for example: **Intertype**, **Linotype**, and **Monotype**.

composing room That part of a typesetting shop or a printing plant in which type is composed.

composing stick A metal tray that holds and arranges type while a line of type is being set by hand. It is adjustable so that a line can be set to the desired **measure**.

composite display A low-resolution screen that has a single input connector through which a composite signal, comprising red, green, and blue color information, and synchronization signals flow into the display. Circuitry inside the display separates all the components of the signal and routes them to their proper areas.

composition (1) Setting type. (2) Laying out text and images so that they fit into a design. *See also* **cold type**; **computer-assisted composition**; **display composition**; **hand composition**; **hot-metal composition**; **machine composition**; **photocomposition**; **photomechanical composition**; **reproduction copy**; **reproduction proof**; **typewriter composition**.

composition, computer-assisted *See* **computer-assisted composition**.

compositional grid An arrangement of horizontal and vertical lines—used as a basic constraint upon the organization of images and text—so that the two-dimensional surface (of an electronic display, or a page) is subdivided into rectangular modules of the same size. Used by graphic **designer** in composing page **layouts**. *See also* **constructional grid**.

compositor (1533) A person who sets and arranges type, either by hand or machine. Also called *typesetter*, *typographer*. Abbreviated *comp*. *See also* **operator**.

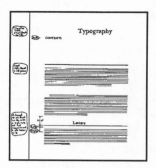

Fig. C-7   A comprehensive layout.

comprehensive A handmade, approximate **facsimile** of a **layout** showing type and illustrations in position and suitable as a finished presentation. Also called *comp, pencil rough. See also* **designer**.

comprehensive layout *See* **comprehensive**.

compressed print *See* **compressed type**.

compressed type Type with a thinner face than that of normal type, permitting more material to be set in a line of the same **measure**. Also called *compressed print*. Compare **expanded type**.

Compute! (1979) A monthly magazine devoted to home and educational uses of computers.

computer Device for performing the sequences of arithmetic and logical processes used in typesetting to store information and make the mathematical, grammatical, and typographic spacing and end-of-line decisions, i.e., hyphenation and justification. *See also* **analog computer; digital computer; home computer; laptop computer; mainframe; microcomputer; personal computer; transportable computer**.

computer-aided design A design developed with the aid of a computer. Abbreviated *CAD*.

Computer Aided Publishing Report A monthly trade newsletter on computer-aided publishing.

computer-assisted composition Digitized type recorded on a **magnetic medium** and run through a computer, where line-ending, hyphenation, justification, and other typographic decisions are carried out. *See also* **CRT composition; photocomposition; photomechanical composition**.

computer bureau An agency that runs other people's work on its own computer and often provides other consulting and assistance services. *See also* **service bureau**.

computer data-storage device Any device—a **disk** or **tape**, for example—used to store **data**.

computer graphics The creation, storage, and manipulation of models of pictures or diagrams— as opposed to letters and numbers— on the **display screen** or **hardcopy output device**. *See also* **bit-mapping**; **graphics characters**; **high-resolution graphics**; **low-resolution graphics**; **user-defined graphics characters**.

Computer Graphics World (1978) A monthly magazine covering all aspects of computer graphics technology.

computer-human interface *See* **human-computer interface**.

computer language A system of signs and symbols for **programming** and interacting with a computer. *See also* **assembly language**; **Beginner's All-Purpose Symbolic Instruction Code**; **C**; **FORTRAN**.

computer network A computer communications system consisting of: (1) one or more **terminals** communicating with a single **host computer** which acts as the **controller** for the **network** system, or (2) one or more intelligent nodes that are able to communicate without a central machine (server) for sharing of resources such as data, programs, large disk storage units, fast or high-quality printers, etc.

computer operator A person skilled in the operation of the computer and associated **peripheral device equipment**. Also called *operator*.

computer peripherals The auxiliary devices— high-speed **printers**, **scanners**, and **laser printers**— under control of a computer.

Computer Pictures (1983) A bimonthly publication for business, broadcast, advertising, and production executives and technical and engineering specialists who communicate using computer graphics.

computer program The series of **instructions** that cause a computer to perform a particular operation or task.

Computer Publishing and Advertising Report (1983) A biweekly newsletter for publishers of computer magazines and

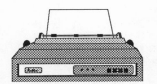

Fig. C-8   A printer is a computer peripheral.

books and computer advertisers and marketers.

computer security The preservation of computing resources against abuse or unauthorized use, especially the protection of data from accidental or deliberate damage, disclosure, or modification.

computer system Refers to the hardware components, such as the CPU, screen, keyboard, etc.

computer user group (1955) A group whose members share— via meetings, newsletters, trading equipment, and sharing programs— the knowledge they have gained and the programs they have developed on a computer or certain brand of computers. Also called *user group*.

computer vendor An organization that manufactures, sells, or services computer equipment.

Computeriter A monthly newsletter for **microcomputer** news and views for writers and editors.

computerized composition *See* **computer-assisted composition**.

computerized hyphenation A feature applying standard rules of grammar to automatically **hyphenate** words at the end of a typing line.

computerized typesetting *See* **computer-assisted composition**.

Computing for Business (1975) A monthly publication for the buyer and user of microcomputer hardware and software for business and professional applications.

CON The standard device name— an abbreviation for the **console**— by which **PC/MS-DOS** refers to the **keyboard** and **display** of IBM PC and **compatible** microcomputers. It embodies both the standard input and output devices.

concatenate (1598) To collect separate elements— such as files— into one.

concertina fold *See* **accordion fold**.

concordance (14c) An alphabetic list of words appearing in a document, with an indication of the place where they appear. Compare **index**.

condensed (15c) A narrow version of a regular typeface, which permits more material to be set in a line of the same width. About 60% of the width of standard characters.

condensed print *See* **condensed**.

condensed type *See* **condensed**.

CONFIG.SYS A **PC/MS-DOS** file containing statements specifying how the system defaults should be modified at **bootstrap** to create a particular system **configuration**. *See also* **buffer**; **BUFFERS**; **file**.

configuration (1) The arrangement of a computer system or network as defined by the nature, number, and the chief characteristics of its functional units. May refer to hardware configuration or software configuration. (2) The devices and programs that make up a system, subsystem, or network. (3) A program used to inform the application program what equipment is being used.

configure To set up or integrate the needed component parts of a computer system to fulfill the requirements of a specified application or group of applications.

confirmation letter A letter of agreement between a client and the writer spelling out terms of the writing **assignment, deadline,** rate and date of payment, etc. *See also* **letter of assignment**.

connect time The amount of time one has been connected to a **bulletin board** or **network**.

connector A coupling device that provides an electrical or mechanical junction between two cables, or between a cable and a chassis or enclosure.

consignment The placing of books in a store in which the publisher is paid only upon the sale of books.

console That part of the computer used for communication between the **operator** and the computer. Also called *keyboard.* Abbreviated **CON**.

console operator *See* **computer operator**.

constraint A type of **accuracy aid** that forces an **interactive input** into regular patterns. *See also* **axis constraint**; **gravity field**; **grid constraint**; **point constraint**.

constructional grid A two-dimensional array of vertical and horizontal lines, forming rectangles of varying size, into which a graphic **designer** may place either images or blocks of text. Frequently used ratios in making the subdivisions are: 1:1, 2:1, 3:2, and 5:3. *See also* **compositional grid**; **grid**.

consultant (1697) A person outside the company who is called in to give professional or expert advice.

consumer magazine General-interest magazine aimed at the **mass market**.

contact print (1890) Print or copy made in the same size as the original negative or master copy without the benefit of **enlargement** or **reduction**. It is made on sensitized paper by direct contact with the master or original. Also called *contact sheet.*

contact screen **Halftone** screen made on a film base with a graduated-dot pattern. The screen is placed in direct contact with the film or plate to obtain a halftone pattern from a **continuous tone** original. *See also* **crossline screen**.

contact sheet A sheet furnished by a photo lab on which the exposed frames from a roll of film are printed, usually in reduced size. Also called *proof sheet.*

contact size Size of a print or an image reproduced or copied in the same size as the original, without enlargement or reduction.

content editing The process of evaluating a manuscript for **style**, organization, and large general revisions. *See also* **copy editing**; **edit**; **levels of edit**.

contents (15c) *See* **table of contents**.

contents list *See* **index**.

context sensitivity A software technique that selects from a range of available information only that which is relevant to a user while he or she is in a particular location in the program.

contextual editing An editing technique in which a pattern is introduced into a text passage through repeated key words or phrases, allowing the reader to guess what will be said next. *See also* **edit**; **levels of edit**.

continued line *See* **jump line**.

continued story *See* **jump**.

continued table A **table** that involves the turning of a page or more to complete its reading. Also called *divided table*. *See also* **broadside table**; **doubled table**; **parallel table**.

continuous form One set of forms joined to another in a series of accordion-pleated folds. The sheets are fed into a printing press or other device, such as a computer printer, and are separated into individual sheets by tearing them apart along the lines of the perforations.

continuous paper Paper with rows of holes on each side and perforated between pages. The hole are grabbed by a **pin-feed platen** to feed the paper through a **printer**. Also called *fanfold paper*.

continuous-tone art A piece of **artwork** having gradations of tone from dark to light. Compare **line art**.

continuous-tone copy Any image—photographs, drawings, and paintings—that has a complete range of tones from black to white.

continuous-tone image *See* **halftone**.

continuous-tone negative A **negative** made in a camera without the use of a screen.

contour (1862) (1) Form of an object drawn in **outline**. (2) A photograph from which all the background has been removed. Compare **square up**.

Fig. C-9   Chanel, an image file provided with Ventura is a continuous-tone image.

contract An agreement between two or more persons that is legally binding. Compare **farm out**.

contraction (15c) Shortening a word by omitting letters other than the first and last.

contrast The amount of differentiation between dark areas and light areas. *Low contrast* indicates that tones are slightly defined; *high contrast* indicates tones readily identified from white through black.

contributing editor An out-of-the-office, regular or occasional staff writer or editor who is often paid a regular stipend or retainer, but may be paid only for contributions actually published.

contributor's page A page in a publication on which the editor discusses the writers contributing to that particular edition. *See also* **bionote**.

control ball *See* **track ball**.

control character An **ASCII** character that represents an action— such as a **backspace** on the screen, a **form feed** on the printer, or the ringing of a bell— rather than an **alphanumeric** character. They are typed by pressing a key down while the **Ctrl** key is depressed.

control code The **ASCII** codes— for printable characters and 33 other codes— for such functions as sounding the beeper and performing a **carriage return**.

control key A special function **keyboard** shift key, labeled **Ctrl**, which, in conjunction with another key, usually causes something to happen, rather than displaying a character on the screen.

control panel An **applications program** used to add or delete **fonts** and **printers**, change print connections and settings, and adjust **mouse** and screen settings on graphic user interfaces.

Control Program for Microcomputers (1977) The first **operating system** for general-purpose microcomputers developed by Digital Research. Abbreviated *CP/M*.

control word The basis for determining the sequence of the items. For example, to alphabetize a database by city using the "city" **field** as the control word. Also called *key*.

controlled field test A **documentation** test conducted within the unit or organization originating the documentation, or the close observation of a simulated use of the documentation. Compare **external field test**.

controller A device required by the computer in order to operate **peripheral equipment**. Also called *adapter card, board, controller card, interface card*.

controller card *See* **controller**.

controlling dimension Dimension, either horizontal or vertical, that determines the **enlargement** or **reduction** of an **image**.

conversational style A writing style using first- and second-person pronouns and contractions in an attempt to emulate human conversation.

cooperative advertising (1883) A program in which a **publisher** and a bookstore share the cost of book advertising, with the publisher paying the major share. Also called *allowance*.

cooperative publishing (1883) Several people— or more than one company— working together to put out a book. Also called *copublishing*.

coordination edit An editing activity in which an **editor** expedites the movement of a document through **production** and **distribution**. *See also* **edit**; **levels of edit**.

copper space Space one-half **point** thick, in various point sizes. Also called *hair space*.

coprocessor An auxiliary processor that performs time-consuming (usually higher mathematical computation) tasks to free the **central processing unit**, thus resulting in a faster execution time for the overall system.

copublishing *See* **cooperative publishing**.

COPY A **PC/MS-DOS** command that copies and combines files.

copy *v.* (1) To read data from a source, leaving the source unchanged, and to write the same data elsewhere in a physical form that may differ from that of the source. (2) A command to leave the original text where it is but take a snapshot of it and be ready to **paste** that copy elsewhere. *See also* **duplicate**. *n.* (1) Matter to be set or photographed for printing. (2) Any matter—including photographs, rules, designs, and text—used in any manner in reproduction for printing. (3) The original **manuscript** or **typescript** from which text is to be **keyboarded**. (4) The text of a book. *See also* **camera-ready copy**; **castoff**; **copyfitting**.

copy block A number of contiguous lines of type treated as a unit in **design** or in **makeup**.

copy casting Determining the number of words or characters in a given **manuscript**. *See also* **castoff**; **copyfitting**.

copy clarification edit An editing step that ensures that **instructions** to the **compositor** for typesetting or to the graphic artist for graphics are clear. *See also* **edit**; **levels of edit**.

copy desk (1921) A desk at which copy is edited.

copy edit (1899) Checking facts for accuracy and correcting such things as spelling, punctuation, and grammar.

copy editing (1899) Includes rewriting, revising, and polishing a **manuscript**, checking copy for fact, spelling, grammar, punctuation, clarity, and consistency of style before it goes to the **typesetter**. Usually the last editing of a manuscript before it is set in type. Compare **content editing**. *See also* **edit**.

copy editor (1899) In the traditional publishing process, one who **edits** and otherwise processes copy, controls grammar, and maintains consistency standards. Also called *copy reader*.

copy paper *See* **duplicator paper**.

copy reader (1892) One who edits and otherwise processes copy. Also called *copy editor.*

copy scaling *See* **copyfitting**.

copy to come An **instruction** to a compositor or operator that copy is missing from a particular place in the **manuscript** and will be sent later. Abbreviated *CTC*.

copy to go An **instruction** to a compositor or operator that the copy so marked is to be placed in a particular place in a **manuscript**'s final layout. Abbreviated *CTG*.

copyfitting (1) Making copy fit a predetermined space. (2) To determine the amount of copy that will fit in a given area on a page or in a publication. Also called *copy casting, copy scaling, castoff, casting up. See also* **character count**; **characters per pica**.

copyholder (1874) (1) Person who holds and reads aloud the original copy during **proofreading** while the proofreader marks the **proof** or the reproducible **camera-ready copy**. (2) A frame for holding copy. (3) A device that holds copy, especially for a **typesetter, compositor, or operator**.

copyreader *See* **copy reader**.

copyright *v.* (1806) To secure a copyright. *n.* (1735) The right of a person to retain or to sell copies of artistic work that he or she has produced. *See also* **copyright infringement**; **copyright notice**; **fair use**; **Universal Copyright Convention**.

copyright infringement (1735) Unauthorized and illegal use of **copyrighted** material. *See also* **fair use**; **plagiarism**.

copyright notice A notice required by law to protect publicly distributed information. It must include the symbol ©, the word *copyright* or the abbreviation *copr*. The first year in which the work is published follows. Next comes the name of the copyright holder.

copyright page The page of a book bearing the **copyright notice**.

copywrite (1) The initial writing of a manuscript. Compare **copy editing**. (2) To write

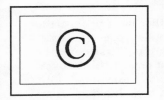

Fig. C-10 The copyright symbol is a notice of copyright protection.

advertising copy, literature, or short items needed in the composition of a publication—captions, explanatory notes, filler, etc.

copywriter (1911) A writer of advertising or publicity copy.

corner style *See* **rounded-corner tool**.

correction fluid A liquid cover-up, applied over an error, that blends into the paper.

correction marks Conventional signs used by printers, editors, and designers to indicate typographic changes. *See also* **proofreader's marks**.

correction overlay An **overlay** containing corrections.

corruption The mutilation of **code** or **data** caused by hardware or software failure.

COSMEP *See* **Committee of Small Magazines, Editors, and Publishers**.

counter (15c) In typography, the space within a character that is enclosed—wholly or partly—by the strokes of a letter, such as the **bowl** of the *b, d, p*.

counting keyboard In phototypesetting, an input **keyboard** that adds up the unit widths of the characters and spaces set and indicates the space used and the space remaining on a line. The keyboard operator must make all **end-of-line decisions** regarding **hyphenation** and **justification**. The counting keyboard produces a perforated paper tape used to drive a typesetting machine. Compare **noncounting keyboard**.

COUNTRY A **PC/MS-DOS** command that selects the date and time format in a **configuration file** used at system boot-up.

courtesy line *See* **credit line**.

cover (14c) *v.* To gather facts or report on an event. *n.* (1) The outer pages of a magazine. *See also* **cover plug; first cover; fourth cover; second cover; third cover**. (2) The outside pages of a document. (3) The two hinged parts of a book binding, front and back. Also, the four surfaces making up the covers in this sense.

cover letter The letter that accompanies a **manuscript** and explains the nature of the **submission** and any conditions arising from the author's dealings with the publisher.

cover materials Flexible **paper** and **boards**, such as leather, cloth, paper, or plastic, used to form the cover in **case binding**.

cover paper Heavy, decorative paper used for covering publications.

cover plug Special emphasis on the first cover for one or more stories.

cover stock Paper, generally thicker than book paper, used for the covers of pamphlets, brochures, paperbacks, etc.

cpi *See* **characters per inch**.

CP/M *See* **Control Program for Microcomputers**.

cpp *See* **characters per pica**.

cps *See* **characters per second**; **cycles per second**.

CPU *See* **central processing unit**.

CR *See* **carriage return**.

crash An uncontrolled system **shutdown**—possibly destroying data and software and even equipment—caused by a hardware malfunction or a software mistake. *See also* **head crash**.

crash finish Linenlike paper **finish**, whose appearance is generally considered one of good taste.

creasing (1588) Breaking fibers of heavy paper and cover stock with a blunt rule in a straight line. The fold resulting therefrom will not break the fibers too much and cause an uneven fold. Creasing improves the endurance of sheets that must be folded. *See also* **crimping**.

credentials (1674) (1) Writer's identification papers, used to establish credibility with subjects to be interviewed or with editors. (2) Press cards.

credit line (1926) A line, note, or name that acknowledges the source of an illustration. Also called a *courtesy line*.

credit memo A statement that shows customers they have credit for returned merchandise.

credits A list of a writer's or artist's published material. Compare **portfolio**.

crimping (14c) Creasing paper, especially at a **binding edge** where pages fold, so that the pages will be exposed and the book will open easily. *See also* **creasing**.

cromalin A **proof**, resembling a color print, that enables a quality check of a **four-color separation** before printing.

crop To eliminate part of a **photograph** or **illustration** by trimming its edges to make photograph or illustration fit in a given space, or to remove unnecessary parts of the a photograph or illustration. *See also* **crop mark**.

crop mark Cross marks at the outside of a **photograph** or **illustration**, usually placed on the mounting of the copy that designates the area of the copy to be used. They should appear on all illustrations at each of the four corners, marking the vertical and horizontal dimensions of the image area. Especially useful on pages that are **backed up**. Also called *trim marks, register marks*.

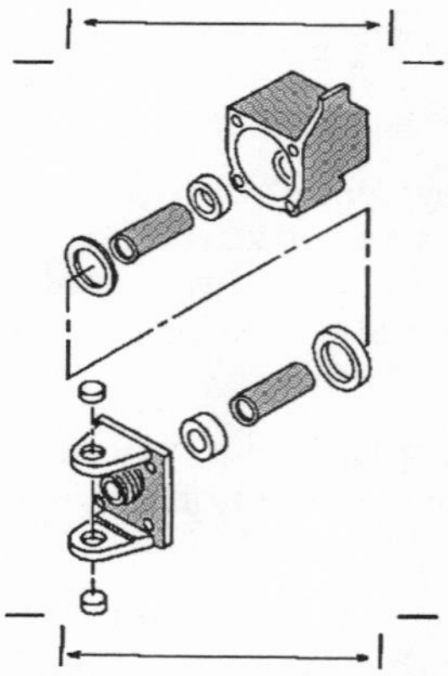

cropping tool Tool used to trim a graphic.

cross-grain binding *See* **against the grain**.

cross-grain folding *See* **against the grain**.

cross hairs (1884) Two lines intersecting at right angles to assist in precise aiming or centering of an instrument.

cross-index (1892) To **index** an item under a second or under more than one **heading**.

cross-reference (1834) A direction to a reader to refer to related matter in another part of a publication.

cross-section grid *See* **square grid**.

Fig. C-11   The arrows point to the four sets of crop marks, which delineates the page area to be used.

cross-section view (1844) Technical illustration of an object in which all or part of the object is cut away to show the shape and construction of the cutting plane and the relationship of adjacent parts.

crossbar The shape of the pointer in **PageMaker** when the tool for drawing lines and shapes has been selected.

crosshatching (1822) Shading consisting of crisscrossed sets of parallel lines applied to an area of an image.

crosshead (1827) A centered **subhead**. *See also* **bank head**; **main head**.

crossline screen Older type of screen used in halftone platemaking. Also called *ruled glass screen*. *See also* **contact screen**; **halftone screen**.

CRT *See* **cathode-ray tube**; **cathode-ray tube display**.

CRT composition Typesetting in which type images are electronically produced and displayed on a **cathode-ray tube display** from which they are transferred to film or photosensitive paper or a laser printer.

CTC *See* **copy to come**.

CTG *See* **copy to go**.

Ctrl *See* **control key**.

Ctrl-Break The **PC/MS-DOS** key combination that causes some programs in progress to terminate. Entered by holding down the **Ctrl** key and pressing the **Break** key.

Ctrl-C Same as **Ctrl-Break** in **PC/MS-DOS** microcomputers.

Ctrl-Num Lock The key combination that shifts the **numeric keypad** on **PC/MS-DOS** keyboards between the **cursor** control and numeric entry modes.

Ctrl-P *See* **Ctrl-Print Screen**.

Ctrl-Print Screen The **PC/MS-DOS** key combination that controls simultaneous displaying and printing (out of LPT1) of characters sent to the screen (console). Also called *print echo*. Pressing *Ctrl-Print Screen* once causes PC/MS-DOS to begin echoing everything that is sent to the display; pressing *Ctrl-Print Screen* again causes DOS to stop echoing.

Ctrl-Z The key combination (or the F6 function key when issued from the **PC/MS-DOS** command line) that creates the special character (displayed as ^Z) that DOS uses to mark the **end of file**.

CTTY A **PC/MS-DOS** command that assigns **console** control to a **remote device**.

cumulative index (1605) An **index** showing all items appearing in a number of separate indexes.

cumulative supplement A **supplement** that includes all information contained in the preceding supplements of a publication and, therefore, supersedes them.

current directory The **directory** in which the **disk operating system** looks for files unless otherwise instructed.

current drive The **drive** containing the disk on which the **disk operating system** looks for a **directory** or file unless otherwise **instructed**.

current line The line on which the **cursor** is located.

current selection box In **Ventura**, an indicator that shows what item from the **assignment list** is currently assigned to the selected frame, paragraph, text, or graphic.

cursive (1861) Typeface resembling handwriting, but in which the letters are disconnected.

cursor (1) A position indicator. (2) In computer graphics, a movable marker used to indicate a position on a **display space**. (3) A displayed symbol that acts as a marker to help the user locate a point in text, in a system command, or in storage. (4) A movable spot of light on the screen of the **display device**, usually indicating where the next character is to be entered, replaced, or deleted. *See also* **physical input device cursor**.

cursor arrow The keyboard keys, also called *directional arrows*, that direct movement of the cursor on the screen:

- cursor down— move the cursor down
- cursor left— move the cursor to the left
- cursor right— move the cursor to the right
- cursor up— move the cursor up

cursor control The ability to move a **cursor** or video display **prompt** character to any position on the screen.

cursor control keys The keys that control the movement of the cursor.

curve chart Graphical representation that uses curves to reflect values such as time, distance, or any other condition desired. *See also* **bar chart**; **column chart**; **pie chart**; **surface chart**.

curve-linear graphics Images that are defined by a series of equations that describe the length, shape, and direction of a line to be drawn. Also called *vector-based graphics*. Compare **bit-mapped graphics**.

custom In **PageMaker**, describes unequal columns, which can be created by **dragging** column guides into the desired position.

custom software Software designed and created specifically for the user to satisfy a particular function. Compare **canned software**.

cut *v.* (1) To remove text or pictures from one location, perhaps to move them to another spot, perhaps to eliminate them. *See also* **paste**. (2) To shorten copy. *n.* A **letterpress printing** term originally referring to a *woodcut* but now generally used to denote a zinc etching, halftone engraving, or other illustrative matter. *See also* **engraving**.

cut and paste (1) In **computer graphics**, moving an item or text to a new location on the **display device**. (2) In conventional layout, cutting copy or artwork from one place and pasting it down on another page to fill a defined space. (3) In **desktop publishing**, to move text from one place to another but deleting it from the original place and then inserting it in its final resting place.

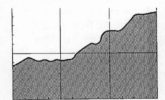

Fig. C-12   A curve chart uses curved lines to show progressions.

cut card Cardboard die-cut to standard and exact sizes.

cut dummy Cut **proofs** of **illustrations** arranged in sequence to facilitate page **makeup**.

cut flush Trimming the **cover** of a document at the same time and to the same size as the inside pages.

cut-in initial (1883) *See* **initial down**.

cut-in head (1) A **head** set on a horizontal space that cuts across the full width of a table and is often set off by rules. Also called *table spanner*. (2) A head that is cut into the first line of type, much as are the entries in this dictionary.

cut-in sidehead A **subhead** cut into a block of text so that text wraps around the subhead.

cut-off rule A **rule** used to separate **advertisements** in publications.

cut-out halftone *See* **outline halftone**.

cut-out lettering Self-adhering transfer type carried on **acetate** sheets that is cut out and placed on the working surface.

cut-sheet feeder An optional device that automatically feeds single sheets of paper into a printer.

cutline (1943) (1) An **instruction** to the printer to insert an illustration during **makeup**. (2) A **legend**, or explanation, that accompanies an illustration or photograph. Also called *caption*.

cutting copy *See* **copyfitting**.

cyan (1889) A greenish blue color, one of the four colors used in **process color printing**.

cyberphiliac A compulsive computer programmer.

cyberphobia A fear of computers.

cycles per second In electricity, the number of complete alternations of a current that changes from positive to negative and back again. *See also* **alternating current**; **direct current**.

cylinder press Style of **letterpress** machine that prints by the action of a cylinder on a flat type **form**. *See also* **flatbed press**.

Notes and New Words

D

dagger (14c) The symbol †, used to key text or tabular matter to a footnote. It is the second of a series of **reference marks**. Also called *diesis*. *See also* **asterisk; double dagger**.

daisy wheel (ca. 1978) The printing element in a **daisy-wheel printer**: a serrated plastic or metal disk around which is arranged a set of fully-formed print characters that are embossed on spokes radiating from a central hub.

daisy-wheel printer A computer printer that uses a metal or plastic **daisy wheel**. *See also* **dot-matrix printer; impact printer; letter-quality printer**.

dandy roll On **papermaking** machines, a wire gauze cylinder that imparts the laid lines or **watermark** into the partially formed paper.

dash (14c) (1) A punctuation mark used as a **hyphen** for dividing words. (2) A punctuation mark used to make a dotted line for coupons and the like.

data (1954) General term for any collection of information (facts, numbers, letters, symbols, etc.) used as **input** for or desired as **output** from a computer.

data bank *See* **database**.

data base *See* **database**.

data bit A signal used in **serial communications** to represent the transmission of a character. Seven or eight data **bits** can be used to represent one character. Also used to reference a specific bit, such as "data bit 7." *See also* **byte**.

data bus A **bus** that interconnects the **central processing unit**, storage, and all **input/output devices** of a computer system for the purpose of exchanging data. *See also* **address bus**.

data channel A communications link between two devices or points.

data communication equipment Any device employing an **RS-232** serial communication link whose port connector is wired in a particular fashion. **Data terminal equipment** is wired in the opposite configuration. Abbreviated *DCE*.

data compression A technique that saves computer storage space by eliminating empty fields, gap redundancies, or unnecessary data to reduce the size or the length of records.

data conversion The process of changing data from one form of representation to another.

data dump A **troubleshooting** feature wherein each code that a computer or printer receives in the data dump mode is printed in hexadecimal notation. Also called *hex dump*.

data entry The method of entering data into a computer system for processing, usually via terminal applications.

data entry device Any equipment used to prepare data so that the computer can accept it.

data entry operator A person who uses a **keyboard** device to transcribe data into a form suitable for processing by a computer.

data field The column or consecutive columns used to store a particular piece of information.

data file A **file** that contains the data needed by a program. The data may be numbers, text, or a combination of the two.

Data Interchange Format A standard format that allows files created on one system to be retrieved by another. A type of output used by many spreadsheet programs. Abbreviated *DIF*.

data leakage Illegal removal of data from a computer facility. *See also* **data security**.

data points Symbols for plotting events or other information on **graphs** and **charts**. A **legend** or **key** explains the meaning of each point.

data processing (1954) In computer technology, handling stored information so as to produce some intended result, as combining keyboarded text copy and **makeup** instructions with font data to produce a typeset page. Abbreviated *DP*.

data protection Measures to safeguard data from undesired occurrences that intentionally or unintentionally lead to destruction, modification, or disclosure of **data**. *See also* **data leakage; data security**.

data rate The transfer rate at which a **channel** carries data.

data security The protection of data from accidental or malicious destruction, disclosure, or modification. *See also* **computer security; data leakage; data protection; disk library**.

data storage The use of any medium for storing data.

data tablet The flat working surface used in **computer graphics** for the input—with a **stylus** or a **puck**—of coordinate information. Also called *digitizing tablet*.

data terminal A point in a computer system or data communications **network** at which data can be entered or retrieved. *See also* **terminal**; **video terminal**.

data terminal equipment Any device employing an **RS-232** serial communication link whose port connection is wired in a particular fashion. **Data communication equipment** is wired in the opposite configuration. Abbreviated *DTE*.

data transfer The movement, or copying, of data from one location and the storage of the data at another location.

data transfer rate The average number of **bits**, **characters**, or **blocks** per unit of time transferred from one data source to another.

databank (ca. 1966) *See* **database**.

database (1967) (1) Generally, the mass storage of information which may be selectively retrieved from a computer. (2) A computer **file** containing a wide range of information on a single subject or related subjects, organized in such a way that it can be **accessed** according to a number of different criteria, or by **key words** or phrases. (3) A program that keeps track of such information. Also called *databank. See also* **online database**.

database management The creation, updating, organizing, and accessing of database files.

database, online *See* **online database**.

database publishing The process of distributing information that has been generated from a computer database.

DATE A **PC/MS-DOS** command that displays and sets the system date.

date line Printing of a date on any page.

dateline (1888) A line in a written document or a printed publication giving the date and place of composition or issue.

daughter board A **printed circuit board** that plugs into a **motherboard**.

OAKLAND, Calif.—The Oakland Athletics beat the Boston Red Sox 4-1, winning the American League pennant and earning its first trip to the World Series since 1974.

Fig. D-1   This story is introduced by a dateline.

DB-25 A style of cable connector often used for **RS-232** printers or other peripheral device connections.

dba *See* **doing business as**.

DC *See* **direct current**.

DCA *See* **document conversion architecture**.

DCE *See* **data communication equipment**.

de-select *See* **deselect**.

dead matter In **hot-metal composition**, lead type masses, plates, cuts, etc., that are no longer required and may be melted down for reuse of the lead. Also called *dead type*, *killed matter*. Compare **alive matter**.

dead time *See* **downtime**.

dead type *See* **dead matter**.

deadline (1864) The last day or hour on which a **manuscript** or **artwork** must be in the hands of the publisher. The cut-off date by which a task must be completed.

deadwood (1) Superfluous verbiage in a manuscript. (2) Useless information in files.

deaerate In printing and reproduction work, to remove the air between sheets of stock, particularly by the use of **joggers**.

DEBUG A **PC/MS-DOS** command that provides facility for displaying and modifying files directly.

debug To trace and correct defects in a computer system. *See also* **bug**; **DEBUG**; **glitch**; **structured programming**.

decimal (1651) The numbering system most commonly used in counting, which uses the ten digits from 0 to 9. *See also* **base**; **binary digit**; **hexadecimal**; **numbering system**; **octal**.

decimal tab A tab that **aligns** a column of numbers on their decimal points, making it convenient to add or compare them.

decision In computer technology, a choice or series of choices, between alternatives, made by comparing new data with stored **in-**

structions, such as a hyphenation and justification program for **typesetting**.

decked heads Used in **tables** to categorize certain groupings of columns and to avoid repeating words in **column heads**. *See also* **spanner head**.

deckle (1816) In hand **papermaking**, a frame that keeps the liquid pulp from flowing over the side of the wire mold. In machine papermaking, a moving rubber *deckle strap* serves the same purpose.

deckle edge A natural uncut feathery edge of paper as it comes from the machine or the rough natural edge of handmade paper. Also called *featheredge*.

deckle strap *See* **deckle**.

dedicated Programs, machines, or procedures that are designed for a special use.

dedicated computer A computer whose use is reserved for a particular task.

dedicated computer system A computer and all of its related equipment that is used for a specific task.

dedicated device A device that is designed to perform only certain functions and cannot be programmed or changed to perform other functions.

dedicated lines (1) Telephone lines leased for exclusive use by a group or individual for **telecommunications**. The user pays a set fee rather than per-call or per-minute charges for leased lines. (2) Also applies to AC power lines within a building for the exclusive use of a computer system.

dedicated word processor A hardware and software combination intended exclusively for **word processing**.

dedication (14c) Brief inscription in which an author dedicates a book, usually in personal terms, to someone of his family, kin, or acquaintance. The dedication appears on a separate page in the **front matter**.

deep-etch halftone *See* **highlight halftone**.

deep-etch plate In **offset lithography**, a working plate on which the image is etched very slightly below the nonprinting surface. Deep-etch plates give high-quality reproduction of fine detail and permit very long press runs.

deep menu A set of interconnected menus presented as a series of hierarchical user decisions. For example, the first menu might solicit from the user whether he or she wants to inquire about a page; subsequent menus would then allow the user to specify progressively his or her page choice. Compare **wide menu**.

defamation (14c) A legally actionable attack—either written or spoken—that tends to injure a person's reputation. *See also* **libel**.

default Values or settings that take effect when a computer is turned on, reset, or initialized, or when a program is run. Usually, the default settings may be changed by the operator.

degauss (1940) To demagnetize a magnetic tape, disk, heads, or the tape path hardware by use of a **degausser**.

degausser (1940) A coil momentarily energized by an alternating current that rearranges the signals on magnetic media or associated hardware, or the internal shadow mask of a color **CRT**. Also called *bulk eraser*.

dejagging A computer graphics technique for smoothing the lines, characters, and **polygons** to remove the staircase effect caused by insufficient spatial resolution. Also called *antialiasing*.

Del key *See* **Delete key**.

dele *See* **delete**.

DELETE A **PC/MS-DOS** command that deletes files from a disk. Also called *erase, flush. See also* **ERASE**.

delete *v.* (1) In computer file management, to remove, eliminate, or erase an item, record, or group of records. (2) To erase a program from memory. (3) *See* **DELETE**. *n.* A **proofreader's mark** indicating that a letter, word, phrase, sentence, or paragraph is to be deleted. Abbreviated *dele*.

delete character A **control character** used primarily to obliterate an erroneous or unwanted character. Also called *erase*.

Delete key A keyboard key that enables text already recorded on the recording medium or in storage to be erased. *See also* **backspace**.

delimiter (1962) A character that marks the boundary. For instance, the space character is a delimiter because it often sets off one word from another.

delineate (1) In graphic arts, to give depth to line art by making certain outlines heavier. (2) To describe in detail.

delivery (1) The date a manuscript is to be given to a publisher. *See also* **deadline**. (2) The date a printed work is to be ready for pickup.

demographics (1966) A profile of a group (readers, listeners, viewers, etc.) documenting such things as age, sex, marital status, education, socioeconomic level, hobbies, and so forth.

dense writing Writing in which information that would be more effectively communicated in lists or tables is placed in paragraph form.

density In general terms, the relative visual darkness of an image area.

density range Measured difference between the minimum and maximum densities of a particular negative or positive. Also called *density scale*.

density scale *See* **density range**.

department A regular **column** or page.

descender (1802) That part of five **lower-case** letters that fall below the **baseline** of the letter: *g, j, p, q,* and *y*. *See also* **ascender**.

descender line In typography, the hypothetical line that connects the bottoms of **descenders**.

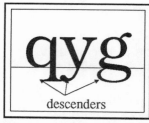

Fig. D-2 Descenders are letters that fall below the baseline.

descriptor (1951) In information retrieval, a word used to categorize or index information. Also called *key word*.

deselect To select another command or option or to click on a blank area of the **screen** to cancel the current selection. To reverse an **icon** from a **selected** (highlighted) state to an **unselected** (normal) **state**.

design (1548) To devise for a specific function or end and to arrange the elements and details in a publication to achieve that function or end. *See also* **layout**; **typography**.

designer In the traditional publishing process, one who makes decisions about **typography**, **layout**.

desired photo area The area of a photograph to be reproduced in a book.

desk accessory **GEM** application— such as graphics, word processing, spreadsheets, etc.— started by choosing its name from the desktop menu or from a comparable menu in another GEM application.

desktop A blank **PageMaker** screen that appears before any publication is brought in.

desktop computer A small, complete computing system consisting of a **microprocessor**, **input** and **output devices**, and storage. Also called *microcomputer, personal computer*.

desktop publish To publish using a **desktop publishing** package.

desktop publisher (1) A page layout application that integrates text and graphics on a **microcomputer**. Examples include Xerox **Ventura** Publisher Edition, Ready,Set,Go!, **PageMaker**, FrameMaker, TeXet, Xyvision, DocuPro, etc. (2) One who uses a desktop publishing application to publish newsletters, books, brochures, etc.

Desktop Publisher... (1986) A newsletter of the International Desktop Publishers Association.

desktop publishing Use of personal computers and software applications that allow integration of text and graphics with true typesetting standards to produce documents faster and cheaper with more control than through the normal publishing process. Also called *electronic publishing, electronic technical publishing, page composition.* Abbreviated *DTP.*

Desktop Publishing and Office Automation A buyer's guide and handbook published monthly for desktop publishing and office automation personnel.

Desktop Publishing Association A professionally managed national user's group for **desktop publishers**.

destructive cursor On a **display device**, a **cursor** that erases any character through which it passes as it is advanced, back-spaced, or otherwise moved.

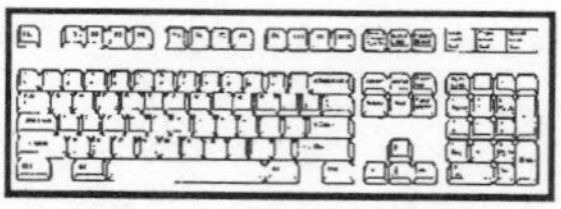

Fig. D-3   A detachable keyboard

detachable keyboard A **keyboard** that is not built into the same case as the video display. It connects to the video display with a cable and allows greater flexibility in positioning the keyboard.

development documentation Documents that function very much like the technical blueprints of a house, designed for an experienced and technical audience.

DEVICE A **PC/MS-DOS** command entered as a command line within the **CONFIG.SYS** file to specify the name of a file containing a **device driver**, which is loaded upon **boot-up**.

device A piece of computer equipment, such as a **display** or a **printer**, that performs a specific task.

device coordinates Coordinates determined and assigned by a user with an **input device**.

device driver A program that controls the sending of information to or receiving it from a hardware device, such as a **mouse** or **printer**, attached to a computer.

device name The name by which the **disk operating system** refers to a device. In **PC/MS-DOS**, PRN indicates the device (usually a printer) connected to the first parallel port (LPT1). Device names are treated like filenames by DOS.

devil The youngest apprentice in a printing shop. Also called *printer's devil*.

diacritic (1866) An accent through or near a character or combination of characters indicating a phonetic value. Common diacritics are:

- acute accent (é)
- grave accent (à)
- circumflex (â)
- tilde (ñ)
- hacek (ô)
- diaeresis (ü)
- cedilla (ç)

diaeresis A **diacritic** that indicates a sound value. For example, the ö in Törangel.

diagnostic A program used to evaluate the condition of a computer or computer device by comparing the hardware against a known set of software instructions.

diagonal *See* **virgule**.

diagonal-line tool Tool used to draw a straight line in any direction.

diagram dummy A draft of a publication that is careful and complete. *See also* **dummy**.

dialog *See* **dialog box**.

dialog box A window or full-screen display that appears in response to a command that calls for setting options. The way most desktop publishing programs communicate with users. *See also* **menu**.

diamond Old type size, now equal to 4.5 points.

diapositive (1893) A positive photographic print on a transparent material, i.e., film or glass, not paper.

diazo proof (1878) Photographic proofing process used to produce **photoproofs** and high-quality **photorepros** from film positives.

dictionary (1) Synonym for **proofreader**, or **spell checker**. (2) In computer-assisted typesetting, an **exception dictionary**, which can be user made or from algorithms. (3) Words of a language, arranged in alphabetical order, with definitions, etymologies, pronunciations, and other information. Also called *lexicon.*

Didot Typographic system of measurement used in most European countries. 12 Didot points = 1 Cicero = 4.511 mm = 12.835 points. Named after Françoise Ambroise Didot (1730–1804), its inventor. Compare **Anglo-American point system; Cicero.**

die cut The process of cutting regular or irregular shapes out of paper by the use of specially fashioned steel knives. The result may be a "door" that can be folded back or a hole in the paper.

die-stamping Intaglio printing done by means of a hard metal die used to color or **blind stamp** covers, cards, letterheads, etc.

diesis (1706) A punctuation mark (‡) used as a **reference mark.** Also called *double dagger.*

DIF *See* **Data Interchange Format**

differential letterspacing *See* **proportional spacing.**

digital computer (1947) A computer that operates with numbers expressed directly as digits. Compare **analog computer.**

digital graphics Artwork, such as **spot art** that identifies new topics in text as a code or symbol would. *See also* **iconic graphics.**

digital image processing *See* **image processing.**

digitize (1953) To convert an image to an array of dots that can be stored in the computer. *See also* **scanned-image file.**

digitizer (1953) A specific input device that converts information into a series of dots, which the eye perceives as shades of gray.

digitizing tablet An input device with a flat surface and a mechanism that converts indicated positions or drawn figures on the tablet's surface into computer-readable information. Also called *data tablet.*

dimension drawing Cross-sectional illustration used in overhaul and maintenance technical manuals to instruct personnel how to inspect, repair, and replace parts of equipment so that the equipment may be kept within designed operating tolerances. Also called *inspection drawing*.

dimension marks L-shaped points or short marks on **mechanicals** or **camera-ready copy** outside the area of the image to be reproduced, between which the size of reduction or enlargement is marked.

dimensioning *See* **scale**.

dingbat (1904) A typographical symbol or ornament. For example, ✠, ☞, ↻, and ❶. Traditionally, these characters are used for decoration or as special characters within text. Usually available as a font, i.e., **Zapf Dingbats**.

DIP switch *See* **dual in-line package switch**.

diphthong (15c) Two vowels joined, as æ and œ.

diploma paper Fine printing paper manufactured especially for greeting cards, official documents, certificates, awards, diplomas, and the like. Also called *art parchment*.

DIR A **PC/MS-DOS** command that lists a **directory** of filenames on the designated **disk** to the **display device**.

dir *See* **directory**.

direct access Entering or retrieving **data** from a **storage device** in such a way that the process depends only on the location of that data and not on a reference to data previously accessed. Compare **serial access**.

direct current (ca. 1889) An electric current, usually constant in value, moving in one direction only. Compare **alternating current**.

direct-entry keyboard A **keyboard** connected directly with a typesetting device, used primarily in connection with **computer-assisted composition**, but it implies equally

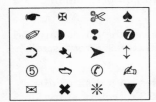

Fig. D-4   Examples of dingbats.

to a **typewriter** or **Linotype** keyboard. *See also* **offline keyboard**.

direct-image composition Any form of **typesetting** that produces an image directly, such as **typewriter**, **filmset**, or **laser printing**.

direct impression A printing impression in which the printing surface comes into direct contact with paper. Compare **offset impression**.

direct mail (1923) Literature or promotional material mailed by an advertiser directly to an addressee, usually to promote or sell a product or a service.

directional arrow Moves the **cursor** around the screen. Also called *cursor arrow, scroll arrow*.

directory A list of **files** on a **disk** or **diskette**. The **PC/MS-DOS** directory entry for each file includes the file's name, extension, size, date and time it was created or last changed, and the location of the beginning of the file. All but the last item are displayed by the **DIR** command. Abbreviated *dir. See also* **directory pathname**; **parent directory**; **root directory**; **subdirectory**.

directory pathname The complete name by which the directory is known. The pathname gives the sequence of directories by which the directory is linked to the **root directory**.

dirty copy Heavily edited or **marked-up copy** or **proof** that is difficult to read and heavy with errors or corrections. Compare **bad copy**. Compare **clean copy**.

dis *See* **distribute**.

disc *See* **disk**.

discount books *See* **remainders**.

discrete justified tape In photocomposition, a tape that indicates the widths of space required within each line **measure** as well as the ends of lines. Compare **range justified tape**.

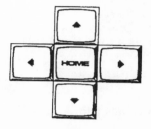

Fig. D-5   Directional arrows on the keyboard.

discretionary hyphen A **hyphen** inserted by an **operator** to divide a word when there is insufficient space to produce the whole of that word at the end of a line. The hyphen appears on the screen and on the printed page only if the hyphen falls at the end of a line. *See also* **hyphenation**.

disk (1962) A magnetically-coated, data storage device. Loosely refers to either a **hard disk** or a **diskette**. The information is stored and recalled with the aid of a **disk drive**. *See also* **disk pack**; **fixed disk**; **floppy disk**; **disk operating system**; **operating system**.

disk accessing The process used in transferring data to and from a **disk file**. *See also* **read**; **write**.

disk directory A list of all the files, containing either programs or data, on a computer **disk**. Ordinarily, the disk directory also contains information required by the computer's **operating system** for accessing the files, such as the specific **track** and **sector** of the disk at which a given file begins, how many sectors constitute the file as a whole, and whether or not the file is password-protected. *See also* **disk operating system**.

disk drive A storage device for holding electronic text. The mechanism for moving a **disk pack** or a **magnetic disk** and controlling its movement in order to read information from or write information to a computer disk. *See also* **drive letter**; **read**; **write**.

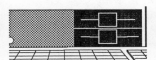

Fig. D-6   Two disk drives, one above the other.

disk file An associated set of records of the same **format**, identified by a unique **label**.

disk library A repository for dismountable recorded media, such as magnetic **disk packs** or **magnetic tapes**.

disk operating system A computer **program** containing routines that allow the computer user, and various programs, to interact with a computer's disk system. Abbreviated *DOS*. *See also* **Apple DOS**; **CP/M**; **disk directory**; **disk drive**; **TRS DOS**.

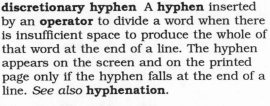

disk pack A removable assembly of flat, circular magnetic recording surfaces.

disk sector A pie-shaped area of disk storage containing some number of bytes of data.

DISKCOMP A **PC/MS-DOS** command that compares the contents of two **floppy disks**. It is used to verify a **DISKCOPY** operation.

DISKCOPY A **PC/MS-DOS** command that makes an exact duplicate copy of a disk.

diskette (1973) A flexible disk for storing files, made of thin plastic and enclosed in a protective jacket. Data is stored magnetically on the diskette's surface. A **floppy** is an 8-inch diskette; a **minifloppy** is a 5.25-inch diskette that holds 1.2 Mbytes; and a **microfloppy** is a 3.5-inch diskette that holds 1.44 Mbytes. *See also* **double sided, double density; double sided, high density; double sided, quad density; double sided, high capacity.**

diskette drive A disk drive used for diskettes.

diskette sleeve An envelope used to store diskettes to prevent accidental contact with the exposed surface. Also called *jacket.*

display (1) The screen on which the computer shows both what is typed at the **keyboard** and the result of its work. Also called *cathode-ray tube, video display unit. See also* **monitor.** (2) An instruction to a printer to set copy on its own line, apart from other copy. (3) *See* **display type.**

display advertisement An advertisement not placed under a **classified** heading with word-line advertisements. It may include **artwork** in addition to text **copy.**

display attribute In computer graphics, a particular property assigned to all or part of a **display,** for example, low density, green color, blinking status.

display blank Paper manufactured especially for show cards, posters, outdoor advertising, etc.

Fig. D-7   A display.

display board Heavy blank paper used for **display advertising**.

display column *See* **addressable vertical point**.

display composition Laying out text and graphics on a screen so that they fit into a design.

display device In computer graphics, a device capable of presenting **display elements** on a display surface such as a **cathode-ray tube, plotter,** or **printer**.

display element In computer graphics, a basic graphic element used to construct a display image, such as a dot, a line segment, or a character. Also called *graphic primitive*.

display field In computer graphics, an area in a display **buffer** or on a display space that contains a set of characters that can be manipulated or operated upon as a unit.

display group In computer graphics, a selectable portion of the **display field** that can be manipulated or operated upon as a unit.

display image *See* **screen image**.

display outer A package containing a number of smaller unit packages, whose outer one's main purpose is to be seen. Compare **shipping outer**.

display panel *See* **panel**.

display space In computer graphics, that portion of a **display surface** available for a display image. The display space may be all or part of the display surface. Also called *operating space*.

display surface In computer graphics, that medium on which display images may appear, such as the entire screen of a **cathode-ray tube**.

display type (1) Typefaces designed for use in **headlines** or other nontext— not for continuous reading— positions. (2) The larger sizes of any typeface (greater than 14 points), as distinct from **body text** sizes, which extend up to 12 or in some contexts, 14 points. (3) Advertisements including pictures and large sizes of type. Compare **classified advertisements**. (4) Materials for use in shops, showrooms, or exhibit displays.

diss *See* **distribute**.

distance roundoff An input technique to ensure accurate drafting, causing all design points to have coordinates measured in even increments. *See also* **accuracy aids**.

distribute (1) To take the individual pieces of type out of the **chase** one by one and distribute them to their proper compartments in the **case** to be used again. (2) To melt down machine-set **hot metal type** and Linotype **slugs** after they have served their purpose. Also called *kill*. (3) The process of placing a printed work into the hands of a likely reader. Abbreviated *dis*, *diss*.

distributor (1526) In the traditional publishing process, a person or group who sells or **distributes** copies to an audience. *See also* **jobber; wholesaler**.

dither matrix *See* **halftone cell**.

dithering (1) An **antialiasing** technique, used in **raster displays** in which color or intensity variations are introduced in order to create smooth lines or edges. (2) Descriptive of the transitional emotional state of a potential user who is becoming an actual user of computer graphics. (3) An image-processing technique that, when used by a printer or computer, produces **halftone** images that appear to have shades of gray.

divided table *See* **continued table**.

divider An **index guide**, such as stiff boards, serving as a partition between areas. Used as an aid for quick referencing.

document (1) Any writing created using **word processing** or **desktop publishing** programs. (2) A unified collection of information pertaining to a specific subject or related subjects. (3) In word processing, a collection of one or more lines of text that can be named and stored as a separate entity. (4) Text stored on disk and displayed on the screen, edited, and printed. Also called *copy*, *file*.

document assembly In word processing, a printing process of **merge** and **output** of recorded text in a predetermined sequence to form a complete, distinct document.

document conversion architecture A **document** format commonly used by systems such as DisplayWrite. Abbreviated *DCA*.

document directory *See* **directory**.

document format (1) Defines the way that text and image documents are stored. (2) The **layout** of a particular document.

documentation (1884) (1) A collection of documents on a given subject. (2) Any written or printed matter concerning the operation and internal functioning of a computer or computer program. (3) The management of documentation that may include the actions of identifying, acquiring, processing, storing, and disseminating them.

dodger Small **handbill**.

dogleg (1889) A **lead line** drawn off in one direction and turned at an angle to point to or indicate an item or to "callout" an item or part on an illustration, and, in most cases, ended in a **arrowhead**. Also called *bent lead line*.

doing business as A term used when a name other than one's own is the business' name. Abbreviated *dba*. *See also* **also known as; fictitious name statement**.

DOS (1977) (1) *See* **TRS DOS**. (1981) (2) *See* **PC-DOS**. (3) *See* **disk operating system**.

dot area Halftone pattern consisting of dots and the clear spaces between them. The area occupied by the dots is known as the *percentage of dot area*. In a checkerboard pattern the percentage of dot area is 50%.

dot chart *See* **scatter graph**.

dot density The number of dots per unit of measure in **dot-matrix printing**, usually expressed as **dots per character** or **dots per inch**.

dot graphics A graphic design formed by patterns of dots.

Page........... 12

Fig. D-8   Dot leaders lead the eye from one place to another.

dot leaders A line of dots used to guide the eye from one point to another. *See also* **leader**.

dot matrix (1963) A two-dimensional pattern of dots used for constructing a display image.

dot-matrix printer An **impact printer** that creates characters on a sheet of paper by printing only selected dots out of a rectangular matrix of dots, in a pattern that forms the desired letter or image. Most dot-matrix printers have 9-pin heads to form the letters. Newer ones have 24-pin heads. Also called *stylus printer*. *See also* **daisy-wheel printer; dot density; dots per character; laser printer; letter-quality printer; matrix**.

dots per character The number of dots in a **dot matrix** used to make a character.

dots per inch The method of measuring the **resolution** of **pixels** on a monitor screen or laser charges on paper. Abbreviated *dpi*.

double-click To click the **mouse button** twice in rapid succession Double-clicking is a fast way to open an **icon**.

double-coated paper Heavily coated paper not necessarily coated on two sides but may be double-coated on one side only.

double-column printing A page format in which two solid columns of text are printed on a page or in which a solid column of text and a column for side headings are printed on a page.

double dagger *See* **diesis**.

double-density A system of recording to a higher density in order to put more data on a given size of medium. For example, a double-density diskette stores twice as much information as a **single-density** diskette.

double-headed arrow The shape of the pointer tool when a handle, ruler guide, or column guide is being dragged.

double hyphen (1893) An editorial mark (=) that is used to make it clear to the **type-setter** than a **hyphen** is being asked for.

double image Two impressions of an entire image or of a portion of an image. The undesirable double image may be caused by pages touching each other during the press run while the ink is still wet.

double-page spread Two facing pages of text or pictures or both. Also called *center spread.*

double-panel A cartoon that comprises two **boxed in** illustrations. *See also* **multi-panel**; **single-panel**.

double quote A quotation mark ("). Compare **single quote**.

double-sided disk A disk with both surfaces available for the storage of data.

double-sided, double density A **floppy disk** that can be read from or written to on both sides, holding about 376,000 characters. Abbreviated *DSDD.*

double-sided, high capacity A **floppy disk** that can be read from or written to on both sides. Abbreviated *DSHC.*

double-sided, high density A **floppy disk** that can be read from or written to on both sides, holding about 1.2 million characters. Abbreviated *DSHD.*

double-sided page An option in **desktop publishing** programs for creating a publication to be reproduced on both sides of the sheets of paper. *See also* **facing page**; **single-sided page**.

double-sided publication A publication with pages reproduced on both sides of each sheet. *See also* **single-sided publication**.

double-sided, quad density A **floppy disk** that can be read from or written to on both sides. Abbreviated *DSQD.*

double spread *See* **center spread**; **double-page spread**.

double strike In **impact printing**, typing each character twice, which gives a darker, more solid impression. *See also* **boldface**.

double truck An editorial or advertising **layout** covering two pages made up as a single unit. *See also* **center spread**.

double width In **dot-matrix printing**, a print width in which each character is twice as wide as normal characters.

doubled table A table so long and narrow that it may be divided into two or more sections that are run side-by-side below the captions. *See also* **broadside table**; **continued table**; **parallel table**.

down A computer that is not running. It may be shut down for maintenance, there may be a hardware failure, or the operating system may have been disarranged by a runaway program.

downtime (1928) (1) Time when equipment is not in use due to malfunction. (2) Time spent waiting for materials, instructions, etc., during which printing is held up. (3) Time when personnel are not working and are charging time against an assignment or a work-order number. (4) Time spent waiting for materials, instructions, OKs, etc., during which work is held up. (5) Time when a supplier is not busy and may give better prices. Also called *dead time*.

download To temporarily **load** data into a device, usually loading software from one computer to another or loading fonts from a computer to a printer.

DP *See* **data processing**.

dpi *See* **dots per inch**.

draft (1) In writing, a preliminary version, used as a **rough draft** or **first draft** of a **manuscript**. (1714) (2) In layout, to compose a drawing or an illustration, usually with the intention of adding refinements after examination. (3) In dot-matrix printing, the use of a minimum number of **dots per**

character for high-speed printing. Compare **letter-quality printer**.

draft copy *See* **draft**.

drag In computer graphics, moving all or part of a **display group** in a **display space** in such a way that the group continuously follows the **pointer** as though it were attached.

drag-place To **drag** a **mouse** diagonally to define the width of a graphic or text while placing it and so override the **column guides**.

DRAM *See* **dynamic random access memory**.

drawn-on cover A card cover fixed to the **spine** of a publication.

draw-type graphics *See* **object-oriented graphics**.

dress The appearance of a publication.

Driography A 3M Company trade name for a method of **offset lithography** without moisture.

drive letter The letter that identifies a **disk drive**.

drive *See* **disk drive**.

drop (1) Generally, the vertical distance (as on a page) from one typographic or design element to another. (2) The distance from a chapter title to the first line of text.

drop cap *See* **drop initial**.

drop-down menu The **menu** commands that "drop down" in a list below the **menu bar** when touched by the **pointer**. Also called *pop-down menu*.

drop folio Page number appearing at the bottom of a page. *See also* **folio**.

drop initial An **uppercase initial letter** of a larger point size than the text, often **aligning** with the first two or three lines of text type. Also called *drop cap*. *See also* **baseline**; **hung initial**.

drop-out *See* **dropout**.

D esktop publishing is in its infancy.

Fig. D-9   A drop initial is aligned with the first two or three lines of text.

drop-shadow A tint or solid laid to one side of an illustration or type form to give a shadow effect.

dropout (1) **Halftone** negative, print, or plate from which certain areas in the original have been removed by **masking** or **opaquing**. A *silhouette dropout* is one in which the entire background has been removed to emphasize the central image. (2) A photograph reduced to black and white with no intermediate tones so that a line reproduction can be made from it. Also called *bleach-out*. (3) Blocking or masking out any undesirable or unwanted image area.

drum In older computer systems, a magnetic-surface shaped like a drum and used, like **disks**, for storing information.

drum printer (1966) A **line printer** in which the printing characters are part of a revolving drum.

dry finish A paper finish created using a dryer on the papermaking machine.

dry ink Very fine powder that forms the image in some copying processes and in **electrostatic screen printing**. In all cases, the ink must be fused by heat or chemical means to fix the image. Also called *powder ink, toner*.

dry offset A combination of the **letterpress** and **offset** methods of printing wherein a relief plate cylinder prints on a **blanket cylinder**, which then offsets the image onto the paper. Also called *letterset printing*.

dry printing *See* **blocking**.

dry-transfer Adhesive lettering or symbols added to **artwork** by hand.

DSDD *See* **double-sided, double density**.

DSHC *See* **double-sided, high capacity**.

DSHD *See* **double-sided, high density**.

DSQD *See* **double-sided, quad density**.

DTE *See* **data terminal equipment**.

DTP *See* **desktop publishing**.

dual disk drive A computer system that has two **disks** installed, but both cannot be used at the same time.

dual in-line package switch One of the small switches in an electronic device that controls various functions. Abbreviated *DIP*.

dull-coated paper Paper that has a dull finish on one side and a highly polished coat on the other. *See also* **coated paper**; **finish**.

dull coated-two-sides paper Paper having a **dull finish** but coated on both sides.

dull finish Matte paper finish without gloss or luster.

dull seal Typesetter's term for **stock** having an adhesive back.

dummy (1) Hand-drawn layouts that show the size, shape, and general style of a planned publication, including the positions of text, artwork, and captions. (2) A bound, unprinted, or only partially printed sample of a planned publication to show its size, shape, and general appearance. (3) A sample book made up to show bulk, size, binding, paper, etc. For example, a dummy book consisting of blank pages and cover can be used to determine the size of the jacket. *See also* **bulking dummy**; **diagram dummy**; **paste-up dummy**.

dummy device A device name used to simulate program operations. The **disk operating system** uses **NUL** as a dummy device name.

dummy publication (1928) Traditionally, a pencil **mock-up** of the pages of a publication, folded or stapled into a booklet, which the printer uses to verify the correct sequence of pages and positions of photographs. *See also* **template**; **thumbnail sketch**.

dummy signature sheets Blank **signature** sheets with numbers indicating where page **boards** should be placed.

dump *v.* To move the contents of a computer's memory for fault isolation purposes. *n.* (1) A display unit used in bookstores. *See also* **point-of-purchase**; **point-of-sale**. (2) The place where type matter is placed.

duotone A process for producing an illustration in two colors from a one-color original, giving a quality of added depth and texture. Also called *duplex halftone. See also* **moiré pattern**; **halftone**.

duplex *See* **full-duplex**; **half-duplex**; **modem**.

duplex board Heavy paper that is colored on one side and white or a different color on the other side.

duplex halftone *See* **duotone**.

duplex paper Paper having a different color or finish on each side of the sheet.

duplicate (1532) Identical copy of an original. Also called *reproduce. See also* **enlargement**; **reduction**.

duplicator (1893) (1) Any machine that makes copies of typed, drawn, or printed matter. (2) One who **duplicates**.

duplicator paper (1893) Paper designed specifically for use in **duplicators**. Also called *copy paper, master paper*.

dust cover (1899) *See* **dust jacket**.

dust jacket (1926) (1) A protective and attractive cover for hardback books, providing space for visual display and promotional copy. Also called a *dust cover*. In the rare-book trade usually called *dust wrapper*, abbreviated *dw. See also* **back flap**; **flap copy**; **front flap**. (2) Now archaic, blank page inserted at the end of a coverless book for the protection of the last page that contains copy.

dust wrapper (1932) *See* **dust jacket**.

Dvorak keyboard A keyboard arrangement that is easier and faster to use than the standard **qwerty keyboard**. *See also* **azerty keyboard**.

dw *See* **dust jacket**.

Fig. D-10 The Dvorak keyboard places the QWERTY letters on the row below the numbers.

dynamic random access memory A low-power semiconductor memory that retains its contents only by periodic, time-consuming refresh cycles from the **central processing unit**. Compare **static random access memory**. Abbreviated *DRAM, dynamic RAM.*

Notes and New Words

E

earmark character A distinctive letter in any typeface, which enables it to be easily recognized. For example, the flourished italic capital *Q* in Bookman or the *z* in Zapf Chancery. Also called *spot letter*.

EBCDIC *See* **Extended Binary Coded Decimal Interchange Code**.

echo To repeat a stream of characters. For example, the commands you type to the computer are echoed on the screen.

ed page *See* **editorial page**.

edit (1791) To modify or revise existing text or to prepare a **manuscript** for publication. It may include revision, rewriting, and checking for accuracy, as well as checking numerical sequence, marking for type, and making the style of the manuscript consistent. Spelling, punctuation, and grammar are also corrected. Modified **proofreader's marks** are used in editing the manuscript. *See also* **coordination edit; copy clarification edit; format edit; integrity edit;**

language edit; levels of edit; mechanical style edit; policy edit; substantive edit.

edited copy Copy marked up with corrections or amendments. *See also* **draft copy**; **final copy**.

editing and correcting terminal *See* **editing terminal**.

editing terminal In phototypesetting, a tape-operated **video display terminal**, using a cathode-ray tube on which the result of keyboarding captured on tape is displayed for editing purposes via its attached input keyboard prior to processing the copy in a typesetting machine. Also called an *editing and correcting terminal.*

edition One or more printings of a work that are basically the same. When a book is published for the first time, all copies are said to be the first, or original, edition. When an edition has been revised substantially, it is a second edition as well as the first revised edition. *See also* **copyright page**; **first edition**; **limited edition**; **reprint**; **revised edition**; **simultaneous editions**.

editor (1649) (1) In the traditional publishing process, one who controls the quality, content, and audience standards. (2) A program used to create or change text files. Also called *text editor.* Compare **copy editor, proofreader**.

Editor and Publisher: The Fourth Estate (1884) A weekly magazine focusing on journalism, advertising, and printing equipment.

editor-in-chief (1873) The top editorial executive in a publishing program, setting policy for that program and directing acquisitions.

editor's query A question to the author posed by the editor about points in a **manuscript** that are unclear or insufficiently developed.

editorial (1830) An article in a publication that expresses the views or opinions of the publishers or editors.

editorial page A page in a publication dedicated to personal expressions and observations and to disseminating a publication's **editorial slant**.

editorial planning Working out the details of a publication, including its page size, illustrations, use of color, printing process, editing, artists, and distribution.

editorial policy *See* **editorial slant**.

editorial slant A publication's viewpoint. Also called *editorial policy*.

editorialist (1901) One who writes **editorials**.

editorialize (1856) (1) Inserting one's opinion in a report of the facts. (2) To write one's opinion, as in an **editorial**.

EDLIN The **PC/MS-DOS** line editor used to create and edit files. It is a simple line editor provided as a standard DOS **utility**.

Education Press Association of America (1895) An association of editors of educational publications.

EEPROM *See* **electrically-erasable programmable read-only memory**.

EF *See* **English finish**.

EGA *See* **enhanced graphics adapter**.

eggshell finish A paper **finish** similar to the texture of an eggshell, applied to books or **boards**.

egoless writing The attitude a professional documenter should take on during the **review** and **field test** stages of documentation. An egoless writer seeks feedback as a necessary step for document creation.

Egyptian A family of type styles more frequently called **square serif**.

eject key A control that releases or moves the recording medium to a position for easy removal from the equipment.

electrically-erasable programmable read-only memory Semiconductor memory that retains its contents until subjected to a special erase signal. Once so erased, it can be reprogrammed. Abbreviated *EEPROM. See also* **erasable programmable read-only memory**.

elastomer keyboard *See* **tactile keyboard**.

electronic bulletin board A computerized telephone answering system that allows callers or **user group** members equipped with computers and **modems** to leave written messages, read messages left by earlier callers, and take advantage of other electronic services, such as access to free programs. *See also* **bulletin board system**.

electronic disk *See* **virtual disk**.

electronic filing The storage of information on magnetic media.

electronic mailing (1967) The ability to transmit documents over cables or phone lines via direct connections or **modems**. *See also* **bulletin board system**.

electronic publishing Publishing using a computer to enter text and graphics and to integrate them to produce typeset copy. Generally reserved for large systems. On microcomputers, also called *desktop publishing*.

Electronic Publishing and Bookselling A monthly newsletter providing information on computer systems that are serving publishers, booksellers, and information professionals.

Electronic Publishing and Printing (1986) A magazine about computer systems for businesses, educational institutions, nonprofit organizations, and government units that perform publishing and information distribution functions.

Electronic Publishing Business (1983) A monthly magazine devoted to electronic publishing.

electronic technical publishing The production and distribution of technical documents containing both text and graphics using **desktop publishing** systems. Abbreviated *ETP*.

electrostatic discharge The release of static electricity from a charged object to a grounded object. Abbreviated *ESD*.

electrostatic process A copying or printing process in which an image is deposited on a material by means of electrostatic forces. Common to all electrostatic methods is the **toner** that is used to form the image instead of the wet or paste ink used with conventional printing presses. *See also* **xerography**.

electrostatic screen printing A pressureless printing process in which a charge is placed on the printing element and an opposite charge on the plate, thus creating a field of attraction. The receiving substratum or article imposed within that field intercepts the **toner** as it travels to the opposite charge. *See also* **dry ink**.

electrotype (1840) A metal printing plate cast from a wax, lead, or plastic mold of type or illustrations, on which has been deposited by electrolysis a copper, nickel, or steel shell, which thus forms a hardened metal face on the softer backing.

element (1) In **layout**, any of the parts, such as **display type**, **text** copy, **line art**, or **continuous-tone art**, that compose a page. (2) In **book makeup**, any of the components of the **front matter**, **body**, and **back matter** of a publication.

elite type A typewriter type providing 12 characters to the linear inch and 6 lines to the vertical inch. Type size for typewriters approximating 10-point printing type. Also called *12-pitch type*. *See also* **pica**; **pitch**.

ellipse *See* **ellipsis**.

ellipsis (1) A regular-shaped oval. Also called *ellipse*. (2) Three dots (...) in text, used to indicate that some of the text—usually from a quotation—has been deleted.

em (13c) (1) A unit of measure equaling the point size of the type; for example, a 12-point em is 12 points wide. Also equal to two times the width of an **en**. (2) The width of an **em dash** or an **em space**. *See also* **en**; **measurement**; **quad**; **spacing**.

Ask not what your country can do for you, but what you...

Fig. E-1 An ellipsis indicates text that is missing.

em dash A dash (—) that is as wide as the point size of the type, which is equal to the **uppercase** *M* in the current point size. For example, a 12-point em dash is 12 points wide because the *M* is 12 points wide. An element of punctuation that helps set off a word or phrase— such as this one— from the main part of a sentence. Also called *long dash.* In a **manuscript** it is represented by two hyphens. Compare **en dash**.

em quad *See* **em space**.

em space A space as wide as the point size of the type, which is equal to the width of the **uppercase** *M* in the current point size. For example, a 12-point em space is 12 points wide. Most frequently used as a **paragraph indent**. Also called *em quad.* See also **figure space**; **thin space**. Compare **en space**.

embedded code A **command** (in abbreviated form) inserted within the running text. A standard way of including commands for the **typesetter**.

embossing (15c) Producing raised letters or designs on paper or other material with a brass or bronze die.

embossing press A printing press capable of embossing work as well as regular printing.

en (1792) (1) A unit of measure equaling one-half the point size of the type; for example, a 12-point en is 6 points wide. Also equal to one-half the width of an **em**. (2) The width of an **en dash** or an **en space**. (3) Abbreviation for *en-quad.* Also called *nut.* *See also* **em**; **measurement**; **quad**; **spacing**.

en dash (1) A dash (–) that is half as wide as the point size of the type, which is equal to the **uppercase** *N* in the current point size. For example, a 12-point en dash is 6 points wide. (2) An element of punctuation that separates numerical values or years in a range as in 1978–79 and Figure 5–35. Also called *short dash.* (3) Denotes the arithmetic minus sign. Compare **em dash**.

en quad *See* **en**; **en space**.

en space A space as half as wide as the point size of the type, which is equal to the width of the **uppercase** *N* in the current point size. For example, a 12-point en space is 12 points wide. Also called *en quad. See also* **figure space; thin space**. Compare **em space**.

enameled finish (15c) Paper coated with clay, glue, and other substances, having a glossy finish. *See also* **coated paper**.

encapsulated PostScript format An image document format used with **PostScript** printing devices for embedding PostScript graphics images (made up of formats other than PostScript) within text. Abbreviated *EPSF*.

End key A keyboard key that moves the **cursor** to the last line on the screen.

end matter *See* **back matter**.

end of file (1) Text files are terminated with a particular "end of file" character that tells the system it has reached the end of the text file. (2) On a tape, it is usually a physical marker. Compare **magnetic tape trailer**. Abbreviated *eof. See also* **end-of-tape marker**.

end-of-line decisions Decisions, made by either the **keyboard operator** or by the **computer**, generally concerned with when and where to **hyphenate** and **justify** text at the end of a line.

end-of-tape marker A marker—such as a transparent section of tape or a photo-reflective strip—that indicates the end of the recording area on a **magnetic tape**. Abbreviated *EOT marker*. Compare **beginning-of-tape marker**.

end-user The person who uses **software** or **hardware**. Also called *operator*.

endleaf (1888) Paper at the beginning or end of a book, half of which is pasted to the cover. It must have sufficient strength to hold the inside of the book and the cover together, and it must accept paste without crinkling. Also called *book lining, endpaper, endsheet, flyleaf, self-ends*.

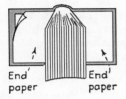

Fig. E-2   An endleaf is pasted to both the signatures and cover.

endnote A note placed at the end of an article or chapter or any text.

endpaper *See* **endleaf**.

endsheet *See* **endleaf**.

engineering document Any specification, drawing, sketch, list, standard, pamphlet, report, or other written information on the design, procurement, manufacture, test, or inspection of equipment or services.

english Old type size, now equal to about 14 points.

English finish Paper finish smoother than **machine finish**, but not so smooth as that of **supercalendered** stock. It is popular for magazines, brochures, and illustrated booklets for which **halftone** screening is employed and for which paper must be of reasonably good quality. Abbreviated *EF*. *See also* **finish; uncoated paper**.

engraver's proof *See* **proof**.

engraving (1601) (1) The cutting of a design into a block of material, resulting in a pattern from which a print can be made. (2) Process engraving is an alternative term for **platemaking**. (3) In fine arts, a print from an **intaglio printing** plate prepared by cutting below the surface with a **burin**. (4) In the graphic arts, short for *photoengraving*, a metal plate with a relief printing surface prepared by acid etching. (5) An illustration printed from such a plate. *See also* **continuous-tone; halftone; line copy**.

engrossing (1825) The hand-lettering done on diplomas and citations. *See also* **calligraphy**.

enhanced graphics adapter (1984) A **printed circuit board** in the system unit of a **PC/MS-DOS** microcomputer that controls the display. Shows both text and graphics at medium to high resolution in up to 64 colors. Abbreviated *EGA*.

enlarge To blow-up, or make an image that is larger than the original. Compare **reduce**. *See also* **scale**.

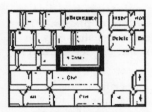

Fig. E-3 The Enter key, shown in the thick black box, is also called a Return key.

enlarged photo size The size to which a photo must be **enlarged** to appear in a publication.

enlargement An item that has been **enlarged**, such as a photograph or a **graphic**.

enlarger font Negative film font used to produce type sizes larger than 16–18 points.

enter To transfer a message from a terminal to the computer.

Enter key A **keyboard** key used to confirm the selected options in a **dialog box**, initiate a **command**, or process an operator's input. Causes previously typed information to be entered into computer memory. Also called *Return key, carriage return.*

entry The individual line or item of data found in an **index**. Also called *heading.*

envelope A **diskette sleeve** used to store disks to prevent accidental contact with the exposed surface. Also called *jacket.*

envelope corner card An address printed at the left of an envelope.

eof *See* **end of file**.

EOT marker *See* **end-of-tape marker**.

epigraph (1624) A quotation placed at the beginning of book or a division of it. Its purpose is to suggest the theme of the book or division.

epilogue (15c) A concluding section that rounds out a story and often updates the reader. Part of the text, not of the **back matter**.

EPROM *See* **erasable programmable read-only memory**.

EPSF *See* **encapsulated PostScript format**.

Epson Standard Code for Printers A set of **commands** developed by Epson and supported by almost all application software for personal computers.

equivalent weight (1929) In the paper industry, the weight of 500 sheets of paper in a size either larger or smaller than the **basic size**.

erasable programmable read-only memory
Semiconductor memory that retains its contents until physically exposed to ultraviolet light. Once so erased, it can be reprogrammed. Usually contains **BIOS** or other **firmware**. Abbreviated *EPROM*. *See also* **electrically-erasable programmable read-only memory**.

ERASE A **PC/MS-DOS** command that **deletes** files from a **disk**.

erase (1) In computer **painting**, to delete parts of an image by switching **pixels** to the background color. Selective erasing can be achieved by using a **brush**. (2) *See* **DELETE**. (3) *See* **ERASE**.

erection drawing Engineering drawing that shows the procedure and sequence for the erection or assembly of individual items or subassemblies of items.

ergonomics (1949) The science of the adaption of work, the equipment used in work, and the workplace environment, to meet human physical and cognitive strengths, capabilities, and limitations. Also called *human factors*.

errata (1589) (1) Error in writing or printing. (2) An acknowledgment of such an error. *See* **errata sheet**.

errata sheet Loose pages with revised text that are often sent to recipients of technical books to correct technical, typographical, or other errors. Errata sheets are usually sent prior to the book's next printing.

error message An indication that an error has been detected, commonly received when an operator error, such as a **typo** or incorrect command format, is encountered.

Esc *See* **escape**; **Escape key**.

escape A special **control code** used to begin most printer commands. Abbreviated *Esc*.

Escape key A **keyboard** key labeled **Esc** that cancels a line typed in— but not yet entered— on the **PC/MS-DOS** command line, suspends the correct activity, regresses to a previous level, or exits a program.

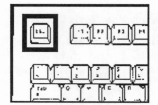

Fig. E-4   The Escape key, shown in the thick black box, on the IBM AT keyboard.

ESD *See* **electrostatic discharge**.

estimate *v.* To determine the cost of a particular job before it is undertaken. *n.* A cost so determined. Also called *price estimate*.

etch proof *See* **reproduction proof**.

etching (1634) Acid corrosion of a metal plate to produce an illustration.

ETP *See* **electronic technical publishing**.

etymology (14c) The study of the history of a language. *See also* **lexicon**.

excelsior Old 3-point type size, now seldom used.

exception dictionary In **computer-assisted composition**, a list of **exceptional words** that is consulted by the computer if the **hyphenation routine** does not make **end-of-line decisions**.

exceptional word A word that does not **hyphenate** in accordance with the logical rules of hyphenation. For example, *in-kling* would be an exceptional word since computer hyphenation logic would break it *inkl-ing*. *See also* **exception dictionary**.

excerpt (15c) A portion of text taken from a longer work. Also called *extract*.

exclamation point (1824) A punctuation mark (!) used after an utterance of force or strong feeling. Also called *bang*.

exclusive (1533) A news or feature story or television appearance printed or aired by one media source substantially ahead of its competitors.

EXE *See* **executable file**.

EXE2BIN A **PC/MS-DOS utility** program that converts some types of **.EXE** program files to **.COM** program files.

executable file A file that carries an *EXE* file extension and is used to initiate a program.

execute The computer's performance of an operation or command in a program.

exit To close a program and leave it to do another task. Compare **open**.

exit button Rectangle on a screen on which a **mouse button** is clicked to permit a user to remove a dialog box from the screen.

expanded type Type with a wider face than that of normal type which permits less material to be set in a line of the same **measure**. Also called *extended type*. Compare **compressed type**.

expert reading (1889) A reading of a book done by an authority on the book's subject to determine accuracy and completeness prior to a publication.

expert user A **user** who has a great deal of experience with a particular software system and who wants any information he needs to be communicated quickly and succinctly without extensive explanation or examples. Compare **novice user**.

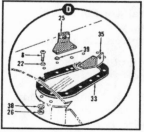

Fig. E-5   In an exploded view, parts are drawn separately to show their relationship to each other.

exploded view (1944) **Line drawing** or photograph of a piece of equipment, an article, or a component or part of an article in which the parts are drawn separately in perspective or isometric projection to show their relationship to each other. Each part is identified by a number that is **keyed** to a parts list or **legend**. They are also used in conjunction with text matter for the disassembly, inspection, repair or replacement, and reassembly of parts. Also called *illustrated parts breakdown*.

exposé (1803) Sensational revelation of hidden elements in a situation of public importance or in the life of a celebrity.

expressed folio Any page number that is printed. Compare **blind folio**. *See also* **folio**.

Extended Binary Coded Decimal Interchange Code A code often used for storage of **alphanumeric** information in large computers. Abbreviated *EBCDIC*.

extended characters Special characters such as foreign letters, mathematical symbols, and graphic characters.

extended guide A divider that is slightly larger than the printed page and extends above or outside the normal dimensions of the page as a visual aid in locating information. *See also* **index guide**.

extended type *See* **expanded type**

extension One to three optional characters that are at the end of a **PC/MS-DOS filename** (the part of the filename to the right of the period). For instance, the extension in the filename DESKTOP.DOC is DOC.

external command Any **PC/MS-DOS utility** program kept on a disk. For example, **CHKDSK, FORMAT, BACKUP,** and **RESTORE.** Compare **internal command**.

external documentation Documentation produced by a company or unit of a company for use outside of the company or unit. Often more care and attention is paid to this type of documentation than to **internal documentation**.

external field test The part of a **field test** performed outside the company or unit that produced the documentation. It is the portion of field testing in which actual users report on how difficult or easy it is to use the documentation. Also called *beta test.* Compare **controlled field test**.

external memory A device or medium for the storage of computer information separate from the computer itself, as opposed to **internal memory** storage. An external memory storage device is usually nonvolatile and has a much larger capacity than the internal storage of the computer. Also called *mass memory, auxiliary storage. See also* **disk; disk drive; floppy disk; memory; nonvolatile memory; transfer; volatile memory**.

extra-condensed A very thin **typeface**.

extract A long quotation set off from main text by a smaller size type, narrower measure, or by space above and below, or a combination of these techniques. Also called *excerpt.*

eyeball Colloquial term meaning to draw lines and objects without reference to scale.

eyeletting The process of reinforcing a punched hole.

Notes and New Words

Notes and New Words

Desktop Publisher's Dictionary

F

F&Gs *See* **folded and gathered pages.**

face (1) The part of a type piece that receives the ink and comes in direct contact with the printed surface, thus forming the image. Also called *typeface.* (2) *See* **type style.**

facing page The two pages that face each other when a publication is open. Facing pages have an even-numbered page on the left and an odd-numbered page on the right. *See also* **double-sided page; double spread.**

facsimile (1691) (1) Generally, any exact reproduction of an original. (2) A machine capable of sending written messages, photographs, or drawings over telephone lines. (3) An item so transmitted.

failure *See* **malfunction.**

fair use The limited use of quotations from previously copyrighted material, in a manner not considered a violation of **copyright**, and not requiring permission.

faking *See* **carding.**

family In typography, a series of alphabets in different weights—roman, italic, bold, condensed, expanded, etc.—with the same design characteristics. *See also* **font**; **type style**.

fanfold paper Continuous sheets of paper joined along perforations and folded in a zigzag manner. Usually used with printers as it can be continuously fed and folded without ongoing operator participation. Also called *continuous paper.*

farm out (1849) To sublet a process in printing, as the binding, composition, or presswork. Compare **contract**.

FASTOPEN A **PC/MS-DOS** command that stores the location of a specified number of files in memory to increase disk **access** speed.

FAT *See* **file allocation table**.

fat (1) Oversize copy. (2) Type that is wide. (3) *See* **file allocation table**.

fatigue a loss of mental aquity stemming from poor **readability** factors.

fatting pattern In scanning, a **halftone** pattern that gives better resolution than **course fatting**, but has fewer shades of gray.

fault *See* **malfunction**.

FDISK A **PC/MS-DOS** command used to divide a **fixed disk** into two or more **partitions**. Allows two or more **operating systems** to be used on the same fixed disk.

feasibility study A study made to determine whether conversion to a particular **desktop publishing** system can improve production or office operations.

feather *v.* To insert extra **leading** between lines to lengthen a page or column. *n.* In a printed or duplicated image, an undesirable bleeding effect in which a microscopic featherlike fringe surrounds the characters. Particularly noticeable on copies from **laser printers**. Also called *fuzz.*

featheredge *See* **deckle edge**.

feature *v.* To play up or emphasize. *n.* An article, usually human interest, related to, but not necessarily, news.

feeder (1) A device for automatically delivering the sheets of paper to a press. (2) A person who hand-feeds sheets of paper to a press.

feet The two lower projections of a piece of hand-set type. *See also* **off its feet**.

felt finish Finish applied by a special marking felt on a web of paper as it goes through the papermaking machine. *See also* **finish**; **marking felt**.

felt side Printing side of paper. The felt side is the top side of the paper as it comes off the papermaking machine; it is the opposite of the **wire side**.

fictitious name statement A notice published in a local newspaper announcing that you are doing business under a name other than your own. *See also* **doing business as**.

field (1) A subsection of a line. (2) One or more items of **data** that comprise a **record**. (3) A subgroup of characters in a group of characters.

field delimiter In a sequential **database** file, it is a single character surrounding each **field**.

field separator The character used to separate one **field** from the next; a **string** of one or more spaces is the usual field separator.

field test A user test of **documentation** in an actual or simulated working environment before the final release of a document. It is part of the **review** process.

The Fifth Mode (1987) A quarterly newsletter for **Ventura** users that contains software release information, design techniques, and operation tips.

figure (1) General term for any form of drawing, diagram, halftone, or color image that serves to enhance a printed piece. Also called *illustration. See also* **artwork**; **graph**; **photograph**. (2) An **Arabic numeral**. Abbreviated *fig.*

Fig. F-1   The first issue of *The Fifth Mode*, a newsletter for Ventura usrs.

figure number (1) Number assigned to an illustration in a publication. (2) In **Ventura**, a tool that automatically assigns the correct figure number to each picture and puts the number on the page.

figure space A space equal to the width of a number in the current point size. Use figure spaces between numbers in tables to keep tabular information aligned properly. *See also* **em space**; **en space**; **thin space**.

figure title In a technical work, the title of an illustration, usually preceded by a figure number. *See also* **legend**.

file A document, program, or other collection of information stored under a **filename** on a computer disk or in the computer's internal memory, where it is available to be processed by a computer program. A file is often structured as a series of **records**.

file allocation table An area on **PC/MS-DOS** disks (duplicated in another location for safety) in which a list of sector addresses is kept, each designated as "available," "in use," or "bad." When DOS writes a file to disk, it controls the file allocation table to locate available sectors for data storage, then marks them as "in use" as it writes out data. Abbreviated *FAT*.

file control block Information on a file's name, location, and size is maintained in a file control block.

file laminate A plastic film bonded to a **jacket** or paperback cover to protect the surface. *See also* **lamination**.

file management Handling the electronic form of documents— saving them, measuring their length, combining them, or moving them from one place to another.

file name *See* **filename**.

file number *See* **art file number**.

FILES A **PC/MS-DOS** command that specifies the maximum number of **files** that may be open at any given time.

filename A 1- to 8-character name used by **PC/MS-DOS** to identify a computer **file**.

An optional 1- to 3-character **extension** may be used. For example, if a document file named DESKTOP has a file extension of DOC, then the full filename for the file is DESKTOP.DOC. *See also* **disk operating system**.

filename expansion The process by which a **disk operating system** matches **filenames** with **metacharacters** to actual filenames. For example, matching *.DOC for any document with a *DOC* filename **extension**.

filespec The complete specification of a file, which may include a **drive letter**, **pathname**, **filename**, and **extension**.

fill In graphics, to pour a **pattern** or **texture** into a closed **figure**, such as a box or circle.

fill area An area, defined by a set of coordinates, that is to be filled with a solid color or **crosshatching**.

fill-in The name, address, and salutation that are typed at the top of a **form letter**.

fill pattern *See* **fill**.

filler (1) Short pieces of information— poems, witticisms, parables, proverbs, jokes, cartoons, crossword puzzles, photographs, and public announcement advertisements— used by editors to fill small blank spots in the pages of a publication. (2) **Typeset** copy for use in emergencies. (3) Any copy used to fill in a blank area.

Filler for Publications (1959) A newsletter that provides four monthly editorial services: copy, cartoons, **clip art**, and crossword and word games.

fillet Line impressed on the cover of a book for decorative purposes.

filling Adjusting the line lengths in text so that all lines have about the same length.

film Plastic film made of cellulose acetate, polyethylene, polypropylene, etc., used in photographic typesetting and photography. *See also* **metal foil**.

Fig. F-2   A roll of film showing the sprockets and exposure areas.

film advance The control on a **filmsetter** or **phototypesetter** by which the spacing between lines can be adjusted. Equivalent to **leading**.

film mechanical A **mechanical** made with text, halftones, and display elements all in the form of film **positives stripped** into position on a sheet of base film. Equivalent of a complete type **form**; from the film mechanical **photorepros** or contact films are made for the platemaker. Also called *photomechanical*.

film processor Machine that automatically processes sensitized and exposed film or paper: develops, fixes, washes, and dries.

filmset *See* **photoset**.

filmsetter (1961) A machine that sets copy automatically on film or on photographic paper. Also called **photographic typesetter**.

filter (1) In **Ventura**, the specification on the directory line in the item selector that determines which files are displayed. The asterisk character (*) indicates that any set of characters can be displayed; the question mark (?) indicates that any single character can be displayed in that position. For instance, *.STY will display any filename with the extension STY. GRAB????.IMG will display all eight-character filenames starting with the letters GRAB and having the extension IMG. (2) The use of a weighting function to interpolate the value of a **pixel** from the **polygons** intercepting it to solve **aliasing** problems. (3) *See* **FILTER**.

FILTER A **PC/MS-DOS utility** that processes data in some way (for example, sorts it in alphabetic order) and writes the result to **standard output**.

final copy The final version of the text. Also called *final draft*. *See also* **draft copy**; **edited copy**.

final draft *See* **final copy**.

final proof A **proof** made by the **compositor** from the film that is sent to the printer for the making of printing plates.

FIND A **PC/MS-DOS** filter **utility** that finds and displays or writes all lines from a specified **filename** containing a specified text **string**.

fine arts (1767) Arts created with concern for aesthetic values rather than for utility. Among them are architecture, sculpture, drawing, painting, and ceramics.

fines (1909) In paper, blemishes formed of clumps of fibers that remain stuck together through the papermaking process.

finish (1779) The character of the surface of paper. *See also* **calender**; **coated paper**; **machine finish paper**; **supercalender finish**.

finish size The size of a book after it is trimmed and bound at the **bindery**. *See also* **trim size**.

finishing processes The processes used to finish a book, including:
- **eyeletting**
- **graining**
- **laminating**
- **perforating**
- **punching**
- **varnishing**

firmware (1967) Programming, generally in **read-only memory**, that cannot be altered without changing the computer's **hardware**.

first draft The author's first version of a **manuscript**.

first edition (1828) The entire original **printing** of a work from the same plates.

first proofs Proofs submitted for checking by proofreaders, copy editors, etc.

first serial rights The right to serialize a forthcoming work prior to the publication date. Often sold to only one magazine or one newspaper. *See also* **rights**; **second serial rights**.

fit (1688) Space relationship between two or more letters. The fit can be a "tight fit" or a "loose fit."

fitting copy *See* **copyfitting**.

5.25-inch disk A **floppy disk** that can be read from or written to on both sides. These disks can hold from 350,000 characters to more than 1.2 million characters. Also called *minifloppy*.

five-em space *See* **hair space**.

five-to-the-em space *See* **hair space**.

fixed disk A disk that cannot be removed from its drive as a permanent storage medium for data. Generally, a fixed disk has much greater capacity, speed, and reliability than a **floppy disk**. Also called *hard disk*.

fixed-length record A **record** having the same length as all other records with which it is associated.

flag *v.* To mark a correction or question on the **mechanical**. *n.* (1) An **argument** to a command indicating a particular option, modification, occurrence, or state. (2) *See* **nameplate**.

flap copy The material describing a book and its author which appears on the inside folds of a **dust jacket**. *See also* **back flap**; **front flap**.

flat Assemblage of various film negatives or positives **stripped** in correct order and orientation, in **register**, to a piece of **film**, **goldenrod**, or suitable **masking** material ready to be exposed on a plate.

flat bed press *See* **flatbed press**.

flat cathode-ray tube A **cathode-ray tube** screen having a relatively flat design to reduce the bulk of the conventional **cathode-ray tube**.

flat fee A onetime payment for a job or task, such as the preparation of text or artwork.

flat-panel display A **visual display unit** that reduces the bulk of the conventional **cathode-ray tube displays**, increases portability, and reduces electromagnetic interference. The most widely used are *plasma panels, liquid crystal displays,* and *electroluminescent displays.*

flatbed press A press in which the type or plates lie flat. Compare **rotary press**. *See also* **flexography**; **letterpress printing**; **relief printing**.

flatbed scanner A **scanner** with a glass surface on which is placed the material to be scanned. The results are more precise than those from a **sheet-fed scanner**.

fleurons In **hot metal composition**, ornaments cast on bodies of specific type sizes.

flexible disk *See* **floppy disk**; **diskette**.

flexible hours *See* **flextime**.

flexo *See* **flexography**.

flexography (1954) A **relief printing** method in which rubber plates having a **relief** image are used to make an impression. The rubber plate is mixed with a liquid ink instead of paste ink, such as that used in **letterpress** printing. Such items as food cartons, candy and gum wrappers, cellophane bags, and waxed papers are ideally suited for this type of printing. Also called *flexo*. *See also* **flatbed press**; **printing methods**; **rotary press**.

flextime (1973) A working schedule chosen by the worker rather than the company. Also called *flexible hours*.

flicker The perception by the **user** of rapid, rhythmic fluctuations of the **luminance**, **hue**, or **saturation** of a **video display unit**.

flier An inexpensive promotional piece— such as a broadside, announcement, handbill, or circular— often printed on an 8.5-in x 11-in sheet of paper of inferior quality and printed on one side of the sheet.

flippy disk A diskette physically configured so that it can be inserted upside-down in single-sided **disk drives** so that both sides of the disk can be used. *See also* **floppy disk**.

flock application *See* **flocking**.

flocking (1874) Minute fiberlike particles of wood or cloth in various colors that are blown onto printed matter or painted objects

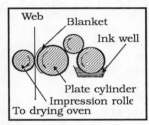

Fig. F-3   In flexography, rubber plates with a relief image are used to make an impres-

blown onto printed matter or painted objects having an adhesive ink. The particles adhere to the ink or paint, producing a decorative effect. Also called *frost printing, flock application, glitter application.*

flong A plastic mold in which stereotypes are cast. *See also* **matrix**.

flop To turn over an image, such as a **halftone**, so that it faces the opposite way when printed. Also called *flop-over*.

flop-over *See* **flop**.

floppy disk (1973) A flexible disk coated with magnetically sensitive material, widely used for storage of information in computer technology. Also called *flexible disk, metafloppy*. While *floppy disk* specifically refers to an 8-in diskette, it is a generic term used to identify a **minifloppy** (5.25 in) and **microfloppy** (3.5 in). These portable disks come in varying densities, from less than 360,000 characters to more than 1.4 million characters. *See also* **disk**; **disk drive**; **diskette**; **hard disk**.

Fig. F-4   Floppy disks are also called flexible disks or metafloppies.

flow *v.* To load text into a multicolumn layout. *n.* Writing that reads easily and smoothly with continuity is said to *flow*.

flow diagram (1943) Schematic diagram indicating the direction of flow of a material through a system and the relationship of the components. Compare **flowchart**.

flow line Line that indicates the physical relationship of parts of an object when the parts are separated in the drawing. It is broken into alternate short and long lines. *See also* **exploded view**.

flow text *See* **flow**.

flowchart (1920) A diagram that shows step-by-step progression through a procedure or system. Also used to explain how a program makes decisions or how computer hardware works.

flush *v.* To make even with. *n.* (1) In typesetting, lines set **flush left** are **aligned** vertically along the left-hand margin while lines set **flush right** are aligned vertically along the right-hand margin. *See also* **align-**

This is an example of a flush-and-hang indention. Notice that there are two outdent lines at the top.

Fig. F-5   An example of the flush-and-hang indention.

ment; justify; paragraph; ragged left; ragged right. (2) *See* DELETE.

flush-and-hang indention To set copy **flush** with a **hanging indention**.

flush blocking Mounting a **cut** on a wooden block with a double-sided adhesive. This replaced the older method of **tacking**, which required a margin of wood all around.

flush cover Book cover having the same dimensions as the inserted book.

flush left (1594) Text of a column or page that is **aligned** vertically along the left margin, leaving the right edge **ragged**. Also called *left-justified*. Opposite of **ragged left** and **right-justified**. Compare **flush right**.

flush right Text of a column or page that is **aligned** vertically along the right margin, leaving the left edge **ragged**. Also called *right-justified*. Opposite of **ragged right** or **left-justified**. Compare **flush left**.

flyer *See* **flier**.

flyleaf *See* **endleaf**.

FOB *See* **free on board; front of the book**.

foil (1611) Very thin sheet or leaf of metal, such as gold or silver, that is used to embellish designs and lettering in a stamping process. *See also* **metal foil**.

foil stamping Method of using metallic foil to impress an image on a surface. The foil, or leaf, is stamped and affixed to the surface by using heat in the relief **matrix**. Also called *hot foil stamping*.

fold (before 12c) *v.* To bend or press something so that one part is placed over another part. (13c) *n.* A crease made by folding something. (2) Any part that is doubled or laid over another part.

folded and gathered pages Printed sheets that have been folded into **signatures** and collected into the correct order for binding. These are unbound book pages. Often sent as a **review copy**. Abbreviated *F&Gs*. *See also* **galley**; **proof**.

folder (1) Area on a disk to store information such as documents, applications, and other files. When a folder is opened in a graphic user interface environment, its contents are displayed in a window. Also called *filename, directory, subdirectory.* (2) A machine that folds printed sheets into **signatures** for binding, often attached directly to the press at the delivery end. (3) Printed circular folded and used as a mailing piece.

foldout An oversize **leaf**, often a map, an illustration, or a table, folded to fit within the **trim size** of the book and **tipped in**. Also called *gatefold.*

Folio A monthly magazine devoted to magazine publishers.

folio (1533) (1) In papermaking, a paper size measuring 17 in x 22 in. (2) In printing, a sheet of paper folded once. (3) A large book, about 12 in x 15 in. (4) In a publication, a page number. *See also* **blind folio**; **drop folio**; **expressed folio**; **running foot**; **running head**. (5) In a descriptive bibliography, a leaf of a manuscript or early printed book, the two sides being designated *r* (**recto**, or front) and *v* (**verso**, or back). (6) Formerly, a book made from standard-size sheets folded once, each sheet forming two leaves, or four pages.

folio line *See* **running head**.

follow copy Direction to compose or type **copy** exactly like the **manuscript copy** without making any changes.

font (1683) All the type—including capitals, small capitals, lowercase, numbers, and punctuation marks—in one size of one **typeface**. For example, 12-point Times Roman is a different font than 12-point Times Italic, 14-point Times Roman, or 12-point Helvetica. Special characters (those not in a font) are called **pi characters**. Screen fonts (**bitmapped fonts** used to display text accurately on the screen) can differ slightly from printer fonts (**outline fonts** used to describe fonts to the **laser printer**) because of the difference in resolution between screens and printers.

Fig. F-6   A foldout is folded to fit within the trim size of a book and tipped in.

font metric In **Ventura,** the width and height information for each character in each font. This information is stored in a **width table.**

font module In some printers, a device that plugs in to add character fonts.

font size The **point size**, measured by the distance from the lowest descender to the highest ascender.

foolscap (1632) Any of various sizes of paper measuring from about 12 in x 15 in to about 13.5 in x 17 in.

foot The bottom of a book page or job of printing. Compare **head.** *See also* **running foot.**

foot margin The margin at the bottom of a page. Also called *bottom margin, tail margin.*

footer Repetitive words, phrases, or sentences placed at the bottom of each page of a document. Also called *trailer. See also* **folio; running foot.** Compare **header.**

footnote (1822) A comment, explanation, or other note placed below the text on a printed page. It is usually set in smaller type than the text or table on which it comments. Footnotes are usually referred to in text by **superior** numbers and in tables by **reference marks.**

fore edge The trimmed outer edge—the edge opposite the spine—of the leaves of a book. *See also* **fore edge margin.**

fore edge margin The **margin** at the trimmed outer edge, opposite the spine. Also called *outside margin.*

foreground Running under direct control of the terminal. The terminal cannot be used for anything else until a foreground job finishes or is halted.

foreground print A printing job that takes over the program or equipment such that no additional work can be done at the same time. Compare **background print.**

foreign rights The **subsidiary rights** that allow a work to be published in other countries or translated into other languages. *See also* **rights**.

foreword (1842) Statement forming part of the **front matter** of a book, often written by an expert (other than the author) to give a book greater promotability and authority. Compare **afterword; preface**.

form (1) In printing, the assemblage of type pages or **cuts** that are to be printed on one side of one sheet of paper. (2) The printing surfaces—type, cuts, metal plates, offset plates, etc.—so ordered as to produce the foregoing. (3) Equivalent to a page. *See also* **chase; imposition; makeready; quoin; signature; strip**.

form feed (1) In a printer, the mechanism used to bring an assigned part of a form to the printing position. (2) A **control code** or a button that advances the paper in a printer to the top of the next page. (3) In word processing, a function that advances the typing position to the same character position on a predetermined line of the next form or page.

form letter The same basic letter to be sent out to a number of different people, usually prepared in advance and duplicated.

form stop A device that automatically stops a printer when the paper has run out.

form tractor Optional equipment for a printer that provides controlled feeding of blank or preprinted forms to the printer from a supply located under or behind the printer. Also called *tractor feed*.

FORMAT A **PC/MS-DOS utility** that prepares a new disk for use to receive and hold information by organizing the disk into magnetic **tracks** and **sectors**, by creating a **directory** and **file allocation table**, and by testing the surface for defects.

format (1964) A contraction of "*format of material*." (1) The shape, size, style, and overall appearance of a publication. (2) Formerly, the size and proportion of a book as determined by the number of times the sheets have been folded, as **folio, quarto, octavo**, etc. (3) *See* **format a disk**. (4) *see* **FORMAT**. (5) In **phototypesetting**, translating the designer's **type specifications** into format or command codes for the phototypesetting equipment. Formatting is gradually replacing **markup**.

format a disk To prepare a **magnetic disk** for use in conjunction with a specific **disk operating system** on a specific computer. This generally involves placing information on the surface of the disk in electromagnetic form. The task is usually performed automatically by the disk operating system. Also called *initialize the disk*.

format edit An editing activity in which page layout is examined to ensure its effectiveness. *See also* **edit; levels of edit**.

format of material *See* **format**.

Formula Translation (1954) A high-level programming language. Abbreviated *FORTRAN*.

FORTRAN *See* **Formula Translation**.

forwarding The process of binding a book after the sheets are fastened together.

foul proof Type **proof** from which corrections have been made and approved by the author or the editor.

foundry proof Last or final **proof** of type and material locked in a **form** before making the **electrotype** or **stereotype**.

foundry type Hand-set metal type cast by **type founders** in individual characters with a special hard metal. This type, used in **hand composition**, is kept in a **case**, each character in its own compartment. It is reserved for display material or other small jobs.

four-color process The printing process in which full-color reproduction is obtained by printing successive images from photographic plates in cyan, magenta, yellow, and black. *See also* **process color printing**.

four-color separations For a full-color picture, separate negatives showing the printer what to make black, magenta, yellow, and cyan. With those colors, the printing press can generate surprisingly lifelike images.

Fourdrinier machine (1839) A papermaking machine whose name is derived from two brothers, Sealy and Henri Fourdrinier of London. The machine was built in 1803.

four-em space *See* **thin space**.

four-to-the-em space *See* **thin space**.

four-headed arrow Shape of the **pointer** when used to **drag** a selected text **block** or **graphic**.

four-up In **offset lithography,** to duplicate the printing image on the plate so that four copies of the piece are printed at the same time, side-by-side. **Compare** two-up.

fourth cover Exposed back cover of a book or magazine.

fractals Mathematically generated shapes, first developed by **Benoit B. Mandelbrot**. Fractals have an irregular surface or other properties similar to objects in nature.

fraction (14c) A quantity less than a whole number. In typography, these come in three **type styles**: **built-up fractions** (also called *adaptable*), which are made up of three separate characters— two text size numerals separated by a slash; **case fractions**, which are small fractions available as a single character; and **piece fractions**, which are small fractions made up of two characters— a nominator and slash or separating rule as one character and the denominator as the second character.

Fraktur (1904) Once a widely used type in Germany, a lighter version of **Old English** type. For example, ℜ and ℑ. *See also* **Gothic**; **typeface nomenclature**; **type style**.

frame A box or container that provides boundaries for text and graphics. A frame can be any size up to the size of the entire page.

frame mode In **Ventura**, an operational mode involving the creation, editing, and positioning of **frames**.

This
is a
frame

Fig. F-7   A frame.

free on board When books are shipped from the manufacturer *free on board*, the publisher must pay shipping costs to the destination. Abbreviated *FOB*.

free sheet Paper free from **mechanical wood pulp**.

free-lance (1902) *v.* To write as a free-lancer. (1820) *n.* Writers, photographers, artists, editors, or consultants who are self-employed, and not on the regular payroll of a publication or organization.

freelance *See* **free-lance**.

freeware Free software, usually obtained from **user groups**. *See also* **shareware**.

French fold A piece of paper folded twice, with the second fold at right angles to the first, creating an uncut eight-page folder.

French Japon *See* **Japan paper**.

friction feed Method of feeding sheet paper into a printing press or other device in which rubber rollers are used to transport the paper in its initial progress through the press. Compare **hand feed**, **suction feed**.

friction-glazed finish Highly polished finish given to **coated papers** by using wax and processing the paper through the friction rollers.

frisket (1) In hand printing, a piece of paper with holes cut in it placed between the inked form and the paper to keep unwanted ink from getting on the paper. (2) A paper or plastic film stencil used in preparing **artwork**.

front cover Face of a book or magazine. The cover may be soft and flexible or hard, as in a **casebound** book. *See also* **cover**.

front flap The inside fold of a **dust jacket**. *See also* **back flap**; **flap copy**.

front list *See* **frontlist**.

front list books *See* **frontlist books**.

front margin The outside margin of a page.

front matter (1585) Everything before page one of a book, including: **abstract**; **acknowledgment**; **copyright**; **dedication**;

Fig. F-8 The front cover of the October 1988 issue of *Publish!* magazine.

foreword; frontispiece; half-title page; introduction; preface; table of contents; table of illustrations; table of tables; title page. Usually numbered with lowercase roman numerals, but printed numbers do not appear until after the **copyright page**. Also called *preliminaries*.

front of the book Designation used by periodical editors for articles to be placed in the opening pages of the magazine. Abbreviated *FOB*.

front plate *See* **frontispiece**.

frontispiece (1597) Formerly, the first page or title page of a book. Now a photograph, sketch, drawing, portrait, or other illustration prefacing and facing the title page of a book or other publication. Also called *front plate*. *See also* **front matter**.

frontlist A publisher's list of books just published or about to be published. *See also* **lists**. Compare **backlist**.

frontlist books Books published within the last two seasons. The term is used when calculating **remainders** and **returns** to and by bookstore owners. Usual rate of returns is higher on frontlist books than on **backlist** books.

frost printing *See* **flocking**.

fulfillment The filling and shipping of book orders or serial subscriptions.

full box In **Ventura**, a diamond-shaped box in the upper right corner of the screen that is used to change the window's size from small to full. *See also* **size box**.

full binding (1) All-leather binding of a book. (2) Using the same **cover material** all the way around a book. Compare **quarter binding**; **three-quarter binding**.

full-duplex Transmitting or receiving data over a **modem** in which the receiver and the transmitter can communicate with each other at the same time. Compare **half-duplex**.

full measure Text set to make a line of type the full width of a column, **flush** with both margins. Compare **narrow measure**. *See also* **indent**; **justification**; **measure**.

full measure left Text set to the left-hand edge of the column, without indent.

full-returns policy A publisher's agreement with bookstores and **wholesalers** that they may return any unsold volumes for a full credit within a prescribed period of time after publication.

full-tone A **halftone**, or screened **continuous-tone copy**.

function An action the software can carry out, usually initiated by a single command.

function key (1) A **keyboard** key other than standard typewriter keys. (2) One of several keys, usually labeled F1, F2, and so on, that cause the **disk operating system** (or an applications program) to perform a certain function, such as copying characters in a line of text or boldfacing copy. (3) On a terminal, a key, such as Enter or F6, that causes the transmission of a signal not associated with a printable or displayable character. Detection of the signal usually causes the system to perform some predefined function for the operator.

furnish The specific combination of materials, including the type of pulp, fillers, size, pigments, etc., that goes into making a particular type of paper.

furniture Pieces of wood or metal (greater than 12 points in thickness) used to fill out large blank spaces in a type **form** that are locked in a **chase**. Thin pieces of furniture are called **reglets**.

fuzz (1) Loose or projecting fibers on a paper surface. (2) In a printed or duplicated image, an undesirable bleeding effect in which a microscopic featherlike fringe surrounds the characters. Particularly noticeable on copies from **laser printers**. Also called *feather*.

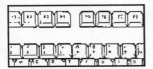

Fig. F-9   The top row are some of the function keys on the IBM AT keyboard.

Notes and New Words

G

GARF *See* **Graphic Arts Research Foundation.**

gag (1553) A comic idea that may be put to use in a variety of ways. The gag idea need not be submitted in final form.

gage *See* **line gauge.**

gagging The words usually printed directly beneath a cartoon. Also called *caption.*

galley In metal composition, a long, shallow metal tray used by **compositors** to hold type after it has been set. The type is later divided into pages. *See also* **author's alterations; folded and gathered pages; galley proof; printer's error.**

galley press A proofing machine for type and plate.

galley proof (1) Long sheets of typeset copy pulled from **galleys** and used by **editors** and writers for last-minute revisions and checked by **proofreaders** for **printer's errors.** (2) In cold-composition work, the first printing of the copy as it comes from the typesetting machine. It is usually not **paginated**. Also called *rough proof.* A **review copy** may be sent to important reviewers. *See also* **page proof**; **proof**.

gang printing Printing of several jobs on the same sheet, to be cut later.

gang shooting In photolithographic plate making, photographing several pages of original copy, such as pages of a book or booklet at the same time.

garbage in, garbage out Programming slang for bad input produces bad output. Abbreviated *gigo*.

gas discharge display (ca. 1961) A **video display unit** that produces images by the control of light generated by an interaction of electric current and inert ionized gas, such as neon. Generally limited to a single (orange) color. Also called *plasma panel.*

gate page Page having a **gatefold**.

gatefold (1946) *See* **foldout**.

gather In the binding process, to put **signatures** in proper order. *See also* **collate**; **folded and gathered pages**.

gauge A measuring rule in picas. Also called *line gauge.*

gazetteer (1611) Portion of dictionary that lists names of places as well as information on their location and population.

GBC binding *See* **comb binding**.

GEM file A **file** that contains **object-oriented graphics**.

generic font A screen representation of alphanumeric characters, which may not look like the printed characters. See also **font**.

get (1) To obtain a record from an input file. (2) In word processing, the act of retrieving a defined block of text from a document and inserting it into the document being created or revised.

ghost Unavailable options in a **menu**.

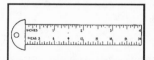

Fig. G-1   A gauge is a ruler that measures picas as well as inches.

ghost writer (1927) One who writes for others without receiving public credit. *See also* **as told to; ghostwriting; work for hire**.

ghosting (1957) A condition in which the printed image is faint, caused by faulty distribution of ink on rollers.

ghostwriting (1927) Writing intended to be published as the work of another, on which the actual author's name will not appear. *See also* **ghost writer**.

gigo *See* **garbage in, garbage out**.

gilding The application of gold leaf to the edges of book paper for the purpose of decoration. *See also* **staining**.

glitch (1962) In computer terminology, something that causes a system to malfunction, such as a mechanical defect or a programming error. Usually transient in nature. Also called *bug*. *See also* **debug**.

Glitches (1981) A newsletter for users of Compugraphic phototypesetting equipment.

glitter application *See* **flocking**.

global Applying to an entire **file** or **disk**.

global search and replace A **command** to search for repeated occurrences of a **character string** and then replace that character string with another.

glossary (1) A function of a word processing system that stores repetitive keystrokes for later retrieval and use by an operator. (14c) (2) List of terms in a particular field with their definitions. *See also* **back matter**.

glossy *See* **glossy finish; glossy print**.

glossy finish (1) *See* **glossy print**. (2) **Coated paper** with a shiny **enameled finish** rather than a **matte finish**.

glossy print A photograph with a hard, very shiny finish, preferred for reproduction work. Compare **matte finish**. Also called *glossy*.

golden section (1875) The ratio 1:1.618 when a line or rectangle is divided. This harmonious proportion, considered to be mystically significant by Renaissance painters, is derived geometrically.

goldenrod Orange-colored **masking** paper used in **layout** and **makeup** work for **stripping** in line and halftone negatives for lithographic reproduction. *See also* **flat**.

Gothic (1644) A **typeface** that is square-cut, **sans serif**, and without hairlines. *See also* **typeface nomenclature**.

grabber hand An **icon** shaped like a hand that permits the moving of elements in a **window** or **frame**.

gradation (1549) Variation in tonal values from white to black; also, the passing of one tint or shade gradually into another. The tones between the two extremes are called **middle tones**.

GRAFTABL A **PC/MS-DOS** command that loads the graphics table providing access to **ASCII** characters 128 through 255.

grain In machine papermaking, the fibers tend to align themselves longitudinally with the web as it moves through the machine, thus establishing the *grain* of the paper. Grain may be determined by tearing the paper; if the paper tears easily with relatively few broken edges, it is torn with the grain. A smooth and even crease results when paper is folded with the grain. *See also* **against the grain**; **grain long**; **grain short**.

grain long Grain running the long way of the sheet

grain short Grain running the short way.

graining (1) Roughening the surface of a metal offset-lithographic press plate by means of marbles and an abrasive to increase its water-carrying capacity during the press run. (2) A process applied to **cover papers** in the finishing process of papers.

grammage In the metric system for specifying the **basis weight** of paper, the weight in grams of one square meter of the paper, i.e., *grams per square meter*, abbreviated g/m^2 or *gsm*.

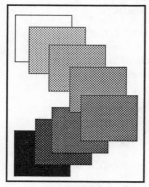

Fig. G-2   Gradation is shown in these screens.

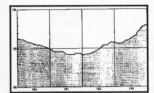

Fig. G-3   A surface
chart.

grammar (14c) (1) The study of the classes
of words, their inflections, and their functions and relations in the sentence. (2) The
facts of language with which grammar deals.

graph (1878) A diagram representing varying relationships between two or more factors by visual means. The term is used in
preference to **chart** in scientific and technical work.

graphic (1944) (1) A symbol produced by
handwriting, drawing, or printing. Also
called *graphic symbol.* (2) An image other
than text that can be displayed on a computer screen or printed by a computer.

graphic arts (1882) Arts represented by
drawing or imposing on a flat surface an
image that communicates a message. Also,
the methods, processes, and techniques
employed in these arts.

Graphic Arts Monthly (1929) A monthly
magazine featuring printing and graphic
arts information.

Graphic Arts Research Foundation (1949)
Association to advance printing technology
by focusing on developments of text processing and typesetting machines for multiline
writing forms. Abbreviated *GARF.*

Graphic Arts Technical Foundation (1924)
A scientific, technical, and educational organization serving international graphics
industries to conduct research in all graphic
processes and applications.

Graphic Communications Association
(1966) A national association of printers,
publishers, advertising agencies, manufacturers, fulfillment houses, and service
bureaus who are interested graphic communication.

graphic primitive *See* **display element.**

graphic symbol *See* **graphic.**

GRAPHICS A **PC/MS-DOS** command that
is loaded prior to printing graphics. To take
effect, a graphics printer and a color/
graphics monitor adapter are required.
Upon using Shift-Print Screen, graphic im-

ages, like those used to produce a pie or bar chart, are reproduced on the printer.

graphics Refers to anything in computers that is not text. *See also* **computer graphics**.

graphics application A software application that is used to edit graphic images.

graphics card Hardware device installed in a computer so it can display graphics.

graphics characters Symbols in the character set of some computers that can be used to construct graphics images. These **low-resolution graphics** are rather like pieces of a jigsaw puzzle; though meaningless in themselves, they can be put together to form a picture. *See also* **character set; computer graphics; high-resolution graphics; user-defined graphics characters**.

graphics file A **file** containing a graphic.

graphics mode In Ventura, an operational mode used to add graphics such as boxes, circles, and lines.

graphics resolution The amount of detail that a computer can generate in a graphics image. The more **pixels** that can be included in a picture generated on the computer's video display, the higher the resolution of the computer and the more realistic the picture. The fewer the pixels, the lower the resolution, and the "blockier" the picture.

graphics set A set of **graphics** containing international characters with accents and graphics characters.

graphics tablet A peripheral device that allows a user to input positional information to a computer by touching a pressure-sensitive surface; commonly used in the creation of graphic images.

grave accent (1620) A diacritical mark that indicates a sound value. For example, the è in *après*.

graver *See* **burin**.

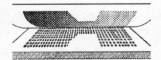

Fig. G-4   Gravure printing uses a plate in
which the image is sunk
below the surface in ink-
filled depressions.

gravity field A technique used to facilitate cursor positioning. Placed around a line, the gravity field will attract, or **snap**, the cursor to an exact point on the line.

gravure ink A special ink used in gravure printing.

gravure printing (1893) A **printing method** using the **intaglio** process that is done from a plate in which the image is sunk below the surface in ink-filled depressions. *See also* **rotogravure**.

gray goods Undyed, unfinished book cloth as it comes from the loom.

gray scale A logarithmic scale of **gradations** of gray from white to black, used to measure tonal range and contrast of copy to be photographed. Data representing different shades of gray.

gray-scale scan A type of **scan** that registers more information about the actual values in an image than a **bi-level scan** and are device independent.

great primer Old type size, now equal to about 18 points.

greeked text *See* **greeking**.

greeking Traditionally, a block of text used to represent the positioning and point size of text in a designer's **comp** of a design. Standard greeked text used by typesetters actually looks more like Latin. In **desktop publishing** applications, used to increase screen drawing speed.

green copy One of the first copies to come off a printing press.

grid (1839) In graphic design, grids enable a designer to compose a page layout by entering images, blocks of text, and headlines into predetermined boxes displayed on the screen. They promote clean, consistent, and coherent designs. *See also* **compositional grid**; **constructional grid**.

grid constraint An **accuracy aid** that acts as a lock on the movement of the design system's positioning input device. It causes the screen cursor to jump to the nearest grid intersection whenever a point is entered. Also called *snap-to*.

grid snap The effect of various types of non-printing guidelines— margin guides, ruler guides, and column guides. These guides exert a magnetic pull on the cursor, text, or a graphic that comes close to the guides. Useful for aligning text and graphics accurately. Also called *snap-to*.

gripper On a printing press, a finger that seizes the edge of the paper and pulls it through the press. *See also* **gripper edge**.

gripper edge The edge of the sheet that enters the printing machine first and is held by **grippers**. On this edge, gripper area (about 3/8 in to 5/8 in) must be allowed beyond the printed area. Also called *gripper margin*.

gripper margin *See* **gripper edge**.

grotesque (1561) Another name for **sans serif** typefaces. *See* **typeface nomenclature**.

groundwood pulp (1917) Inexpensive wood pulp, such as that used in the manufacture of newsprint. Also called *mechanical wood pulp*. Compare **chemical pulp**.

groundwood paper (1917) Paper used originally for newsprint. It is manufactured from **groundwood pulp** and bleached or unbleached **chemical pulp**.

groupware A software application program designed to allow a group of workers to accomplish a specified task.

guide (1) A nonprinting line (**margin guide**, **ruler guide**, or **column guide**) created to help **align** objects on a page. (2) Sheet-feed gauges against which paper is fed on printing presses.

guide words (1928) Words at top of page to indicate first and last tagged words on page. Used in dictionaries and glossaries, in particular. *See also* **header**.

gussets *See* **buckles**.

gutter (1) The inner margin of a single-column page, which makes an allowance for

gutter (1) The inner margin of a single-column page, which makes an allowance for the binding in a book. See also **margin**. (2) The area between columns. Also called *alley*.

gutter margin *See* **gutter**.

Notes and New Words

H

H&J *See* **hyphenation and justification**.

hacek (1953) A **diacritical** mark that indicates a sound value. For example, the ê in *être*.

hack (1721) A writer who writes for others without receiving public credit. *See also* **ghost writer**.

hacker A computer hobbyist or industry professional with the inclination and talent to modify computer hardware and software, sometimes out of necessity, but more often just to see if he or she can do it.

hair space A space that is one-fifth of an em, one-sixth of an em, or one-half point in size used to **letterspace** words and to justify lines of type. Also called *copper space, five-em space, five-to-the-em space*. Compare **figure space**; **thin space**.

hairline (1846) The finest of an assortment of printing **rules**— usually 0.25 point— used to describe lines and typefaces.

half-diamond indention When successive lines are **indented** each slightly more than the ones above in type composition.

half-duplex A mode of transmitting or moving data with a **modem** in which only one computer at a time can communicate. *See also* **full-duplex**; **modem**.

half-title page (1879) A page on which the title stands alone with no other information, usually immediately following the front **fly-leaf** and preceding the full **title page**. Also called *bastard title, panel title page, short title page*.

halftone A process whereby a **continuous-tone** image, such as a photograph, is broken up into a pattern of dots of varying size from which a printing plate is made. When printed, the dots of the image, though clearly visible through a magnifying glass, merge into varying grays to give an illusion of continuous tone to the naked eye. *See also* **continuous-tone art**; **dithering**; **half-tone screen**; **highlight halftone**; **moiré pattern**; **outline halftone**; **vignette**.

halftone art Consists of figures that contain not only black and white but also varying shades of gray. Compare **line art**.

halftone cell The number of dots per inch that a printer can print divided by the number of lines per inch in a **halftone** results in a number that defines the size of a halftone cell. When all the printer dots in a cell are on, the cell is black; when they are all off, the cell is empty, or white. Also called *dither matrix*.

halftone paper Smooth paper prepared especially for the reproduction of **halftones**.

halftone screen A screen placed in front of a negative material in a process camera to break up a **continuous-tone image** into a dot formation. The fineness of the screen is denoted in terms of lines per inch, as a *133-line screen*. There are two types of halftone screens: **crossline screen** and **contact screen**. *See also* **halftone**.

hammerhead A headline that contains two lines; the top line is **flush left** and twice the

Hammerhead

Smaller headline

Fig. H-1   A hammer-head headline contains a top headline that is much larger in size than the lower headline.

size of the bottom line, which is **flush right** and indented from the left. A rule may be placed between the two lines. Compare **kicker**.

hand composition Setting type by hand. The type is set on a measured **composing stick**. *See also* **full measure**; **justification**; **justify**.

hand cursor A hand-held device for inputting coordinate data, used in conjunction with a **data tablet**. Also called *puck*. *See also* **cursor**.

hand feed Method of feeding sheet paper into a printing press or other device in which an individual feeds each sheet by hand to transport the paper in its initial progress through the press. Compare **friction feed**; **suction feed**.

handbill (1753) A printed sheet, usually containing advertising, that is circulated by hand. *See also* **brochure**; **circular**; **flier**.

handle (1) A small black rectangle enclosing a selected shape, which can be dragged to change the size of the selected object. (2) The feel or handling quality of materials, such as paper.

handout (1877) Publicity release.

handshaking The interaction between two devices where the transfer of information between two computers requires a continuous exchange of signals between them.

hanging figure Like lowercase letters, these numerals have **ascenders** and **descenders**, thus *1 2 3 4 5 6 7 8 9 0*. Also called *old style figure*. Compare **aligning figure**.

hanging indent (1904) In composition, a style in which the first line (or more) of copy is set **full measure** and all the lines that follow are indented. Also called *flush-and-hang indention*. *See also* **flush left**; **flush right**; **indentation**; **run out**.

hanging paragraph *See* **hanging indent**.

hanging punctuation In justified type, punctuation that falls at the end of a line

The first (and, in this example, the second) line of a hanging inden is full measure; the remaining lines are indented.

Fig. H-2   An example of a hanging indent.

and is set just outside the measure in order to achieve optical alignment.

hang-up A computer that is frozen up due to a **malfunction** of software or hardware.

hard carriage return A return entered when the **Enter key** or some other key is pressed to force a new line. Compare **soft carriage return**.

hard copy (1890) (1) General term for original or other copy. (2) A printed copy of machine output in a visually readable form, for example, printed report, listing, **document**, summary, **camera-ready copy**, **reproduction copy**, original typewritten manuscript copy, or computerized **output** on **laser**, **dot-matrix**, or **letter-quality** printers. Compare **softcopy**.

hard cover (1949) Stiff-covered book. The cover is manufactured separately, and the sewn book is inserted and affixed to the cover. Also called *case bound, hardback,* and *hardbound. See also* **boards**; **bookbinding**.

hard disk A data-storage device using rigid disks of magnetic material turning at high speed, usually permanently encased in its drive unit. Also called *fixed disk. See also* **external memory**. Compare **floppy disk**.

hardback (1952) *See* **hard cover**.

hardbound *See* **hard cover**.

hardware The *hard* or physical components of a computer system, e.g., **disk drives**, **keyboard**, the electronic computer, **CRT**, **memory**, used in data processing. Compare **software**. *See also* **firmware**.

harmony In **layout**, the state of a pleasing relation between elements in a printed piece.

hatching (1658) Evenly spaced parallel line shading applied to a bounded area to identify the area. Compare **crosshatching**.

head (1) The top of a book page or job of printing. Compare **foot**. (2) The name, headline, or title of a story. Also called *heading*. *See also* **subhead**; **running head**. (3) A small electromagnetic device that reads, writes, or erases data on a magnetic storage medium.

head crash Impact by the read/write head to a magnetic disk surface resulting in damage to the surface. *See also* **crash**.

head margin The top **margin** of a page. Also called *top margin.*

head to come A note to the printer that the headline is not accompanying the copy, but will be supplied later. Abbreviated *HTK*.

head to foot Arrangement of copy on both sides of a sheet with the foot of the opposite page aligned with the top of the first page. It is necessary to flip the sheet to view the opposite page for normal reading. Compare **head to head**.

head to head Arrangement of copy so that the top of the page is at the same end on both sides of a sheet. Compare **head to foot**.

headband Decorative band at the top and bottom of the **spine** of a book, originally intended to take the strain of a person's finger as a book is removed from the shelf.

header Repetitive words, phrases, or sentences placed at the top of every page of a document. Typically contains **titles** or **guide words**. Compare **footer**. *See also* **folio**; **running foot**; **running head**.

heading (1935) (1) *See* **head**. (2) Caption or title of a division of a brochure, book, or other publication. (3) A main entry in an index. *See also* **entry**; **sidehead**.

headless paragraph Paragraph that stands alone without the support of a **sidehead**.

headline (1824) (1) A head of a newspaper story or article, usually printed in large type and giving the gist of the story or article. (2) Words set at the head of a passage to introduce or categorize. (3) Major caption set above a newspaper or magazine article or advertising text. *See also* **banner**; **hammerhead**; **kicker**; **sidehead**.

headliner ruler A transparent ruler with horizontal and vertical lines.

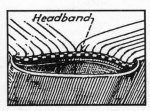

Fig. H-3   The decorative headband at the top of a book.

headnote (1855) (1) In a **table**, a brief explanation of a table title. For example, a common headnote is the phrase *(in thousands)*. (2) Short text accompanying the **head** and carrying information on the story, the author, or both. (3) A note of comment or explanation that prefaces a text.

headpiece (1535) Illustrative image used to decorate a chapter or section heading.

head trim The side of gathered **signatures** that is **trimmed** before being bound.

height Distance between two points along the **vertical dimension**. It is perpendicular to the **width**. When measurements are given for **line art** and **continuous-tone copy**, the width is stated first, and the height second.

Heintz Dinter On Desktop Publishing A monthly publication that covers problem solving and improving productivity and business image in the PC publishing marketplace.

hell box A place where broken or worn-out type and material is placed.

help message Information displayed on a screen to assist the user in small tasks. Compare **tutorial**.

Hercules Developer and manufacturer of board-level products for personal computers, including the popular Hercules graphics board for the IBM-PC.

hertz (1928) An international unit of measurement equal to one cycle per second. Abbreviated *Hz*.

hex *See* **hexadecimal**.

hex dump *See* **data dump**.

hexadecimal A numbering system that uses 16 digits: the numerals from 0 to 9 and the letters of the alphabet from A to F, which allows numbers to be stated in a much more compact form than the **binary notation** system. Any decimal number between 0 and 255 can be expressed by a two-digit hex number. Abbreviated *hex*. *See also* **decimal**; **numbering system**.

HFR *See* **hold for release**.

hickey (1) In **offset lithography**, a blemish in the impression caused by dirt, a blob of ink, etc., on the **printing plate** or **blanket**. (2) A speck or blotch in a photographic negative.

hidden file A file, usually used only by **disk operating system**, that is not listed when a **directory** is displayed. Hidden files cannot be erased, copied, or otherwise affected by DOS commands.

hidden line In computer graphics, a line segment that represents an edge obscured from view in a two-dimensional projection of a three-dimensional object. *See also* **hidden line removal**.

hidden line removal A **command** used to remove **hidden lines** in graphic representations.

hierarchical filing system A disk storage system in which files can be stored in separate **directories**, which, in turn, may contain **subdirectories**. *See also* **multilevel filing system**.

high-bulk paper Paper thickened during manufacture by having air blown into it.

high finish A smooth, high-polished paper finish.

high-level language A programming language that allows a user to write **instructions** in an English-like notation corresponding to several machine code instructions.

high resolution Video graphics display systems or printers that reproduce images in great detail with a high degree of accuracy.

high-resolution graphics Graphics produced through **bit-mapping**, whereby the programmer has control over each individual **pixel** on the **video display**. Such graphics show great detail and can look very realistic. *See also* **computer graphics; resolution, graphics; user-defined graphics characters**.

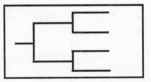

Fig. H-4   A hierarchical filing system stores files in directories, subdirectories, etc.

highlight (1927) *v.* (1) To distinguish visually, usually by reversing the normal appearance of a selected text, graphic, or option (for example, black text on a white background appears as white on black). (2) Several methods of cursor movement used to mark the text that will then be denoted by high-intensity display or reverse display. *n.* That part of a **halftone** in which the brightest sections are represented by opaqueness in the negative and by nearly white paper in the print.

highlight halftone A **halftone** that is cut out on the inside. It is not the subject's background that is cut away, but some part of the subject itself, usually an area that was blank in the original but would appear as pale grey in print. Also called *deep-etched halftone.* Compare **outline halftone**.

hinge In a bookbinding, the connection between the covers and the book proper.

HIS values Values that indicate the **hue, intensity**, and **saturation** of a color.

history A **utility** that maintains a numbered list of previous commands and provides a shorthand notation to let the user repeat or modify previous commands.

hokum Overly sentimental copy or art.

hold Not to be published without release. Also called *hold for release*, abbreviated *HFR.*

hold for release *See* **hold**.

holding lines Lines drawn by the designer on the **mechanical** to indicate the exact area that is to be occupied by a **halftone**, color, **tint**, etc.

Hollerith card (1946) A card that contains data, which is created with holes punched in designated positions. Also called *punched card. See also* **keypunch**.

home The beginning position of a **cursor** on a **video display**, usually in the top left-hand corner of the screen. Also called *home position.*

home computer A **microcomputer** used at home to play games and do small tasks, such as home accounting or checkbook balancing. *See* **personal computer**.

home directory The **directory** assigned to a user by the **system manager**. Usually the same as the user **login directory**.

Home key A **keyboard** key that moves the **cursor** to the top left of the screen. *See also* **directional arrow**.

Home Office Computing (1983) A monthly magazine written for home users of the computer with emphasis on the home office entrepreneur.

home position *see* **home**.

home view In Publish Pac, displays the image so that the width of the image fits into the window. This is how the image is displayed after scanning.

horizontal bar chart *See* **bar chart**.

horizontal justification Determines the length of a line of text, and normally the contour of the right margin of a document. *See also* **justified**; **ragged right**.

horizontal line pattern In Publish Pac, a halftone pattern used to emphasize vertical lines or smooth contours.

horizontal page *See* **broadside page**.

host computer The larger computer, usually stronger and more dominant, in a **network** that acts as the controller for the system.

hot composition *See* **hot metal composition**.

hot foil stamping *See* **foil stamping**.

hot metal type Strictly, type from a casting machine, but widely used for any type set in relief on a metal body. Compare **cold type**. Also called *hot type, metal type*. *See also* **letterpress printing**.

hot metal composition (1963) The setting of cast metal type, either by hand or by machine. *See also* **Intertype**; **Linotype**; **Ludlow**; **Monotype**.

hot type *See* **hot metal type**.

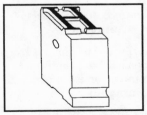

Fig. H-5   An example of a hot metal type.

hot zone The area in which an editing system will decide to return the line and expand it for right-justified text or select a hyphen point in the word which is about to exceed the right margin— or both— to adjust the right-hand margin.

hourglass Symbol that temporarily replaces the **pointer** to indicate that the software is busy completing instructions. No other functions can be performed when the hourglass is on the screen.

house A publishing company.

house ad An advertisement for the magazine in which it appears or for another issued by the same publisher.

house magazine *See* **house organ**.

house organ (1907) Periodical or newsletter issued by a firm or organization for its members, employees, customers, stockholders, dealers, or prospects. Also called *house magazine, company magazine*.

house style The **style guide** adopted by a particular publishing or publishing house. *See also* **style**.

housekeeping Keeping track of what files are where, of who is doing what, disk space used and remaining, and other system monitoring routines.

how-to (1926) Articles and books devoted to explanations of how the reader can accomplish or make something.

HTK *See* **head to come**.

hue One of the three perceived color dimensions, an attribute represented by the infinite combinations of different wavelengths, referred to as **color**. *See also* **brightness; intensity; saturation**.

human-computer interface The means by which information is passed back and forth from a program to the user, for example, **help messages** and **commands**.

human factors Factors to be considered when designing an interactive program or system. Examples include: provision of consistent sequences, avoid overloading the user with too many options, the use of **prompts** to guide the user, making allowances for user mistakes, and provision for adequate feedback information. Also called *ergonomics*.

human interest Feature material designed to appeal to the emotions.

hung initial Display letter that is set in the left-hand margin. Compare **drop initial**.

hype *See* **hyperbole**.

hyperbole (15c) Exaggerated claims intended to sell a product or promote a person. Also called *hype*.

hyphen (1620) A punctuation mark (-) used to divide words, word elements, or numbers. *See also* **discretionary hyphen; double hyphen; hyphenation**.

hyphen drop The function of a program that ensures that a **discretionary hyphen** is not printed when the word concerned subsequently appears elsewhere in the text and no longer requires hyphenation.

hyphenate (1892) (1) To connect (as two words) with a hyphen. (2) To divide (a word at the end of a line) with a hyphen.

hyphenation (1892) Determining where a word should break at the end of a line. In typesetting, computers are programmed to determine hyphenation by the following methods: **discretionary hyphen, exception dictionary**, or true **dictionary**. *See also* **hyphenation routine**.

hyphenation and justification The grammatical and typographic **end-of-line decisions** that must be made by either the **operator** or the computer during the typesetting process. Abbreviated *H&J*.

hyphenation routine In **computer-assisted composition**, a set of instructions for hyphenating words at the end of a line, usually supplemented by an **exception dictionary**. *See also* **hyphenation**.

hypotenuse oblong A book page proportion in which the depth is 50% greater than its width.

Hz *See* **hertz**.

Notes and New Words

Notes and New Words

I

I-beam (1986) In **Ventura,** the shape of the **pointer** when the **text icon** is selected.

IBM PC-DOS (1981) *See* **PC-DOS.**

IC *See* **integrated circuit.**

icon A small representational **graphic** symbol in graphic user interfaces, frequently used for giving a visual indication of the meaning of a **command** on a screen menu. The icon usually stands for **disks, files, documents,** etc.

Fig. I-1   Possible icons for a minifloppy disk and a microfloppy disk.

iconic graphics Artwork such as photographs or line drawings that act as examples of textual information.

identification line The line at the end of a business letter on which the initials of the writer and typist appear.

idiot tape In **computer-assisted composition,** magnetic tape or punched paper bearing only the keyboarded text itself. **Hyphenation, justification,** and other **end-of-line decisions** are added by a computer programmed to perform these functions.

illustrated parts breakdown A list of parts that contains illustrations of those parts. Also called *exploded view, illustrated parts list, provisioning parts breakdown.*

illustrated parts list *See* **illustrated parts breakdown.**

illustration *See* **artwork; figure.**

illustration file number *See* **art file number.**

illustration guide *See* **legend.**

illustration request Form that requests that an individual piece of art be executed. It is usually filled in by the writer of the text that the illustration is to accompany.

illustration title *See* **figure title.**

image Any representation of a concept or an object on a paper sheet, plate, or other material. It may be drawn, typewritten, stamped, printed, marked, cut, carved, engraved, typeset, or photographed and be applied by any method or process. The image may be a **text block**, a **line drawing**, a **photograph**, a **symbol**, or a **dot**, but only if it was made intentionally and communicates a message.

image area (1) In word processing, the area of a display device where characters can be displayed. (2) Square or rectangular area that encompasses a printed, drawn, or photographed **image** and the white or dark background space around the image. It is enclosed by imaginary vertical and horizontal lines. (3) For **artwork**, the four sides of the area are established by using **crop marks** that limit the horizontal and vertical dimensions but are not printed. (4) In text matter, the image area is defined by a line **measure** along the horizontal dimension and a line count along the vertical dimension. (5) Area inside the **margins** of the page.

image enhancement Bringing out all the elements of a picture that may have previously been too small or had too little

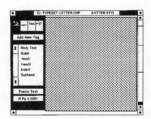

Fig. I-2 The shaded area is the image area in Ventura.

contrast or definition to have been seen without the computer's help.

Image Folio A software program containing photographic images for **desktop publishing** systems.

image graphics In computer graphics, a technique for displaying images without the use of coordinate data. Also called *noncoded graphics*.

image master In phototypesetting, the type fonts, i.e., a disk, filmstrip, etc. Also called *type matrix*.

image printer A printer using optical technology to compose an image of a complete page from digital input.

image processing Changing **images** into a digital format that can be processed by a computer, altered, and restored to an image format. Also called *digital image processing*.

imaging The ability to take information— which would be meaningless if viewed in its raw form—and construct a useful picture.

impact paper (1871) A **coated paper** that may be used to get one or more copies of printed, typed, or handwritten information without the need for a ribbon or other inking device. Also called *carbonless paper*.

impact printer Computer printer that uses arrays of needles (**dot-matrix printers**) or hammers (**daisy-wheel printers**) to print the image. They make direct contact with the printing ribbon and, consequently, with the substrata itself, hence are called *impact printers*. Compare **ink-jet printer**; **letter-quality printer**; **nonimpact printer**.

impose (1) To arrange pages in the proper order and orientation for printing. (2) In typesetting and makeup, the plan of arranging the printing image carrier in accordance with a plan.

imposing table The flat stone or metal-topped table on which **forms** are **locked up** in **chases**.

imposition (1) Arrangement of the pages that are to be printed on one side of a sheet

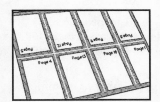

Fig. I-3   The imposition of a porition of a signature.

so that, when cut, folded, and trimmed, they will be right-reading and fall in numerical sequence. (2) The order or arrangement of imposed pages. (3) In **offset lithography** usually called *stripping*.

impression (1) The pressure of type **forms** or **printing plates** on the paper in a printing press. *See also* **kiss impression**. (2) An image of any kind imposed on a surface. (3) The speed of a printing press is given in terms of **impressions per hour**. (4) All the copies made in one **pressrun**. Also called *printing*.

impression cylinder In a **rotary press**, the cylinder that impresses the paper against the **printing plate** or **blanket cylinder** containing the image.

impression paper Paper that receives the image in any duplicating or printing operation. Also called *printing stock, rolled paper, copy paper*.

impressions per hour The number of copies made by a press in an hour. Abbreviated *iph.*

imprint *v.* To print a person's or a firm's name and address on a previously printed piece by running it through another printing press. *n.* (1) The identifying name of a publishing company carried on a published book. (2) A specific line of books within a publishing **house** usually defined by its own name and **colophon**. (1912) (3) The name of a **Monotype** typeface that was first designed and used in mechanical linecasting composition in the short-lived, but influential, magazine, *The Imprint.* (4) Printed bibliographical and copyright information.

imprinter Any device used to produce or impress marks or patterns on a surface, for example, printing presses, typewriters, and pens.

impure page (15c) A page carrying commercial **puffs**.

in-flights Periodicals commissioned or published by airline companies, usually distributed without cost to passengers.

in-house (1956) (1) Those functions performed within a publishing company rather than by outside contractors. (2) Indicates that the finished books have been delivered to the publisher. (3) Periodicals published by and generally, though not always, read only by employees of a company or corporation.

in-house ad agency An advertising agency set up by a firm for which it is the sole client.

In-Plant Printer and Electronic Publisher (1961) A bimonthly publication serving printing, graphics, and typesetting facilities located in business, industry, education, government, hospitals, associations, and nonprofit organizations.

in print (1950) Books that are currently available from publishers. Also called *front-list*. Compare **backlist**.

inch-pica-point conversion chart *See* Appendix 1.

inches per second Usually refers to the speed of tape moving past a recorder head. Abbreviated *ips*.

increment (15c) Distance between tick marks on a ruler. *See also* **measurement system**.

incunabula (1861) Books printed before 1501.

indent A feature applicable to any text creation method that enables blocks of recorded text to be indented with different margins while still retaining the original fixed margin settings. Indention is used to help the reader's eye catch the beginning of each new paragraph. The space used for an indent is usually one **em**. Compare **full measure**. *See also* **hanging indent**; **outdent**; **paragraph indent**.

indention (1763) Moving of one or more lines of printed or typewritten matter in from the **margin**.

index (1571) *v.* In word processing, to move the paper or display pointer in the direction used during normal printout. *n.* (1) A list of the contents of a **file** or of a **document**, to-

This paragraph starts with a 1-em indent.

This paragraph starts with a 2-em indent.

Fig. I-4   Indents helps the reader's eye catch the beginning of each new paragraph.

gether with **keys** or references for locating the contents. Also called *contents list*. (2) A symbol (☞), used to call attention to an item. (3) Alphabetical listing of the important topics of a work, accompanied by the page numbers on which they occur. It is the last element in the **back matter**. Compare **concordance**. *See also* **blind reference**; **scattering**.

index entry The individual line or item of data found in an index, such as an entry in a dictionary. Also called *entry, heading*.

index guide Printed **tab** or other device marking a division of a publication, card file, ledger, or filing system for quick reference. There are three kinds of index guides: **dividers, thumb indexing, extended guides**.

index hole A hole cut in a **floppy disk** showing the beginning of the first **sector**.

index letter (1) Letter of the alphabet, usually a capital letter, used to **key** a part or item depicted in an illustration to a legend or to a discussion in text. **Index numbers** are used for the same purpose. *See also* **key number**. (2) Also, letter of the alphabet used to introduce its following words.

index number *See* **index letter**.

indexer (1720) In the traditional publishing process, one who compiles an **index**.

indexing (1974) **Line spacing** on a typewriter or printer. Some programs and printers will index quarter line, half line, one line, 1.5 lines, and double space. Some are infinitely adjustable. Similar to **leading**.

India ink (1665) Dense, black ink, made of lampblack, and preferred for drawing and ruling in preparing **artwork** for photographic reproduction.

India paper (1768) *See* **Bible paper**.

indicia (1625) Mailing information data required by the post office.

individual document blueprint Writing plan used to communicate the very detailed and specific plans associated with a particular paper or online document.

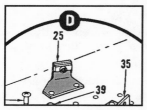

Fig. I-5   An index letter.

inferior character A letter, numeral, or symbol written below the **baseline** and to the right of another character, usually in a smaller type, as 123 or H_2O. Generally used in mathematical settings. Also called *subscript*. *See also* **superior character; superscript**.

inferior figure *See* **inferior character**.

Information and Word Processing (1971) Semimonthly newsletter for word processors.

Information Center (1985) A monthly magazine to serve readers who are responsible for management of end-user computers in business organizations.

information processing A system that integrates **word processing** and **data processing**.

initial A single letter, bigger than the text, usually used to mark the beginning of a chapter or section. Also called an *initial letter*. The large letter used at the beginning of a book page. *See also* **drop initial; initial down; initial up; swash initial**.

initial cap *See* **initial capital**.

initial capital (1) A text style in which the first word has an initial capital letter. (2) A direction to the typesetter to set only the first character of a **heading** or line of text with a capital letter.

initial down A text style in which the top of the **initial** aligns with the top of the first line of type and carryover lines run around the lower part of the initial. Also called *cut-in initial*.

initial letter *See* **initial**.

initial up A large letter used to begin a chapter or section that aligns at the bottom with the first line of text but sticks up into the white space above. Also called *stickup initial*. Compare **drop initial; initial down**.

initialize (1957) Setting a device to its beginning, or initial, state.

initialize a disk *See* **format a disk**.

This initial letter is aligned with the bottom of the first line of type.

Fig. I-6   An initial up.

ink film Ink thickness, varying according to the printing process involved. The following thicknesses refer to ink film on smooth papers:

offset lithography	0.00008 in
flexography	0.00008 in
letterpress	0.00020 in
gravure	0.00050 in
screen process (thin film)	0.00125 in
screen process (thick film)	0.00250 in

ink-jet printer A **nonimpact printer** that forms characters by the projection of a jet of fast-drying ink onto paper. Tiny streams of ink are shot onto the paper to create **dot-matrix** characters. Compare **impact printer**.

ink-jet printing A printing method in which an image is formed as the paper moves past a row of minute jets that squirt ink in response to electronically controlled signals. *See also* **ink-jet printer**.

ink uniformity The degree of light intensity variation over the area of printed characters, specifically within the character edges. *See also* **feather**.

inking In computer graphics, creating a line by moving a **pointer** over the display space leaving a trail behind the pointer in the manner of a pen drawing a line on paper.

input *v.* To enter information, instructions, text, data, etc., in a computer system. *n.* The data so entered. Also called *input process*. *See also* **input device**.

input device A tool used by the **operator** to put data into the computer. A **logical input device** is the **software** and **firmware** routines that perform logical functions. A **physical input device** may be a **locator device** (stylus, light pen, or data tablet), a **pick device** (puck or mouse), a **keyboard**, or a **button device**.

input speed Rate at which the copy is translated into machine form.

input/output (1) A general term for the equipment used to communicate with a computer, commonly called *I/O*. (2) The data involved in such communications. *See also* **input**; **output**.

involved in such communications. *See also*
input; **output**.

input/output device A **physical input device** to enter data or to obtain data from a
computer. A **keyboard** is an input device.
The **screen** and **printer** are output devices.
The **disk drive** is both an input and output
device.

input/output port A **serial** or **parallel** connection that enables the computer to input
or output data.

input primitive In computer graphics, a
basic data item from an **input device**.

input process (1) The process of transmitting **data** from **peripheral equipment** or
external memory to **internal memory**. (2)
The entry of information by an **end-user**
into a data-processing system, including the
conversion of information from a human language into a language that the **system** can
understand. Also called *input*.

insert *v.* To put in text, usually squeezing
it between existing characters. *n.* (1) Additional material added to a **manuscript** by
an author or editor. (2) An extra printed
leaf, sometimes folded, usually of different
paper from the text, which is **tipped in** or
placed loosely between the text pages. (3) Additional matter typed on a separate page
and pinned to the **proof**, to be set in type
and **run in**.

inserting requirements Indicates where **signatures** must be placed within other
signatures during **gathering**.

insertion order A form advertising agencies
use to place advertising in various media.

insertion point The point at which text is
to be typed or pasted.

inside margin Margin along the edge of the
page that will be bound. It is the margin on
a page nearest to the fold. *See also* **gutter**;
margin.

inspection drawing *See* **dimension drawing**.

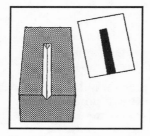

Fig. I-7   Intaglio printing.

Institute for Personal Computing
(1983) An association for individuals with an interest in personal computing.

instruction (1) A computer command in digitally coded form to perform some function in connection with data supplied to it. A computer **program** consists of many such instructions. (2) Directions given to a **typesetter** or **operator** when entering text.

intaglio printing (1644) One of the five basic methods of printing in which the image is engraved on the surface of the **printing plate**. The ink is held in the etched recesses and transferred to paper as an ultrathin coating. Also called *gravure printing*. It is called *photogravure* printing when **photography** is used and *rotogravure* printing when a **rotary press** is used. *See also* **letterpress printing**; **lithography**; **planographic printing**; **relief printing**.

integrated circuit (1959) An electronic device that combines many electronic components such as transistors, diodes, resistors, and capacitors on a small wafer, or chip, of silicon. Such devices are the building blocks of computers. Abbreviated *IC*. Also called *chip*.

integrated modem *See* **internal modem**.

integrity edit A **level of editing** in which cross-references are checked for clarity and accuracy.

intelligence Refers to the level of complexity of automatic functions provided by a system.

intensity The amount of **brightness** of a **pixel**, as opposed to its other color attributes. Also called *brightness*.

intensity level One of a discrete set of brightness levels that can be given a digital definition for display on a **display screen**.

interline spacing *See* **leading**.

interactive Allowing the computer and the user to carry on a dialogue. Compare **stand-alone**.

interactive graphics A mode of operation of a **display device** that allows an online user to alter or interact with a **display image**. Compare **passive graphics**.

interactive program Any program in which the results of an operator's actions are seen immediately. Compare **batch file**.

interactive programming A kind of programming where humans can make changes easily and quickly and the computer can readjust the program to get the change. Such a program may also point out errors as the programmer goes along rather than waiting for the entire program to be run.

interface (1964) The point at which two devices or components come into contact and communicate with each other. A **serial interface** transmits data one **bit** at a time; a **parallel interface** transmits data one **character** or **code** at a time (many bits in parallel). *See also* **human-computer interface**; **user interface**.

interface card *See* **controller**.

interjection (15c) A short utterance usually lacking grammatical connection and expressing an emotion.

interlaced display A video display technique in which the odd lines are scanned and then the even lines are scanned to make a complete image, thus doubling the apparent speed of the display.

Interleaf (1984) An **electronic publishing** program that runs on several computer systems.

Interleaf MilSpec Update A quarterly newsletter that addresses **military specifications** for **Interleaf** users.

interleave To insert unprinted sheets between printed sheets. Also called *slip-sheet*.

interlock (1874) (1) Effect of joining type characters, produced usually in display type set with a photographic typesetter. Similar to **ligature**. (2) A switch that prevents operation of a device until certain conditions are met. For example, a printer paper interlock will not allow a printer to operate unless paper is present.

intermediate user A **user** who has some experience with a particular piece of **software** or with a related piece of software. The intermediate user requires less explanation than a **novice user**, but more than an **expert user**.

internal command Any **PC/MS-DOS utility** that is kept in **random-access memory** (as part of COMMAND.COM) for quick and easy access. For example: **DIR, COPY, CD,** and **ERASE.** Contrast **external command**.

internal documentation Documentation produced by a company or unit of a company for use inside that company or unit. Compare **external documentation**.

internal memory Electronic circuits within a computer that retain information in the form of **binary** numbers. Used to store computer programs or data. There are two types of internal memory: **random access memory**, to which data can be both written and read, and **read-only memory**, which is used for permanent storage of information since data can only be read from it. Also called *main memory*. Compare **external memory**. *See also* **address; address bus; American Standard Code for Information Interchange; binary digit; bus; central processing unit; data bus; machine language; word**.

internal modem A modem that is an integral part of the device with which it operates. Also called *under-the-cover modem*. Contrast **standalone modem**.

International Association of Business Communicators (1970) An association of communication managers, public relations directors, writers, editors, audiovisual specialists, and other communicators who use a variety of media to communicate with internal and external audiences.

International Desktop Publishers Association (1986) An international association of **desktop publishers**.

International Graphic Arts Educational Association (1923) A group of graphic arts and printing teachers who develop an integrated and comprehensive system of graphic arts courses in U.S. schools and colleges.

International Reply Coupon A form that may be purchased from a post office, used in lieu of return postage from foreign countries. Abbreviated *IRC.*

International Standard Book Number An essential identifying number— issued by R.R. Bowker & Co. for a book— used for ordering and cataloging purposes. Abbreviated *ISBN.*

interoperability (1988) The ability of **software** to operate on a variety of **computer systems**.

interpolate To insert a word or words into text or a quotation and enclose in square **brackets**.

Interpress A **page-description language** developed by **Xerox** and used to describe how to print a page that consists of both text and pictures. This description is completely independent of the printing device. *See also* **PostScript**.

interpreter A program that translates each of the statements of a high-level language into **machine language** as they are entered on the **keyboard** or read from a file. **Interactive** languages use interpreters instead of **compilers**.

interrobang (ca. 1967) (1) A single punctuation mark that is made up of two separate characters (? and !) and used with an exclamatory rhetorical question. (2) *See* **overprint**.

Intertype A **linecasting machine**, similar to the **Linotype**, but manufactured by a different company. **Matrices** for the two machines are interchangeable.

interrupt *v.* To break off a **command** or other process and, thus, terminate it. (1957) *n.* A feature of a computer that permits the execution of one program to be interrupted in order to execute another.

introduction (14c) In a book, a preliminary explanatory statement that appears as part of the **front matter**, comments on the scope and content of the book, how it should be used, and the like. This type of introduction may be made by someone other than the author.

inventory Books on hand and available for sale.

invert *See* **reverse**.

invoice A bill sent with an order.

I/O *See* **input/output**.

I/O redirection *see* **redirection**.

iph *See* **impressions per hour**.

ips *See* **inches per second**.

IRC *See* **International Reply Coupon**.

ISBN *See* **International Standard Book Number**.

island An advertisement surrounded by reading matter.

ital *See* **italic**.

italic (1612) (1) A type in which the characters slant to the right, used to emphasize a letter, word, or series of words in text and to print foreign words or phrases. *This sentence is set in italic.* (2) In a **proof**, underscore the word or phrase and write "ital" in the margin for instructions to italicize the word or phrase. Abbreviated *ital.* Compare **roman**. *See also* **type style**.

item selector In **Ventura**, a special kind of **dialog box** used to select files.

Italic type slants to the right, as in this example.

Fig. I-8   Italic type.

Notes and New Words

Desktop Publisher's Dictionary

J

jacket (1) A protective cover for a floppy disk. (2) A **dust cover** for a hardcover book, bearing the book's title, the author's and publisher's name, and other information as desired. Also called *dust jacket, dust wrapper. See also* **back flap; blurb; flap copy; front flap.**

jacket band A strip wrapped around a book **jacket** for sales promotion purposes, such as to emphasize some local or late news tie-in.

jaggies Jagged lines or edges, an **aliasing** problem caused by rendering lines and the edges of surfaces as strings of rectangular **pixels.** They can be overcome by using **antialiasing** routines or using a **high-resolution display** with more pixels.

Japan paper An exceedingly strong high-grade paper made in Japan. Also called *French Japon, Japan vellum.*

Japan vellum *See* **Japan paper.**

Jewish Publication Society of America (1880) An association of Jewish institutions or organizations interested in the publication and dissemination of books on Jewish history, religion, and literature.

job *See* **process**.

job case *See* **case**.

job compositor A **typesetter** who sets commercial printing.

job font A small assortment of type in any one size and style.

job lot A book offered by the **publisher** or **wholesaler** at special low prices to close out or cut down stock. *See also* **remainders**.

job number An identification number assigned to a job.

job press A small **letterpress**, usually a vertical **platen press**, used for printing **letterheads**, circulars, and other small jobs.

job printer A printer who does small commercial printing, such as letterheads and envelopes.

job shop Commercial printing plant. Compare **captive shop**.

job ticket Usually an envelope containing copy and artwork, on which directions are given for the printing of a job. Used in printing shops.

job type Type faces used in printing commercial work.

jobber (1670) (1) In the book business, one who buys in large lots to resell to retailers or libraries. Also called *wholesaler, distributor*. (2) A press used for small work.

jog To align and position any material, particularly paper, for any purpose during **production**.

jogger Vibrating device used to align the edges of **stock** before **trimming**, **folding**, and **binding**.

JOIN A **PC/MS-DOS** command that logically connects a drive to a **directory** on another drive to produce a single directory structure from the two separate directories.

joint The hinge joining the side of a book cover with the **spine**.

joint author A person who writes a book in collaboration with one or more associates.

journalese (1882) A style of writing like that used in newspapers.

journalism (1833) The work of gathering news for, writing for, editing, or directing the publication of a newspaper or other periodical.

journalist One whose occupation is **journalism**, including editor, correspondent, critic, or reporter of a newspaper or other periodical.

journeyman (15c) A printer who has completed his apprenticeship.

joystick (1910) A computer **input device** that is capable of motion in two or more directions. The lever or stick that can be tilted in different directions to change the movement of the **cursor**.

jump (1530) *v.* To continue a story from one page to another. (1552) *n.* A story so jumped. Also called *continued story*.

jump head The title or headline placed over a **jump**.

jump line (1) Text at the end of an article on one page that indicates on what page the article is continued. (2) The text at the top of a continued story, indicating from where the story is continued. Also called *continued line*.

jump the gutter A title or illustration that continues from a left-hand page to a right-hand page. *See also* **gutter**.

junior books *See* **juvenile books**.

junior editor A novice editor, usually just out of school, who assists an editor. The junior editor is usually assigned tasks deemed to be less important.

justification (14c) The adjustment of a line of type so that it fills the line, **flush** from left to right, to a specified **measure**. Compare **unjustified**.

justification range The allowed minimum and maximum space that can be inserted between words within a line.

justification routine The procedures a computer follows in calculating the required spacing to justify a line of type.

justified margin Arrangement of data or type printed on pages such that the left-hand or right-hand characters of each horizontal line lie in the same **column**.

justified text Text that is **flush** at both the left and right edges. *See also* **alignment**.

justified type Lines of type that **align** on both the left and the right of the **full measure**.

justify (14c) To **align** characters horizontally or vertically to fit the positioning constraints of a required **format**. *See also* **flush**; **left-justify**; **right-justify**; **vertical justification**.

juvenile books Children's books or pertaining to them. Also called *children's books, junior books.*

This paragraph is justified. It has a flush left margin and a flush right margin.

Fig. J-1   Justified text.

Notes and New Words

Notes and New Words

K

K Placed after a number it indicates "thousands," as in 128 Kbyte, meaning 128,000 bytes. However, 1 Kbyte is actually 1,024 bytes. Abbreviation of Greek prefix kilo-, meaning "thousand."

Kbyte *See* **kilobyte**.

keep type standing *See* **standing type**.

kern *v.* To reduce the amount of white space between letters— in order to create visually consistent spacing— by tightening the text horizontally. In **phototypesetting**, this is accomplished by deleting one or more units of space from between characters. Composition set this way is often termed *set tight*. (1683) *n.* In metal type, the part of the type face that extends over and from the side of the type body, such as the **descender** of an italic *f. See also* **kerning pair**.

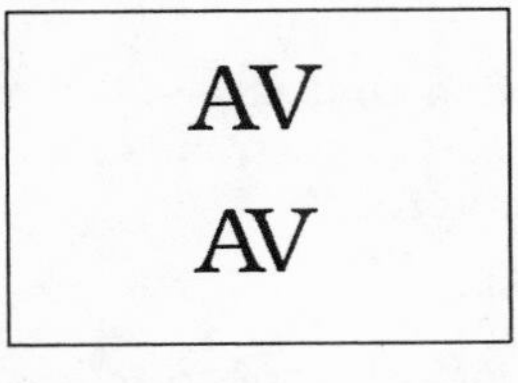

kerning pair Any combination of two characters that may be **kerned**. For instance, a capital **V** following an uppercase **A**

AV

AV

Fig. K-1   The upper pair is not kerned; the lower pair is kerned.

should be placed closer to the **A**: This is not kerned: AV.

This is kerned: AV

key *v.* To enter data via a **keyboard**. *n.* (1) A **keyboard** key. (2) An identifying explanation of coded material, e.g., a color-coded map and its accompanying key indicating what each color represents. (3) A code used in an advertiser's address to identify the publication from which an inquiry originates to determine the effectiveness of an advertising medium. (4) A device for opening and closing **quoins**. (5) In sorting, same as **control word**.

key letters Identifying letters (or words) used in a **comprehensive** or **dummy** to indicate that such letters (or words) are to appear as part of the copy at that particular place. The completed text is furnished separately.

key mat A prepunched plastic user-labeled sheet that fits over a **keyboard** for key identification.

key numbers In technical illustrations, index numbers used in sequence with **lead lines** and **arrowheads** to **key** items on an illustration to an identifying **legend**. *See also* **callout**.

key phrase In **word processing**, a single-key abbreviation for often-used phrases. This feature works like **block moves**, but it involves phrases or sentences instead of paragraphs.

key plate The **printing plate** used to guide the **register** of subsequent color plates in color printing.

key procedures A function that stores frequently used sequences of keystrokes for future replay. *See also* **macro**.

key stroke *See* **keystroke**.

key word (1859) A significant word from a text that is used as an **index** to its content. Also called *descriptor, entry, heading.*

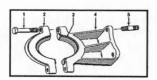

Fig. K-2　Key numbers are used to identify illustrated parts.

key word in context An index prepared by highlighting each key word from a title in the context of words on either side of it and aligning the key words of all titles alphabetically in a vertical column. Abbreviated *KWIC*.

KEYB A load keyboard **PC/MS-DOS** command that allows the user to place a keyboard configuration conforming to a particular language requirement.

keyboard (1965) *v.* (1) To capture or set data or text by means of a keyboard. Also called *typing, entering, keying.* (2) To operate a computer by means of a keyboard. *n.* (1) In **linecasting, phototypesetting**, and **typewriter** or **strike-on composition**, that part of the typesetting machine at which the operator sits and types the copy to be set. (2) Assumed by **PC/MS-DOS** to be the **standard input** unless a different device is specified. *See also* **azerty keyboard; Break key; control character; counting keyboard; Ctrl; cursor; direct-entry keyboard; Dvorak keyboard; Enter; function key; hard copy; noncounting keyboard; numeric keypad; offline keyboard; qwerty keyboard; Return.**

keyboard entry A technique whereby access into the contents of a computer's storage may be initiated at a keyboard.

keypad (1967) A supplementary set of keys, usually numerical and arranged like a calculator and added to a keyboard. Also called *numeric keypad.*

keyline Copy for **offset** reproduction, with outlines showing the placement of **halftones** and type, as well as which parts print in which colors. Also called *layout, paste-up. See also* **markup; mechanical.**

keypunch (1947) A keyboard device containing a mechanism for punching holes in a **Hollerith card** to code information.

keystroke (1910) The operation of a single key on a **keyboard**.

keystrokes per hour A measure of the number of **keystrokes** an **operator** inputs in one hour. Is often used to measure productivity. Abbreviated *kph.*

Top line
Kicker head

Fig. K-3   A kicker contains two lines of type; the top line is half the size of the bottom life. The top line is flush left; the kicker is indented.

kicker A two-line **headline**. The top line is **flush left** and half as large in point size as the bottom line, which is "kicked in," or **flush right**. Compare **hammerhead**.

kid finish Paper **finish** similar to that of kid leather. It is comparatively smooth.

kill (1) To delete unwanted copy. (2) An order to a letterpress printer to break up pages and melt down type. *See also* **standing type**. (3) To terminate a process before it reaches its natural conclusion. (4) To omit, purposely, text or illustrations in revision of **manuscript** or printed matter.

kill fee Money paid to a writer in compensation for time spent working on assignment on a piece the publisher decides not to accept. Also called *salvage fee*.

killed matter *See* **dead matter**.

kilo Metric abbreviation for 1,000.

kilobyte (1970) 1,024 **bytes**. Abbreviated *Kbyte*.

kiss impression (1) In letterpress printing, near-perfect **impression** produced by the ideal contact between printing plate and paper. (2) In **offset lithography** any impression is a kiss impression.

kludge (1962) Programmer's slang for a computer program, or a computer, that has been patched together awkwardly to do a job it was not originally intended to do. It works, but is difficult to maintain and hard to upgrade.

kph *See* **keystrokes per hour**.

kraft paper (1906) Brown paper, used chiefly for wrapping, made from unbleached sulfate pulp. *See also* **chemical pulp**.

KTS *See* **keep type standing**.

KWIC *See* **key word in context**.

Notes and New Words

Notes and New Words

L

LABEL A **PC/MS-DOS utility** program used to create, change, or delete a disk volume **label**, or name.

label (1) A temporary, adhesive-backed card or piece of paper used to identify the contents of a **disk**. (2) A permanent identifier that contains disk manufacturer and capacity information. (3) The name of a **data field** or **disk file**. (4) In structured writing, a **sidehead**.

lacquer *See* **varnish**.

laid paper (1839) Paper which, when held up to the light, shows finely spaced parallel lines and more widely spaced cross lines produced either by a hand process or by laid wires in the **dandy roll** of a papermaking machine. Also called *laid antique paper*. *See also* **dandy roll; wove paper**.

laid antique paper *See* **laid paper**.

lamination In graphic arts, uniting plastic film by heat and pressure to a sheet of paper to protect the paper and improve its appearance.

Fig. L-1   A landscape
page, at top, is wider
than it is long, at bottom.

LAN *See* **local area network**.

landscape monitor A **monitor** that is wider than it is long. Compare **portrait monitor**.

landscape page A page orientation of rectangular format in which the horizontal dimension of the frame is longer than the height of the rectangle. Compare **portrait page**. Also called *broadside page*.

landscape printing Printing in which the printout is sideways on the paper. *See also* **page orientation**; **portrait printing**.

language edit An editing activity in which the editor examines sentences and paragraphs for parallelism, clarity, coherence, and conciseness. *See also* **edit**; **levels of edit**.

Lanston, Tolbert (1844–1913) Inventor of the **Monotype**.

laptop computer A **portable computer** small enough to fit in a person's lap. Compare **transportable computer**.

laser (1957) A device able to emit a tiny beam of electromagnetic radiation in the high end of the spectrum, from visible light to far infrared X-ray frequencies. Acronym for *L*ight *A*mplification by *S*timulated *E*mission of *R*adiation.

laser printer A high-speed computer printer that produces **hard copy** of computer data using laser technology and processes similar to those used in the **electrostatic process**. *See also* **toner**.

laser printing Printing with one of the **toner**-based **laser printers**. These printers use laser technology to project an intense light beam with a very narrow width (1/300th of an inch in 300-dots-per-inch printers). This light creates a charge on the printer drum that picks up the toner and transfers it to the paper. *See also* **phototypesetter**.

lasergravure A printing process in which copper cylinders are etched directly by a **laser** instead of by the conventional combination of photographic plates and chemical baths used in **photogravure**.

LASTDRIVE A **PC/MS-DOS** command used to specify the letter of the last **disk drive** available to a specific computer system.

latency *See* **latent period**.

latent period The time interval between the instant at which an **instruction** control unit initiates a call for data and the instant at which the actual **transfer** of the data is started.

lateral reversal Left-to-right, or mirror-image, reversal of an image.

Latin alphabet (1867) The ancestor of our alphabet, consisting of 21 letters (*j, u, w, y,* and *z* lacking). It is the parent of alphabets used in printing western European languages, including the **Old English**, German **Fraktur**, and Irish forms of letters. Also used to distinguish from such forms as the Greek, Cyrillic, and Semitic alphabets.

lawn finish Linenlike **paper finish**.

lay Character of the **bed** on which paper rests before it enters a **flatbed press**. Register controls, sheet-size alteration, and type of paper **grippers** are considerations of lay.

lay of the case The arrangement of letters and characters in a **type case**.

layout (1888) *v.* To arrange text and graphics on a page. *n.* (1) The designer's blueprint for the printer to follow. It is a drawing— to exact size— of the job to be printed, page by page, showing blocks or columns of type, illustrations, headings, photo captions, pagination, marginal allowances, center headings and sideheads, placement and size of display and body type, and placement of illustrations. Refers specifically to **cold-composition copy**, while **makeup** is used to refer to work handled by printers. (2) In **offset lithography**, a full scale drawing of a proposed press sheet, divided into individual units of the job, containing measurements needed to position correctly the work areas in the unit. *See*

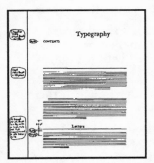

Fig. L-2   An example of a page layout.

also **comprehensive; dummy; footer; header; mechanical; sample page.**

layout board A large piece of paper with **nonreproducing blue** ink grids that are used to position a graphic, but whose lines "disappear" when photocopied. Also called *board.*

layout grid A displayed grid in which horizontal and vertical lines provide guidance for placing **artwork** on a page. *See also* **compositional grid; constructional grid; grid.**

layout typing Typing text for **reproduction copy** while allowing space for illustrations or other material.

l.c. *See* **lowercase.**

LCCN *See* **Library of Congress Card Number.**

ld *See* **lead.**

lead (Rhymes with fed) In **hot metal composition,** thin strips of metal (in thicknesses of 1 to 2 points) used to create space between the lines of type. Leads are less than type-high and so do not print. Abbreviated *ld. See also* **leading.**

lead (Rhymes with feed) The beginning of a book or nonfiction article.

lead-in (1913) First few words in a block of copy set in a different, contrasting **typeface.**

lead line Line that leads to and points out an object or a point of interest or reference. **Arrowheads** may be used with lead lines. *See also* **dogleg.**

leaded matter Text matter in which there is **leading** between lines.

leader (Rhymes with feeder) (1) Leading article in a newspaper. (2) Row of dots, periods, hyphens, or dashes, evenly spaced, used to lead the eye across the page. Specified as 2, 3, or 4 to the **em.** For example:
Table Item 1.....Item 2.....Item 3.....Item 4

leader line *See* **lead line.**

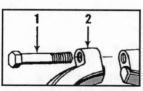

Fig. L-3   The two numbered arrowheads are lead lines.

leading (Rhymes with wedding) (1) In **hot metal composition**, the insertion of **leads** between lines of type. (2) In **phototypesetting**, the placement of space between lines of type. Also called *film advance, line feed, line spacing*. (3) Refers to the spacing between lines of type and paragraphs, measured in points. If 8-point type is set on a 10-point **body** (called "8 on 10" and written 8/10), the effect is of leading 2 points. If no leading is used, the type is said to be **set solid**. *See also* **type specifications; lead; leaded matter; slug; visual space**.

leaf (1) A single sheet of paper, each side of which is a page. Thus, a leaf consists of two pages. (2) A thin sheet of gold or similar material used in **foil stamping** or lettering.

learning curve A theory by which the learning process of an **operator** can be estimated.

leather finish Paper finish giving the appearance of leather. It is made by **embossing**.

leaves *See* **leaf**.

LED (1970) *See* **light-emitting diode**.

left-hand page An even-numbered page. Also called *verso*. Compare **recto; right-hand page**. *See also* **page numbering**.

left-justify To control printing positions of characters on a page so that the left-hand margin of the printing is **aligned**.

left runaround *See* **runaround**.

legal-size paper Paper measuring 8.5 in x 13 in or 8.5 in x 14 in. Compare **letter-size paper**.

legend (1) An explanatory list of the symbols used on a map or chart or in an illustration. *See also* **key**. (2) Identifying words below table, photograph, or art. Also called *cutline, illustration guide*.

legibility That quality in type and its spacing and composition that affects the speed of perception: the faster, easier, and more accurate the perception, the more legible the type. *See also* **readability**.

letter (13c) A graphic character that, when used alone or combined with others, represents in a written language one or more sound elements of a spoken language, but excluding **diacritical marks** used alone and punctuation marks.

letter group A group of entries starting with the same letter in any alphabetical list, including an **index, glossary, dictionary**, etc.

letter of assignment An editor's written confirmation of an **assignment**, which legally serves in lieu of a formal contract. *See also* **confirmation letter**.

letter out To **erase**.

letter paper Paper, regardless of size, that is manufactured for correspondence.

letter-quality printer A computer **printer** that produces type of the quality associated with **typewriters**. Most letter-quality printers use a **daisy wheel** or thimble containing fully-formed characters to produce impressions. Compare **dot-matrix printer, laser printer**. *See also* **daisy-wheel printer; draft**.

letter-size paper Boxed-paper size, ordinarily 8.5 in x 11 in. Compare **legal-size paper**.

letter space *See* **letterspace**.

letterfit In composition, the quality of the space between the individual characters. Letterfit should be uniform and allow for good **legibility**.

letterhead (1887) (1) Information printed or engraved as a heading on a sheet of stationery. (2) The printed or engraved sheet itself. (3) Company stationery that is printed with the name, address, telephone number, and any **logo**.

letterpress printing (1758) A **printing method** based on the relief principle whereby raised surfaces are inked and then pressed against the paper.

letterspace (1917) *v.* (1) To place additional space between letters of words to fill out a line of type to a given measure or to im-

Fig. L-4 Letterpress printing uses an inked raised surface that presses against the paper.

prove appearance, T H U S. (2) In **hot metal type**, letterspacing is achieved by inserting thin paper or metal spaces, which are less than type-high and so do not print, between the letters or increasing the set-width of the face. In **phototypesetting**, letterspacing is achieved either by keyboarding extra space between letters or **kerning**. *See also* **pitch**; **word spacing**. *n.* The space between letters in a line of type.

letterset printing In this printing method, a relief image is produced and then transferred to a **rubber blanket**, from which it is offset to stock. Also called *offset letterpress*, *offset relief*, *dry offset*. The word *letterset* combines the *letter* in "letterpress" and *set* from "offset." *See also* **planographic printing**; **printing method**.

levels of edit Standardization of the documentation editing process into eight discrete steps:
- **coordination edit**
- **copy clarification edit**
- **policy edit**
- **integrity edit**
- **format edit**
- **mechanical style edit**
- **substantive edit**
- **language edit**

lexeme (1940) The written word, particle, or stem that denotes meaning.

lexical (1836) Relating to the words as distinguished from the grammar and construction of a language. *See also* **etymology**.

lexicon (1603) An alphabetical arrangement of a language's words with their definitions. Also called *dictionary*. *See also* **etymology**.

libel (14c) Written **defamation** of character, for which one can be sued.

library (1) A collection of **utility** programs used by certain high-level programming languages. (2) *See also* **boilerplate**. (3) A collection of books. (4) A repository for dismountable recorded media. *See also* **disk library**; **tape library**.

library blueprint A writing plan that communicates the general plan for a group of documents (e.g., reference card, tutorial manual, online help messages) related to a particular **software** product.

Library Journal (1876) A magazine published **semimonthly** to serve library management.

Library of Congress Card Number A number assigned to a book to help catalog it for storage and retrieval in a library. Abbreviated *LCCN*.

lift (1) Greatest number of sheets of paper that can be cut at one time with a paper-cutting machine. (2) The number of sheets that can be handled in an operation of any kind. (3) When each piece of type in a **form** stays in place after being locked in a **chase**, it is said to *lift*.

ligature (15c) A printed character consisting of two or more letters or characters joined together, as *fi, fl, ff, ffi, ffl, æ, œ, Œ*. *See also* **kern**. Older, more decorative forms are called *quaint characters*. *See also* **diphthong; logotype**.

light amplification by stimulated emission of radiation *See* **laser**.

light box *See* **light table**.

light-emitting diode (1970) A semiconductor device that gives off visible or infrared light when a voltage is applied. Abbreviated *LED*.

light-emitting diode display A **display** in which characters are formed from a **dot matrix** of **LEDs**.

light face *See* **lightface**.

light gun *See* **light pen**.

light pen (1958) In computer graphics, a light sensitive **pick** device that is pointed at the **display** surface.

light table A table having a transparent glass top through which fluorescent light is reflected from below. Used to facilitate **paste-up**, **alignment**, and **stripping** negatives into **flats**. Also called *stripping table*.

Fig. L-5   Examples of ligatures.

lightface (1871) A relatively thin **typeface**, lighter than the ordinary variety of **roman** or **italic** type. Compare **boldface**. *See also* **type style**.

limited edition (1903) A specified and limited quantity of books, often numbered and signed by the author.

limp binding (1706) A flexible **cover** such as paper or cloth. Also called *soft cover*, *paperback*. *See also* **self-cover.**

line (1) Publishers often refer to an **imprint** within their **house** as a *line*. (2) A long, thin mark made by a pen, pencil, or by an **input device** using a graphics program. (3) One-twelfth of an inch. (4) A **channel**.

line art A black-and-white original illustration that does not require **halftone** reproduction. In line art there is no in-between tones of gray. Examples include line drawings, charts, maps, and graphs.

line break (1) The end of a line of text, created by automatic **word wrap** and **hyphenation**. *See also* **carriage return**. (2) In **Ventura**, the blank line that separates two paragraphs. Compare **column break**; **page break**.

line copy (1) Original copy that is printed, written by hand, typewritten, or drawn by hand. (2) Composition of solid black lines and masses without **gradation** of tone. In text, line copy consists of letters, numerals, punctuation marks, pen-and-ink drawings, rules, borders, dots, or any other marks in black and white. Compare **continuous-tone copy**.

line cut (1902) *See* **line engraving**.

line drawing (1891) A drawing made with a pen or other pointed instrument in solid black lines, usually with pen and ink. (2) A graphic image composed of rules, grids, screens, and other geometric elements. Compare **halftone art**.

line edit To tighten sentences, smooth over transitions, etc., as opposed to a major overhaul.

Fig. L-6   This is a line drawing of a recriprocating engine.

line editor (1) Editor who specializes in the editing, rather than acquisition, of manuscripts. (2) An editor who **line edits**.

line-ending adjustment A **software** feature that, during printout, automatically adjusts the line endings of edited text to comply, within the **line-ending zone**, with the original margin setting or to changed settings with or without editing.

line-ending zone A predetermined amount of printable space immediately to a left or right margin that is used to trigger semiautomatic and automatic line-ending decisions during adjust text mode operations. Also called *hot zone*.

line engraving (1802) A **printing plate** made up of black-and-white, nonscreened artwork. Also called *line cut*.

line feed A **control code** or **button** that advances the paper in a printer one line space. *See also* **form feed**; **leading**.

line gauge An ruler-like instrument used for **copyfitting** and measuring typographic material. Also called *type gauge, pica pole, pica rule*.

line graph (1914) A **graph** in which points representing values of a variable are connected by a line with values of an independent variable.

line illustration **Artwork** made up of black-and-white lines and solid areas, without continuous tone.

line length Horizontal **measure** of a **column** or a line of text. Usually expressed in **picas** and **points**. *See also* **alphabet length**.

line measure *See* **measure**.

line negative A negative made from **line copy** used to make a line plate, without shooting through a **halftone screen**.

line screen (1) A **screen** that permits varying percentages of color to be printed. (2) Refers to the number of dots per linear inch of a **halftone**.

Fig. L-7   A line gauge, also called a pica pole.

line plotter A printing device with a carriage located above a table. The carriage holds a pen and draws lines on paper according to directions fed to it by a computer.

line printer (1955) A computer **output device** that prints a whole line of characters at once, at speeds of up to 2,000 **lines per minute**.

line printing The printing of a line of characters as a unit.

line spacing (1) In **typesetting**, the consistent baseline-to-baseline distance between horizontal lines of text, measured in **points**. (2) In **phototypesetting**, also called *indexing, leading. See also* **readability**.

line style Appearance of the border of a shape or a line.

line weight Thickness of any line in **artwork** or **rules**.

linecasting machine (1964) A typesetting machine—such as **Linotype** and **Intertype**—that automatically sets lines of type. Before **tape** was used, a linecasting machine was run solely by an **operator** who **keyboarded** the words into the machine.

linen finish Paper or cardboard having a **finish** similar to that of linen cloth.

lines per inch (1) On a printer, the measure of the number of lines per vertical inch of paper. Abbreviated *lpi*. (2) A measure of the frequency of dots on a **halftone screen**. *See also* **screen ruling**.

lines per minute A unit of measure for expressing the speed of a typesetting system. Abbreviated *lpm*.

linescreen *See* **screen ruling**.

lineup table Device designed to facilitate close **register** work and **alignment** of materials before and after **platemaking**. It is used to align the components of a paste-up, such as finished art and nomenclature, and for laying out and stripping negatives into **flats**, ruling and scribing, checking press proofs for dimensional accuracy, handling **imposition**, assuring correct register for complementary and multiple flats, and anything that demands accuracy and precise alignment.

lining See **align**.

lining figure A numeral that **aligns** with the capitals of the typeface to which it belongs: 1 2 3 4 5 6 7 8 9 0. Also called *aligning figure, modern figure*. Compare **hanging figure**. See also **Arabic numeral**.

LINK A **PC/MS-DOS** command that permits programmers to combine individual programs that are in compiled (object) form.

link An entry in a **directory** file that links a system's user-assigned name for a file to the systems identification number for that file.

Linotron Trade name for a high-speed **cathode-ray tube phototypesetting** machine and system manufactured by Mergenthaler Linotype Corporation.

Linotype (1886) A trademark used for a **keyboard**-operated **typesetting** machine, made by Mergenthaler, that uses circulating **matrices** and produces each line of type in the form of a solid metal **slug**. It employs **hot metal composition**. Invented by Ottmar Mergenthaler (1854–1899). See also **Intertype; linecasting machine**.

liquid laminate A liquid coating for book **jackets** and paperback **covers** that when dry gives an effect similar to **laminate**.

list (1) New books published by a particular **house**. Most houses issue two lists annually, in the fall and spring. (2) All the titles a publisher has in print and for sale, made up of **frontlists** and **backlists**. (3) See **list price**. (4) The names of individuals or businesses that make up a specific market area used in **direct mail** advertising.

list box Area in a **dialog box** that displays options.

list broker Someone who handles **direct mail** list rentals for use in direct marketing efforts.

list of illustrations Element in the **front matter** that contains the figure numbers and titles and the page numbers on which the figures appear. Also called *table of illustrations*. *See also* **table of contents**; **table of tables**.

list of tables Element in the **front matter** that contains the **table** numbers and titles and the page numbers on which the tables appear. Also called *table of tables*. *See also* **table of contents**; **table of illustrations**.

list price (1871) The full retail price of a book, without discounts.

listing (1) A **printout** of a **file**. (2) A printout of all the lines in a computer program, often on paper, though a listing can also be displayed on the computer's screen.

literal (1622) (1) A misprint; a literal error. (2) The question mark (?) used within **filenames** to represent any character. Also called *wild card*.

Literary Market Place A comprehensive compilation of **publishers**, **agents**, **book clubs**, **printers**, and everyone else relevant to the book publishing industry, with names, addresses, and phone numbers.

literature search A systematic and exhaustive search for published material on a specified subject, and often the preparation of **abstracts** or summaries on that material.

lithographer One who specializes in the art and process of **lithographic printing**.

lithographic printing Printing from a plane surface, the most popular method of **planographic printing**. *See also* **printing method**.

lithography (1831) A **printing method** in which the surface of a metal plate is treated with chemicals so that some portions will accept ink while other portions will reject it. It is a **planographic process**, the image being flush with the surface of the printing plate. In **offset lithography**, the image is first transferred to a rubber **blanket** before impressions are taken. *See also* **bimetallic plates**; **Driography**.

Fig. L-8   Lithography is a planographic printing process.

live key A **keyboard** key that continues to operate as long as the key is depressed. Also called *automatic repeat key, repeat-action key*.

live matter (1) A printing **form** or **copy** in current use. (2) Type matter that is to be held, or used for printing. Also called *alive matter, alive type*. Compare **dead matter**.

LMP *See* ***Literary Market Place***.

load To move data or programs from an **external storage device**, such as a **disk** or **tape**, to the **internal memory** of a computer.

loading Putting the machine-language **instructions** of a program into memory.

local (1824) Having limited scope. Compare **global**.

local area network A system linking together computers and **peripheral equipment** to create an interoffice, or intersite network. These networks usually provide access to external networks, for example, public telephone and data transmission networks, and information retrieval systems. Abbreviated *LAN*.

location In computer terminology, the particular place in a storage medium where specific data is to be found, identified by an **address**.

locator (1) Information provided with a **reference** or **index entry** that gives the location (as the page, column, paragraph, verse, or line) of the cited material or indexed term. (2) *See* **spot**. (3) *See* **locator device**.

locator device A logical or physical **input device**— for example, a **data tablet**, **stylus**, **light pen**, or **joystick**— that allows a user to specify a position on the screen.

lock In **PageMaker**, a command to **anchor** column guides and ruler guides on the current page or to anchor the **ruler zero point**.

lock up *v.* (1) In **letterpress printing**, to tighten up all the matter (type and blocks) in a **chase** by means of **quoins** to make it into a **form** for printing. (2) To put a disk or a file in a condition whereby it is impossible to write to that disk or file. *See also* **write-protect notch**. *n*. Spelled *lockup*.

lockup *See* **lock up**.

logarithmic scale (1949) Proportional scale often used on a **chart** or **graph** as a vertical scale with lines varying as to distance; the distances so represented have equal ratios.

logged disk The active, current, or default, **disk drive**.

logic (1) The configuration of computer circuits for data processing. (2) The circuits themselves. (3) An analytical, deductive method of reasoning approach in the decision making process.

logical device A portion of **memory** or a **disk** that is named and treated by software as a **physical device**.

login The process of gaining access to the computer system to begin a session. *See also* **logout**.

login directory The **directory** in which the user is placed at login; usually a user's **home directory**.

login name The name by which the computer system knows the user.

logo *See* **logotype**.

logotype (1816) (1) A company **trademark**. Compare **symbol**. (2) The **banner** on the front cover of a magazine or newsletter. Also called *flag, nameplate*. (3) Two or more type characters which are joined as a trademark or a company signature. Compare **ligature**.

logout The process of signing off the system. *See also* **login**.

long dash *See* **em dash**.

long fold Having the **grain** running along the long dimension, said of paper. Compare **broad fold**.

long page In **makeup**, a page that runs longer than provided for in the design to avoid a bad break.

Fig. L-9 The trademark, or logotype, for CONVEX Computer Corporation.

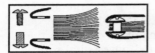

Fig. L-10   In loose-leaf binding, drilled holes have fasteners that are used to bind the publication.

long primer Old type size, now equal to about 10 points.

longhand (1616) Writing in which words are written out in full by hand.

loose-leaf binding (1902) A **binding** style in which pages are trimmed and have holes punched or drilled through them. Pages are held together by a metal or plastic spiral or by plastic fasteners. *See also* **mechanical binding**.

lost cluster A **sector** in a **PC/MS-DOS** disk **file allocation table** that is marked "in use" but does not belong to any entry in the **directory**.

loupe (1899) A small magnifier used to measure **point size** and **line spacing**.

low finish Paper **finish** without **gloss** or **enamel**.

low-level language A machine-dependent programming language translated by an **assembler** into **instructions** and data formats for a given machine. Similar to **assembly language**. Compare **high-level language**.

low-resolution graphics Computer graphic images containing a minimal amount of detail and are often jagged and blocky looking. Also said of **displays**. Compare **high-resolution graphics**. *See also* **high-resolution display**; **pixel**.

lower case *See* **lowercase**.

lowercase (1683) (1) Small letters as opposed to capital letters. Abbreviated *l.c.*, *lc*. Also called *minuscules*. (2) Small roman numerals. *See also* **font**; **small capitals**.

lowercase letters *See* **lowercase**.

lpm *See* **lines per minute**.

LPT1, LPT2, LPT3 The names that **PC/MS-DOS** uses to refer to the three ports to which **parallel printers** can be attached. Short for *line printer*. *See also* **COM1, COM2, COM3**.

Ludlow Trade name for a typecasting machine for which the **matrix** is assembled by hand and type is cast in line **slugs**—principally in display sizes of 18 point or larger.

Notes and New Words

Desktop Publisher's Dictionary

M

M Placed after a number to indicate "millions," as in 10 Mbyte, meaning 1 million bytes. However, 1 Mbyte is actually 1,048,576 bytes. Abbreviation of Greek prefix *mega-*, meaning "million."

Macazine (1984) A monthly magazine for owners of Macintosh computers.

machine-coated paper An inexpensive grade of **coated paper** applied on the paper-making machine itself, not as a separate operation. Also called *process-coated paper*, *roll-coated paper*.

machine code *See* **machine language**.

machine-collating sequence An extended alphabetical sequence that encompasses **uppercase** letters, **lowercase** letters, numerals, punctuation marks, and the various other characters recognized by the **system**.

machine composition Generic term for the composition of metal type matter using mechanical means— as on the **Intertype**, **Linotype**, or **Monotype**— instead of **hand-composition**.

machine copy A copy of anything made on an office copying machine. Often used as a **proof** with **direct-image composition**.

machine-finish paper An uncoated paper that has been **calendered** until it is smoother than **antique**, not as **glossy** as a **supercalendered** paper, and not quite so smooth as an **English finish** paper. Abbreviated *MF*.

machine-glazed paper Paper to one side of which a highly polished finish has been applied during manufacture.

machine language The most basic computer program understood by computer hardware. These instructions are represented internally by means of binary notation. It is the opposite of highly structured programming languages such as **FORTRAN** or **C**. Also called *machine code*.

machine-readable Directly usable by a computer. Said of a text or of data that is recorded in digital form with codes appropriate to the particular computer as programmed.

machining *See* **presswork**.

The Macintosh Buyer's Guide (1984) A quarterly magazine presenting product announcements for business users of Macintosh computers. Topics covered include **desktop publishing**, desktop communications, business productivity, and new technology.

macro A software feature used to store frequently used sequences of **keystrokes**, **commands**, or **instructions** under a single keystroke combination or command for future replay. *See also* **key procedures**. Macros speed up repetitive tasks involving several commands.

macro assembler An **assembler** that interprets an **instruction** set made up of **mnemonics**, and converts it into **machine language**.

macron A **diacritical** mark that indicates a sound value.

MacUser (1985) A monthly publication serving business users who own Macintosh computers. Areas covered include **desktop publishing**, desktop presentations, **networks**, **programming**, and **graphics**.

Macworld (1984) A Macintosh users monthly magazine that services the educated business user with trends, solution analysis, consumer issues, and **how-to** articles.

mag tape *See* **magnetic tape**.

magazine (1583) (1) A *periodical*. (2) In hot metal linecasting machines, a slotted metal container used to store **matrices**.

Magazine Publishers' Association (1919) An association of 3,000 publishers of 800 consumer and other magazines.

magenta (1860) A deep purplish red color, one of the four **primary colors** used in **process color printing**.

magic number 5±1 *See* **magic number 7±2**.

magic number 7±2 The concept that human memory can retain from 5 to 9 distinctly different items for a short period. Now challenged by the notion of the magic number 5±1.

magnetic disk A flat circular plate with a magnetizable surface layer used to store data from a computer. Also called *disk*, *diskette*, *fixed disk*, *hard disk*.

magnetic disk storage Storage in which data is stored by magnetic recording on the flat surface of one or more **magnetic disks**.

magnetic disk unit A device containing a **disk drive**, **magnetic heads**, and associated controls.

magnetic drum A magnetic storage device on which data is stored by magnetic recording on the curved surface of a cylinder that rotates while in use.

magnetic drum unit A device containing a drum drive, magnetic heads, and associated controls.

Fig. M-1   A floppy disk is a magnetic disk used for storing data.

magnetic head (1947) An electromagnetic device that can perform one or more functions of reading, writing, and erasing data on a magnetic data medium.

magnetic tape (1932) A ribbon of thin material with a magnetizable surface layer on which information can be stored or retrieved sequentially, i.e., by searching the tape from one end to the other. *See also* **beginning-of-tape marker; end-of-tape marker**.

magnetic tape cartridge *See* **magnetic tape cassette**.

magnetic tape cassette A container holding **magnetic tape** that can be processed without separating it from the container.

magnetic tape deck *See* **magnetic tape drive**.

magnetic tape drive A mechanism for controlling the movement of **magnetic tape**.

magnetic tape file A reel of **magnetic tape** holding records that are arranged in an ordered sequence.

magnetic tape label One or more records at the beginning of a **magnetic tape** that identify and describe the data recorded on the tape and contains other information, such as the serial number of the tape reel.

magnetic tape leader The portion of **magnetic tape** that precedes the **beginning-of-tape marker**. Compare **magnetic tape trailer**.

magnetic tape strike-on typesetter An obsolete, but once widely used typewriter-composing machine manufactured by the IBM Corporation. Abbreviated *MTST*.

magnetic tape trailer That portion of the **magnetic tape** that follows the **end-of-tape marker**.

magnetic tape unit A device containing a **tape drive, magnetic heads**, and associated controls.

mail A computer system facility that allows the sending and holding of messages via the computer.

mail fulfillment house A company that handles envelope-stuffing, addressing, and mailing for a **direct mail** campaign. Some will also provide **copywriting** and **list** acquisitions.

mail order (1867) A method of merchandising publications directly to the consumer by using **direct mail** and ads in magazines and newspapers.

main head The topmost **headline**, usually in larger point size. Compare **bank head**; **crosshead**; **subhead**.

main memory Usually the main storage device of a computer and the one from which **instructions** are executed. Also called *internal memory*.

main mouse button See **mouse buttons**.

mainframe (1964) In computer terminology, a large **central processing unit**, as distinct from input and other devices attached to it. The term is commonly reserved for powerful scientific and business-oriented computers.

majuscule An **uppercase**, or capital, letter. Compare **minuscule**.

make-ready *See* **makeready**.

make-up *See* **makeup**.

makeready (1887) Preparation of a press for printing. Specifically, the adjustment of the **platen** or **impression cylinder** to compensate for high or low spots in the printing **form**. *See also* **chase**; **lock up**; **quoin**.

makeup (1821) Arrangement of text and illustrations on a page, generally in conformity with standard practices of the industry or with particular publication requirements. In **cold composition**, it is called **layout**.

malfunction A computer's failure to operate in the normal manner. May be caused by hardware failures or software error. Also called *failure, fault, mistake*.

M
m

Fig. M-2   A majuscule is an uppercase letter; a minuscule is a lowercase letter.

management by wandering around A sarcastic way of saying that documentation writers and managers should take the time to know their audience as much as possible before, during, and after the creation of a document. Abbreviated *MBWA*.

Mandelbrot, Benoit B. Developer of **fractals**.

manifold paper *See* **onionskin**.

manipulative indexing Indexing where interrelations of terms are shown by coupling individual words. For example, *markers, end-of-tape* to indicate *end-of-tape markers*.

manufacturing In book production, the complete process of composition, printing, and binding of a book.

manuscript (1600) Any document that is not printed. For example, a typewritten or handwritten piece. Abbreviated *ms* (singular), *mss* (plural).

manuscript copy Text that requires further preparation before it is ready for printing or copying. Generally applied to **copy** in the process of being converted into **camera-ready copy**. Abbreviated *script.*

manuscript preparation Putting a piece of writing in a form convenient for the editorial process, including typing, spacing, punctuation, and legible corrections.

marble finish Paper **finish** resembling the veins of marble.

marbling (1727) Books that have marbled **endpapers** or edges decorated with a variety of colors in an irregular pattern resembling the veins of marble.

margin The distance from the edge of the page to the edge of the **image area** of the page. The four margins are:
- **gutter margin** (also called *back margin*)
- **head margin** (also called *top margin*)
- **outside margin** (also called *fore edge margin*)
- **bottom margin** (also called *tail* or *foot margin*)

See also **bleed; column guides; column rule; gutter; running foot; running head; type page**.

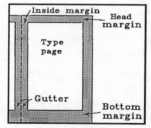

Fig. M-3　　Margins.

margin cut A small illustration set within a side **margin** next to the text.

margin guide On a video **display**, dotted nonprinting lines displayed near the borders of the screen page to mark the **margins** of a page.

marginal head A **headline** that is placed outside the **margin**.

marginal note A note made in a **margin**.

marginalia (1832) Notes or headings written or printed on the **margins** of a page.

mark-up copy (1916) A manuscript that is ready for the typesetter. *See also* **markup**.

marketing plan A publisher's total advertising and promotional plan designed to generate reviews, merchandise **subsidiary rights**, and sell books.

market research (ca. 1937) Information gathering and analysis relating to any aspect of marketing, in order to determine the likelihood that some type of material or publication will be bought.

marking felt In papermaking, a felt containing a pattern with which the paper **pulp** comes in contact. The pattern is impressed on the felt side of the web of paper as it is processed, resulting in a **felt finish**.

markup (1869) *v.* In typesetting, to mark the **type specifications** on **layout** and **copy** for the typesetter. Generally consists of the typeface, spacing, indention, size, line length, leading, etc. (1916) *n.* A manuscript so marked up.

masking (1) Blocking out a portion of an illustration by pasting paper over it to prevent it from being reproduced. Used on **reproduction copy** before exposure. (1897) (2) In color separation, a method used to obtain better rendition of colors in reproduction by means of color-correction as a preliminary to making the plates for color printing.

masking paper *See* **goldenrod**.

Fig. M-4   A marked up manuscript.

mass market The reading public at large, not subdivided by considerations of special interest, education, or taste.

mass market paperback Paperback books, usually 4 in x 7 in, designed for the widest possible distribution and sold in news-stands, airports, drugstores, etc., rather than just bookstores. Compare **trade paper-back**.

mass media *See* **media**.

mass memory *See* **external memory**.

mass storage The storage of large amounts of information on devices external to a com-puter. Also called *bulk storage*. *See also* **external memory**.

massaging Manipulating **input** data to yield a desired effect or format.

master Original typed, drawn, typeset, or hand-lettered copy. It may be produced on film, paper, cloth, or almost any other material.

master items In **PageMaker**, items on a master page, which may include text (run-ning heads), graphics (rules), and nonprinting guides (column guides). *See also* **master page**.

master layout A ruled sheet, usually on white paper, that serves as a guide for strip-ping identical flats in **offset lithography**.

master page In **PageMaker**, a page contain-ing text, graphics, and guides to be repeated on every page in a publication. Called **under-lying page** in **Ventura**. *See also* **master items**.

master paper *See* **duplicator paper**.

master proof A set of **proofs** bearing all corrections and alterations of both the printer and author. Also called *printer's proof, reader's proof. See also* **galley proof**.

masthead (1748) (1) The printed matter in a newspaper or periodical, usually on the editorial page, that gives the title and perti-nent details of ownership, **logotype**, advertising rates, and subscription rates. (2)

The name of a publication displayed at the top of the first page. Also called *banner, flag.*

mat *See* **matrix.**

mathematical symbols Symbols used in mathematical formulas.

matrix (15c) (1) The mold in which **hot metal type** letters are cast in a **linecasting machine.** (2) A rectangular array of mathematical elements that can be combined to form sums and products with similar arrays having an appropriate number of rows and columns. Plural is *matrices.* Abbreviated *mat.* (3) In phototypesetting, the glass plate that contains the **type master**, or film font negative. (4) The paper mold from which a **stereotype** is made. Also called *flong.*

matrix printer *See* **dot-matrix printer.**

matrix sentence (1964) One of two sentences whose essential external structure is maintained even though they are transformationally joined. For example, in "The program that I want is new," "the program is new" is a matrix sentence.

matte finish Dull—without gloss or luster—paper finish on photographs or papers. Compare **glossy finish.**

matte print Photoprint having a dull finish. This finish has ink-absorbing qualities not found in a glossy print with its glazed surface.

MBWA *See* **management by wandering around.**

MCGA *See* **multicolor graphics adapter.**

MDA *See* **monochrome display adapter.**

mean line The line that marks the tops of **lowercase** letters without **ascenders.** Also called *x-line.*

measure In typesetting, the length of a line or width of the column of type, measured in **picas.** The ideal length is about 40 characters of any size. Lines of less than 30 or more than 50 characters should generally be avoided. A good rule to follow is to use 1.5 alphabets of **lowercase** letters, or 39 characters, to the line measure. *See also* **em space**; **full measure**; **narrow measure**; **pica**; **set**; **typographic measurement**; **unit system**.

measurement The printer's basic unit of measurement is the **point**, approximately 1/72 of an inch; 12 points equal 1 **pica**, approximately 1/6 of an inch. Within a font of type of one size the printer commonly measures by **ems**. In 9-point matter, to mark the copy for 1-em paragraph indention means to indent each paragraph 9 points. *See also* Appendix 1, Appendix 2.

measurement system In **desktop publishing** programs, users are usually permitted to choose the measurement system for each publication. Choices are: inch, millimeter, **pica**, **point**, **Didot**, and **Cicero**. The chosen units appear on the rulers and in all dialog boxes that display measurements.

mechanical (15c) A piece of paper or cardboard carrying all the text and graphics for a page, ready to be sent to the printer, often with a protective **overlay**, and instructions to the printer. It is from a mechanical that the negative is made. Also called *board*, *camera-ready copy*. *See also* **keyline**; **layout**; **offset printing**; **reproduction copy**.

mechanical binding Binding by means of metal clasps and prongs, rings, screw posts, or other metal fasteners. Also includes plastic methods of binding (also called *comb binding*). *See also* **post binding**; **saddle-stitched binding**; **side-stitched binding**; **spiral binding**.

mechanical drawing (ca. 1890) A drawing made with T squares, compasses, scales, etc.

mechanical mouse A **mouse** that uses a rotating ball to indicate **cursor** positions. Compare **optical mouse**.

mechanical spacing Equal spacing between all letters. *See also* **optical spacing**.

mechanical screen Thin transparent film printed with white or black dots, placed over **artwork** to simulate **halftone** work. *See also* **Benday process**.

Fig. M-5   Plastic binding is a form of mechanical binding.

mechanical style edit An editing activity in which the editor examines a document for consistency of wording. *See also* **edit**; **levels of edit**.

mechanical wood pulp Pulp for papermaking made by grinding debarked logs. Also called *groundwood pulp*, it contains all the impurities removed from **chemical pulp** and is used chiefly for newsprint.

media (1841) (1) Plural of **medium**. (2) A medium that reaches the largest possible number of people, such as magazines, newspapers, the news services, radio, and television. Also called *mass media*. (3) Actual material or object on which **data** is stored.

medieval laid finish Finish in paper made by chain lines during manufacture. There is an effect of shading adjacent to the vertical chain-line marks.

medium (1593) (1) The physical means by which communication is achieved, for example, paper or video display. *See also* **media**. (2) A device for storing data.

megabyte (1970) A common unit of measurement of data: 1,048,576 **bytes**. Abbreviated *Mbyte*.

membrane keyboard *See* **tactile keyboard**.

memory A **medium** for storing computer data and programs so that they may be retrieved when needed by the **central processing unit** of the computer. There are two types: *internal* and *external*. Data stored in **external memory** must first be transferred to **internal memory** before it can be used by the computer. *See also* **disk**; **minisave**; **random-access memory**; **read-only memory**; **tape**.

memory buffer A storage area used to store data to compensate for a difference in the rate of data flow when transferring data from one device to another.

memory, external *See* **external memory**.

memory, internal *See* **internal memory**.

memory, nonvolatile *See* **nonvolatile memory**.

memory, volatile *See* **volatile memory**.

menu A visual display of alternative choices, composed of elements such as text, colors, or symbols, to help the user perform a task. *See also* **dialog box**; **drop-down menu**; **ghost**; **pop-down menu**; **pull-down menu**.

menu bar In many software applications, the area across the top of the screen where menu choices are displayed.

menu buttons In **PageMaker**, buttons located on the left side of the Edit Window used to expose menu choices.

menu-driven program A program organized around a central **menu**.

menu orientation A way of organizing documentation based on the order of **menus** in a system and the order of items on each particular menu.

menu selection Making a choice from a **menu**.

merge (1) To combine in an arrangement according to some rule. (2) To combine the items of two or more sets that are each in the same given order, into one set in that order. (3) The automatic recording, printing, or sending onto one element of recording medium of selected recorded text, in correct order, from at least two other elements of recording media.

merge sort A **sort** program in which the items in a set are divided into subsets, the items in each subset are sorted, and the resulting sorted items are **merged**.

merge variable The part of a **merge** item that changes from **record** to record.

Mergenthaler, Ottmar (1854–1899) Inventor of the **Linotype**.

metacharacter A character having a special meaning to an **operating system** or **disk operating system**. For example, using

View	
Actual Size	^1
Fit Page in Window	^2
Fit Document in Window	^3
Zoom In	^Z
Previous View	^V
Full Screen	^X
Redisplay View	F3
Preferences . . .	F4

Fig. M-6   A menu from Arts and Letters.

the question mark (*?*) as a **wild card** in a file search.

metafile Application data file containing graphic output from a computer or program. A metafile stores "snapshots" of the graphic image which can be subsequently retrieved and displayed on another computer or program or **telecommunicated**.

metafloppy *See* **floppy disk**.

metal decorating presses Used for printing on tin, aluminum, etc.

metal foil A very thin—0.006 in (0.1524 mm) or less—piece of metal that may be laminated to a plastic film backing.

metal type *See* **hot metal type**.

metallic finish Paper **finish** having a metallic luster.

metaphor (1533) An explicit comparison between a concept or object familiar to the reader and a concept or object not known by the reader.

metric system (1864) System of measures and weights with the meter and the gram as the bases. Some of the more common measures and their equivalents:

kilometer	00.6214 mile
meter	39.37 inches
centimeter	00.3937 inch
millimeter	00.0394 inch
kilogram	02.2046 lbs
gram	15.432 gram (avdp)
inch	02.54 cm
foot	00.3048 meter
yard	00.9144 meter
pound	00.4536 kilogram

MF *See* **machine-finish paper**.

mica finish (1777) Coated paper finish that contains mica particles. It is sometimes used on greeting cards.

microcomputer (1971) A complete, small computing system consisting of hardware and software, with a **microprocessor** as the **central processing unit**. Most commonly used in homes and in small businesses and as individual **workstations** in large businesses. Also called *desktop computer*,

Fig. M-7   A microcomputer with mouse and keyboard.

personal computer. See also **disk; mainframe; minicomputer; modem; printer; random access memory; read-only memory**.

microfiche (ca. 1948) One of three major **microforms** in which information is stored in greatly reduced form on photographic film and read through a special enlarging device. *See also* **microfilm**.

microfilm (1927) A film bearing a photographic record on a reduced scale.

microfilm reader Device capable of projecting an enlarged **microform** image on a screen for viewing.

microfloppy A small **floppy disk** whose diameter is 3.5 in and whose storage capacity ranges from about 800 Kbytes to 1.5 Mbytes. Also called *minidiskette. See also* **diskette; minifloppy**.

microform (1958) (1) A process for reproducing printed matter in a much reduced size. (2) Matter reproduced by microform. (3) Any **microimage** imposed on film, whether a **microfilm, microfiche**, rolled film, individual film, or filmstrip.

micrograph (1909) A device for doing extremely small writing, drawing, or engraving.

micrographics (1969) Pertaining to the study or description of objects too small to be discerned without the aid of a microscope.

microimage (1950 Image produced on **microfilm. A microform**.

microprocessor (1970) A wafer-thin **integrated circuit** (also called a *chip*) performing the computational operations of the **central processing unit** and communicating with the other parts of the system.

Microsoft disk operating system *See* **MS-DOS**.

middle matter Text. Compare **back matter; front matter**.

middle tone Intermediate tones between the **shadow** and the **highlight** in **halftone** illustrations.

mil A measure of the thickness of paper, in thousandths of an inch. *See also* **caliper**.

milestone chart (1746) Chart that lists such information as the elements required to produce an item. By using bars and data points that show scheduled dates in terms of days, weeks, months, or years, production goals can be set and measured.

military specification A set of documentation standards required for any **document** produced for the Department of Defense. Abbreviated *milspec*.

milline (1530) Advertising rate based on the cost of one **agate line** per 1 million copies of a publication's circulation.

milspec *See* **military specification**.

mimeograph (1889) Duplicating machine that employs a direct-plate stencil process. *See also* **mimeograph paper**.

mimeograph paper Paper with good ink-absorbing qualities, available in a **laid paper** or a **wove paper**. *See also* **mimeograph**.

miniature book A book in a small format, usually varying from less than an inch to about 2 in x 1.25 in.

minicomputer (1968) A computer that does not need the closely controlled environment of a **mainframe** and has a richer **instruction** set than that of a **microcomputer**.

minidiskette *See* **microfloppy**.

minifloppy A 5.25-in **floppy disk** generally capable of storing nearly 1.5 characters; used primarily in **microcomputers**. Also called *diskette, metafloppy*. *See also* **microfloppy**.

minion (1548) Old type size, now equal to about 7 points.

minisave In **PageMaker**, an automatic **save** of a **publication** that occurs whenever the user turns a page or clicks a page **icon**. A

Fig. M-8   A minifloppy disk.

minisave creates temporary documents on disk and does not overwrite the publication file.

minus leading *See* **minus linespacing**.

minus linespacing The reduction of space between lines of type so that the baseline-to-baseline measurement is less that the point size of the type. Also called *minus leading*.

minuscule (ca. 1727) A **lowercase**, or small, letter. Compare **majuscule**.

misprint A typographical error. Also called *typo*.

miter In both hand binding and composition, to bring materials together at an angle without overlapping.

Fig. M-9   Mitered corners have two 45-degree corners.

mitered corner A corner that is formed by two 45-degree angles. Compare **rounded corner**; **squared corner**.

mixing (1586) Capacity to mix more than one **typeface**, type style, or size on a line and have them all base-align.

MKDIR A **PC/MS-DOS** command used to create a new **subdirectory**.

mnemonic (1858) (1) Generally, any rule or precept that helps to jog one's memory. (2) Abbreviated **instructions** that are converted into **machine language** by an **assembler**. Mnemonic computer codes are those that are easily memorized, like *tr9* for "9-point Times Roman type."

mock-up (1920) A visual presentation of a proposed page or piece of promotional material. *See also* **dummy**.

MODE A **PC/MS-DOS** command that sets output parameters to **output devices** including **printers, display** units, and asynchronous communications devices (**modems**).

mode (1986) In **Ventura**, the four operating conditions: *frame, paragraph, text,* and *graphics. See also* **mode indication box**.

mode indication box (1986) In **Ventura**, any of a series of four boxes in the upper left corner of the screen that can be activated to perform desired operations.

model release A form giving permission to use a photograph of an individual for publication.

modem (1952) A **telecommunications** device to translate computer signals into a pattern of electrical signals sent over the telephone line, and vice versa. Short for *mo*dulator *dem*odulator.

modern A style of typeface in which there is a marked contrast in weight between thick and thin strokes. *See also* **type style**; **typeface nomenclature**.

modern figure *See* **aligning figure**.

modification level *See* **version**.

modular packaging Packaging chapters so that they stand alone with their own module, **table of contents**, and **index**. All modules within a set also share a master table of contents and a master index. This type of packaging allows a documenter to give readers only the information they need.

moiré pattern (1818) (1) An interference pattern created when two regular dot patterns are asymmetrically superimposed. This effect, which is caused by parallel mesh dots, can be avoided by turning the second screen 15 degrees away from that of the **halftone**. (2) An undesirable grid pattern that may occur when a **bit-mapped graphic** with gray fill patterns is reduced or enlarged.

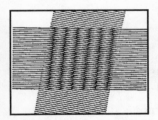

Fig. M-10   A moiré pattern.

mold That part of a **linecasting machine** in which the line of type is cast against a **matrix**.

molly Printer's term for an **em**. *See also* **nut**.

monitor A **video display unit** that does not have any radio-frequency receiving circuits. It is used for displaying text or graphics in many computer applications. Monitors come in two kinds: color and monochrome (white, green, and amber). Also called *cathode-ray tube, display*. *See also* **landscape monitor**; **portrait monitor**.

monochromatic Having a single color.

monochrome (1849) (1) A **continuous-tone** painting or drawing or a printed **halftone** of a painting or drawing having a single color or **hue**. The continuous tone does not become a halftone until it has been **screened**. (2) A computer display capable of displaying one color (white, green, or amber).

monochrome display adapter A **printed circuit board** in a **PC/MS-DOS** computer system that controls a monochrome **display**, which shows text in one color against a black background. Abbreviated *MDA*.

monogram (1636) (1) A combination of letters formed from the initials of a name. Also called *acronym*. (2) Combination of two or more interwoven or overlapping letters to represent a name.

monograph (ca. 1821) A short learned treatise covering a single, specific subject.

monospace **Letterspacing** that is the same for all letters regardless of their shape. Most typewriters and printers produce monospace type, whereas most typeset material uses **proportional spacing**.

Monotype (ca. 1890) Typesetting machine consisting of a **keyboard** and a caster that produces individual characters and assembles them in **justified** lines. Invented by Tolbert Lanston (1844–1913).

montage (1929) In graphic design, a combination of drawings or photographs usually related to one subject and consisting of distinct as well as indistinct images that blend into each other. When only photographs are used, the term *photomontage* is more common. *See also* **collage**.

moonlighter (1957) One who works two different jobs.

MORE A **PC/MS-DOS** filter **utility** that reads data, such as a displayed **directory**, pauses output to the **display** screen when a full-screen condition is detected, and displays the message "More." Pressing any key resumes output until the next full-screen condition is detected, at which time "More" is displayed again.

morgue (1821) A library of clippings from a publication, particularly newspapers.

mortice *See* **mortise**.

mortise (15c) *v.* To cut a hole in two layers of material and replace the undesired cutout piece with the desired cutout piece. *n.* The cutout portion of a mounted **electrotype** or **photoengraving** in which type is set.

mother-of-pearl finish Paper **finish** having the effect of a lustrous change of colors.

motherboard The main **printed circuit board** inside a **microcomputer**, usually containing the **microprocessor** and its associated support **chips** and into which **daughter boards**, or adapter cards, are plugged.

mottled finish (14c) Paper **finish** showing diversified spots or blotches.

mounting and flapping Using a **board** with **artwork** taped on it, covered by a **tissue overlay** to protect line and photographic art and on which **instructions** to the printer may be written.

Fig. M-11   A mouse.

mouse (1983) (1) An small, boxlike, hand-held **input device** with a **light-emitting diode** or a rotating ball on the bottom that are attached to sensors and a taillike connecting wire extending from one end. Used to allow a computer user, particularly a non-typist, to position a **cursor** on the video **display** without using the computer's **keyboard**. *See also* **mechanical mouse**; **mouse buttons**; **optical mouse**. (2) *See* **pickup**.

mouse buttons Buttons on a **mouse** that are depressed in order for the user to choose or manipulate objects on the screen or to communicate **commands** to a computer.

movable type (15c) Type consisting of single pieces, as opposed to **slugs** of type which comprise complete lines cast as one piece. Johann Gutenberg is credited with inventing printing from movable type in the 15th century.

move (1) A process in which text—from a single character to several pages—is relocated within the document. *Block move* involves a block of text; *column move*, a column of text. (2) In computer programming, to copy data from one **storage device** to another. Also called *transfer*.

ms *See* **manuscript**.

MS-DOS Microsoft **disk operating system** for use in IBM-compatible microcomputers. User interface is virtually identical with that of **PC-DOS**.

mss *See* **manuscript**.

MTST *See* **magnetic tape strike-on typesetter**.

multi-panel A cartoon comprising three or more **boxed in** illustrations. Compare **double-panel**; **single-panel**.

multicolor graphics adapter A **display adapter** in a computer system that controls the **display**. Shows both text and graphics at low-to-medium resolution in up to 256 colors; used in some IBM PS/2 computers. Abbreviated *MCGA*.

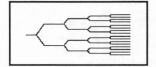

Fig. M-12   A multilevel filing system.

multilevel filing system A computer filing system that lets the user define **directories** within other directories, creating a structure with many levels. Also called *tree-structured* or *hierarchial filing system*.

multilith A printing machine, often used as an office **duplicator**, which operates on the **offset** principle.

multiple-access *See* **multiple-input**.

multiple-input In **computer-assisted composition**, characterized by permitting several input terminals operating simultaneously to serve the same system. Also called *multiple-access, multiterminal*.

multipass Where the printer prints a page with one **typeface** leaving some blank spaces and then, after a printwheel change, makes a second pass to fill in those blanks.

multiple submission The offering of a work to more than one publisher at the same time.

multitasking Pertaining to the concurrent execution of two or more tasks by a computer. Special methods and systems designed to achieve concurrency by separating programs into two or more interrelated tasks that share the same code, buffers, files, and equipment.

multiterminal *See* **multiple-input**.

multiuser Permitting more than one user to use the system at the same time.

must An instruction to the printer that **copy** or **artwork** must appear.

mutton quad An **em space**.

N

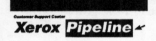

Fig. N-1 The nameplate, or logo, for *Xerox Pipeline*, a Ventura Publisher newsletter.

nameplate (ca. 1864) The publication's name on the cover. Also called *flag*. *See also* **logotype**.

name stripe The black stripe at the very top of a window. It displays the window type, the name of the current document, and other information relevant to the current session.

nano Prefix denoting one billionth. For example, *3 nanoseconds* is three-billionths of a second.

narrow measure A block of copy, such as a long quotation, indented from one or both margins to distinguish it from the surrounding **full-measure** copy.

NASTA *See* **National Association of State Textbook Administrators**.

National Association of Desktop Publishers (1986) An independent, nonprofit trade association for desktop publishing professionals. Publishes a quarterly journal,

Forum, a periodic book catalogue, an educational guide, and a source guide.

National Association of State Textbook Administrators. An association of directors of state educational agencies responsible for the purchase and distribution of textbooks for public schools. It issues specifications, revised periodically, covering manufacturing standards (particularly those pertaining to bindings) required for books intended for sale to schools. Abbreviated *NASTA.*

National Business Publications (1965) A group of business, technical, marketing, scientific, and trade periodicals with audited circulations and independent ownership.

national characters A term for the characters #, @, and $.

National Computer Association (1980) A third-party users group serving primarily users of small vendors' products.

National Printing Equipment Association (1933) An association of companies engaged in the manufacture and distribution of equipment and supplies in the graphic arts industry.

National Scholastic Press Association (1974) A national association of high school newspapers, yearbooks, and magazines that presents All-America awards to outstanding publications.

nationwide marketing plan *See* **marketing plan**.

natural language A software command system approximating human speech or written language patterns.

navigation aids Items such as **headings**, **page numbers**, and **chapter titles** that guide readers through a document.

NCR paper Chemically treated paper that does not require carbons to make duplicates. Also called *carbonless paper, impact paper.*

n.d. *See* **no date**.

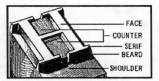

Fig. N-2   The neck is that area of type between the shoulder and the face.

neck The part of a **hot metal type** character between the **shoulder** and the **face**.

negative (1) A reverse image of a page, produced photographically on a sheet of film as an intermediate step in preparing **printing plates** from camera-ready **mechanicals** for **offset printing**. (2) Film used in **photoengraving** and in **photo-offset**.

nested information A software technique that allows the user to access information related to a displayed screen directly rather than referring to a **table of contents** or **index**.

net receipts Moneys received by a publisher on a book's sale after all discounts and returned copies have been deducted. Some authors' contracts specify that royalties are calculated on the basis of net receipts rather than the book's retail price.

network (1940) (1) A group of computers—linked by hardware and network software—that share resources, such as **disk drives** and **printers**. Computers on a network may be in the same room, in different rooms of the same building, or even in different parts of the country or world. They may be connected by cables, by telephone lines and **modems**, or by satellite links. *See also* **node**. (2) A group of editorial contacts, researchers, collaborators, and authorities useful to a writer.

new edition An **edition** containing substantial revisions by the author or editor. *See also* **impression**; **reprint**; **revised edition**.

New England Printer and Publisher (1938) A monthly graphic arts magazine.

New Journalism (1967) Nonfiction writing that relies heavily on fiction techniques.

news cases A pair of type cases in which the **uppercase** letters are kept in the upper case, and the **lowercase** letters are kept in the lower case.

News From the Front A newsletter—published by the **Desktop Publishing**

Fig. N-3   This newsletter is published by Xerox for its Ventura users.

Association— that is dedicated to the issues of desktop publishing services as a business.

news release A one- or two-page story used for promotion, covering the five W's: who, what, when, where, and why. Also called *publicity release*.

news stick A **composing stick** with a fixed **measure**.

newsletter (ca. 1903) A printed sheet, pamphlet, or small newspaper containing news about industry events, trends, and new products of interest chiefly to a special group.

newsprint (1909) A cheap paper made from **groundwood pulp** and varying percentages of **chemical pulp** and used for printing newspapers or ephemeral journals.

newsprint ink A special ink used in presses when printing newspapers.

nick (1) In **hand composition**, a notch in type that acts as a guide to the compositor to help align type properly. (2) In film, a notch or notches in the edge of the film used to identify the type of film when handling in the darkroom.

nixie (1885) A piece of mail that cannot be delivered because of incorrect or obsolete address.

NLSFUNC A **PC/MS-DOS** command that activates the National Language Support for **code page** switching, which selects alternate character sets that correspond to selected national languages.

no date In reference work, indicates that no publication date is printed in the book described. Abbreviated *n.d.*

no place of publication In reference work, indicates that no place of publication is printed in the book described. Abbreviated *n.p.*

no publisher In reference work, indicates that no publisher is printed in the book described. Abbreviated *n.p.*

no year In reference work, indicates that no year is printed in the book described. Abbreviated *n.y.*

node In a **network**, a point where one or more functional units interconnect transmission lines. The term *node* derives from graph theory, in which a node is a junction point of links, areas, or edges.

noise Loosely, any disturbance tending to interfere with the normal operation of a device or system.

nom de plume (1873) A pen name or pseudonym.

nomenclature (1610) In **artwork**, words or symbols used to identify and call out an object. *See also* **call out**.

nomogram (1908) *See* **nomograph**.

nomograph (1909) (1) Graph or chart that enables one to find the value of a dependent variable by aligning a straightedge with the given independent variable. (2) A graphic representation of the relation of numerical values. Also called *nomogram.*

nonbook material Any material that does not meet the definition of a book or periodical, such as audiovisual and vertical file materials.

nonbreaking space A special character inserted between two words so that they are not separated by a line break. *See also* **bad break, orphan, widow**.

noncoded graphics *See* **image graphics**.

noncounting keyboard In **phototypesetting**, a **keyboard** at which the operator types the **copy** to be set, producing a perforated paper tape which is then fed into a computer to determine **line length, hyphenation**, and **justification**.

nondestructive cursor On a **display**, a **cursor** that can be moved within a display surface without changing or destroying the data displayed on the screen. Compare **destructive cursor**.

nonimpact printer A **hard copy** output device that prints graphics and text without impacting or pressing mechanically onto the page. Examples include: **ink-jet printer**, **thermal printer**, **laser printer**.

nonlining figure *See* **lining figure**.

nonpareil Old type size, now equal to about 6 points.

nonprinting master items In **PageMaker**, the **ruler guides** and **column guides** on a **master page**. *See also* **margin guide**.

nonreproducible blue pen Marker whose ink does not photograph. Used on **camera-ready copy**.

nonreturnable Publications that may not be returned for credit or a cash refund.

nonvolatile memory Computer **memory** that does not lose its contents when computer power is turned off. The most common form of nonvolatile memory is **read-only memory**. Compare **volatile memory**.

nonwoven material Class of synthetic **cover** materials for **bookbinding** made by extrusion of felting rather than weaving.

normal view In **Ventura**, a command in the View menu that displays a page approximately the size in which that page will be printed, depending on the screen's characteristics. Same as **actual size** in **PageMaker**.

North American Serial Rights Notation on a **manuscript** that signifies material is being sold or purchased solely for publication in North America. Writer retains the **right** to publish the material in other countries.

notice of copyright (15c) Notice in a book or other printed publication, appearing on the **title page** or on the page immediately following, that alerts all to the fact and date of **copyright** ownership. *See also* **copyright notice**; **copyright page**.

novice user A user who has little experience with a particular software system. The novice user is willing to sacrifice speed and expanded options for frequent explana-

© 1989 by Wordware

Fig. N-4 An example of a notice of copyright.

tions and examples and ready-made program decisions. Compare **expert user**, **parrot user**.

n.p. *See* **no place of publication**; **no publisher**.

nth name Randomly selected names in a mailing **list** (often every tenth), used to test the value of the total list.

NUL A dummy device used by **PC/MS-DOS** when testing a **command**. Input operations encounter an immediate **end-of-file** condition. Output operations are simulated without actual data transfer.

null character An invisible character whose internal code is zero and which occupies no space if printed. Not to be confused with a blank, which is invisible but occupies a space.

NUM LOCK *See* **number lock**.

number lock A **keyboard** key that is used to turn the **numeric keypad** on or off.

numbering system A method of representing numeric values symbolically, as a sequence of digits. Each numbering system uses a finite number of discrete digits to create this representation, though the number of digits varies from one numbering system to another. Three number systems are commonly used:
- **decimal** is base 10 and uses the digits 0, 1, 2, 3, 4, 5, 6, 7, 8, and 9. This is the most familiar system.
- **hexadecimal** (hex) is base 16 and uses the digits 0, 1, 2, 3, 4, 5, 6, 7, 8, 9, A, B, C, D, E, and F. This is frequently used by programmers. Any decimal number between 0 and 255 can be expressed by a two-digit hex number.
- **octal** is base seven and uses the digits 0 through 7.
- **binary** (bit) is base 2 and uses only the digits 0 and 1. All information in computer systems is handled in binary form representing electrical signals that are on or off. Any decimal number between 0 and 255 can be expressed by an 8-bit binary number.

numbering machine A **type high** printing machine that is locked with type in regular printing forms and prints numbers in consecutive order, forward or backward as wanted.

numeral *See* **Arabic numeral; Roman numeral.**

numeric keypad (1967) An extra set of keys often included on computer **keyboards** to facilitate the entry of numeric data. Also called *keypad.*

nut An **en**. *See also* **em**.

n.y. *See* **no year**.

Nyloprint Trade name for a photosensitive plastic plate for **letterpress printing**.

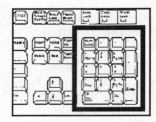

Fig. N-5   The numeric keypad facilitates entry of numeric data.

Notes and New Words

O

o/m *See* **overmatter**.

object file A file created by an **assembler** and containing **machine language** code.

object-oriented graphics A **file** consisting of a sequence of drawing commands stored as mathematical formulas. These commands describe graphics— such as mechanical drawings, schematics, and charts— that are manually produced with a pencil, straightedge, and compass. Also called *draw-type graphics*. Compare **paint-type file**.

oblique (1) In the **sans serif** type faces *oblique* is often preferred to **italic** in describing inclined letters, since true italic type has serifs. (2) *See* **virgule**.

OCR *See* **optical character recognition**.

octal notation (1948) A **numbering system** using the digits 0 through 7. Because of its close mathematical resemblance to **binary notation**, octal is popular among **programmers** for representing numeric values in **machine language** programs.

octavo (1582) (1) An old term for a book made from sheets which have been folded three times, each sheet forming eight leaves or sixteen pages. (2) Any book measuring about 6 in x 9 in.

OEM *See* **original equipment manufacturer.**

off center Any **layout** or design that is not centered in respect to separate line elements, such as **headings, tables,** illustrations, **figures,** and **artwork.**

off its feet Metal type knocked askew on the **proof press.**

off-line *See* **offline.**

off-screen functions The performance of reformat, repaginate, search, etc., over several pages without projecting each page on the screen.

off-the-shelf (1) Pertaining to production items that are available from current stock and need not be recently purchased or immediately manufactured. (2) Computer software or hardware that can be used by customers with little or no adaption.

offline (1950) Unconnected to the central computer. Compare **online.**

offline equipment (1950) Equipment not in direct communication with the **central processing unit.** Also called *auxiliary equipment. See also* **online equipment.**

offline keyboard (1950) A **keyboard** not connected directly with a **typesetter** or **central processing unit.** Material from such a terminal is stored temporarily for later processing. *See also* **direct-entry keyboard.**

offprint (1885) An article, chapter, or other excerpt from a larger work printed from the original type or plates and issued as a separate unit. Also called *reprint.*

offset (1) Unwanted image transferred to the back of a printed sheet by the sheet beneath it as the sheets are stacked after printing. Also called *setoff. See also* **anti-set-off; slip-sheet.** (2) The transfer of the image from the plate to a rubber **blanket** to **stock**

as in **photo-offset** and **letterset printing**.
(3) *See* **offset lithography**.

offset and cut (1) The instruction to be
given to a process engraver to ensure that
printing plates for two printings will fit together exactly—e.g., a **halftone** that is to
print black within a surrounding area of
second-color line. To make the fit optically
perfect, it is usually desirable to include a
very slight overlap. (2) In **lithography**, the
same effect is achieved if the space for the
halftone is burned out of the line color plate.

offset impression A printing impression in
which the printing surface is transferred to
a secondary device which then offsets the
image to paper. Compare **direct impression**.

offset letterpress *See* **letterset printing**.

offset lithography Lithographic printing by
the method of transferring the image to
paper from a **rubber blanket**. The inked
printing plate prints on the blanket, which
then offsets the image to paper. Also called
photolithography, offset. See also **printing
method**.

offset paper An acid-free book paper that
is **coated** or **uncoated**. *Uncoated offset
paper* is used for magazines, advertising
pieces, **house organs, brochures**, and for
color work. *Coated offset paper* is made especially to eliminate fuzz and picking. This
type of paper will reproduce better **halftones** and colors than uncoated offset paper.

offset perfecting press *See* **perfecting
press**.

offset printing A **printing method**
whereby an inked impression from a **printing plate** is made first on a cylinder with a
rubber blanket. The image is transferred to
the paper from the rubber blanket. Also
called *offset lithography, photo-offset. See
also* **camera-ready copy; laser printing; mechanical**.

offset printing press A **rotary press** using
the offset method of **lithographic printing**.

offset relief *See* **letterset printing**.

offset spray *See* **anti-set-off**.

oiled paper Paper treated with oil to give it sealing characteristics, often used as a wrapping paper.

O.K. with changes *See* **O.K. with corrections**.

O.K. with corrections Indicates a **proof** is approved if corrections are made. Also called *O.K. with changes*.

Old English Layman's term for **text** type. *See also* **black letter; type style**.

old style (1617) A **type style** having diagonally-sloping **serifs**.

old style figure A numeral that varies in size, some having **ascenders** and others having **descenders**: *1 2 3 4 5 6 7 8 9 0*. Abbreviated *o.s.* Also called *nonlining figure*. Compare **aligning figure**. *See also* **Arabic numeral; hanging figure**.

omnibus book (1) A collection, in a single volume, of a number of books or stories on a single subject by various authors. (2) A reprint edition of several works of an author, complete or a selection, in a single volume.

on approval A transaction in which a customer is capable of examining a publication before purchasing. If not wanted, the publication may be returned.

on consignment Supplied on an agreement that copies need not be paid for until sold. *See also* **returns**.

on demand A book manufactured as a single copy at the time the customer wants to buy it.

on-line *See* **online**.

on spec *See* **on speculation**.

on speculation An article written that has not been assigned by the editor, who has no obligation to buy the finished work.

once and a half up In drawing, to make the **artwork** 1.5 times larger than it will appear on the printed page.

one-scale chart A **bar chart** that shows only one quantity by using one scale, for ex-

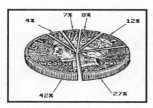

Fig. O-1   A pie chart is an example of a one-scale chart.

ample, a **pie chart**. *See also* **column chart; curve chart; surface chart**.

one-shot (1) In magazine-distribution, a publication of which there is only one issue. (2) A book or pamphlet as opposed to a periodical.

onionskin (1879) A thin, translucent paper used to make a typewriter carbon copy or to serve as a **tissue overlay** for work requiring correction or protection. Also called *manifold paper*.

online Connected to a central computer, in operation, and, by implication, under the computer's control in some way. Compare **offline**.

online database A **database** that can be **accessed** via a computer terminal and with which a user can interact directly.

online documentation Documentation, usually about **software**, conveyed to **users** through a video **display** screen. It is designed for this medium and is not simply a version adapted from paper **documentation**.

online equipment Processing equipment of compatible computer speed that is directly connected to the main processor devices. Generally refers to the operation of **input/output devices** directly controlled by a **central processing unit**. Compare **offline equipment**.

online searching Perusing a **database** while online with a computer.

online storage Storage that is under the control of the **central processing unit**.

onomasticon A list of proper nouns employed as a lookup table to expand titles, for example, for **key words**.

onomastics (1930) The science or study of the origins and forms of the proper names of persons and places.

OOP *See* **out of print**.

OOS *See* **out of stock**.

op-ed (1970) Opposite the **editorial page**. Usually a page of comment by members of the readership and syndicated **columnists**. Style is often more similar to that of a feature than an **editorial**.

opacity (1611) The degree to which paper, ink, or film blocks light.

opaque *v.* (1) To paint portions of a **negative** so it will not reproduce. (2) In **photoengraving**, to paint out on the negative those areas that are not wanted on the plate. (1742) *n.* Water soluble paint used to block out areas on negatives and positives to make them nontransparent.

opaque circular Bond and offset book paper manufactured to provide great **opacity**.

open *v.* To **double-click** on an **icon**, or to select the icon and then *open* a **file**. *n.* (1) Type lines very widely spaced. (2) A **layout** that is not cramped, using **white space** judiciously. (3) A data **file** being used or document being worked on is *open* until exited.

open architecture A computer, such as IBM **compatibles**, that provide room for expanding memory and adding other accessories to increase computing power. Compare **closed architecture**.

open bracket A punctuation mark ([ ) used to start a bracketed expression.

open parenthesis A punctuation mark (( ) that begins a parenthetical expression.

open punctuation A pattern of punctuation making little use of punctuation marks, usually only to separate main clauses and to prevent misreading. Compare **close punctuation**.

open quote (1) To start a quotation with beginning quotation marks ("). (2) The punctuation mark that begins a quotation.

open shop A business operating under the system of employing workers without regard to whether or not they are members of a union. Compare **closed shop**.

opening *See* **spread**.

operating environment The complete range of resources available to a **programmer** or computer **user** in the creation or operation of a computer program, including both **hardware** and **software** resources. For example, amount of available memory, **peripheral equipment**, **operating system**, etc.

operating space *See* **display space**.

operating system (1961) An integrated collection of software procedures that supervises the sequencing and processing of programs in a computer and may provide scheduling, **debugging**, **input/output** control, accounting, compilation, storage assignment, data management, and related services. A special type of operating system is the **disk operating system** (*DOS*), which contains programs to control **disk** operations. Abbreviated *OS*. *See also* **Control Program for Microcomputers**; **housekeeping**; **subroutine**.

operator (1) The person who sets, edits, or prints copy from a **keyboard** in any of the various computerized typesetting processes. Also called *compositor, end-user.* (2) A mathematical sign, such as $= + \times \pm \neq$. *See also* **relational operator**.

operator error An error made by an **operator**.

OPM *See* **other people's money**.

optical center The center of a rectangle as it appears to the eye, usually a point slightly above— about two-fifths from the top of the rectangle— the geometric center of a rectangular plane. Objects placed at the optical center appear to be at the geometric center.

optical character recognition In computerized typesetting, the ability to electronically read typewritten, printed, or handwritten documents with a light-sensitive **input device**, to interpret the typed characters in digital form, and to record them on a magnetic medium for computer input. Abbreviated *OCR*.

optical disk (1980) A plastic-coated **disk** on which information is recorded digitally as tiny pits and read by using a **laser**.

optical mouse A **mouse** that uses an infrared light and a grid pad to indicate **cursor** positioning. *See also* **mechanical mouse**.

optical spacing Arrangement of spacing between letters for **legibility** and appearance. The spacing varies with the shape of the letters to achieve optical equalization. Compare **mechanical spacing**.

option (1) A variation on or modification to a **command**, usually requested by use of a **flag**. (2) The right to purchase or sell something, such as movie **rights**, for a specified price and within a certain length of time. (3) The right a publisher may have, by previous contract, to bid on an author's subsequent books. (4) Displayed in **dialog boxes** when choices are available.

optional argument An **argument** accepted but not required by a **command**.

option button In a **dialog box**, the round area **clicked on** to select an **option**.

order In a manuscript **layout**, the ranking of the various **headings** according to their importance. Desired **typeface**, **point size** and **leading**, **indention**, and the like should be defined for each heading.

ordinal number (1607) A number designating the place (as first, second, or third) occupied by an item in an ordered sequence. Compare **cardinal number**.

organization chart (1881) A block chart or diagram that outlines responsibilities and shows the chain of command, including the names, titles, departments, and responsibilities of personnel in an organization.

orientation *See* **page orientation**.

original (1) A **manuscript** purchased and originated by a paperback house. (2) *See* **master**.

original equipment manufacturer A manufacturer who buys computer components

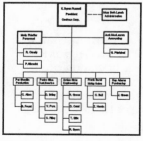

Fig. O-2   A typical organization chart.

from other vendors, assembles them into complete systems, then sells the entire unit. Abbreviated *OEM*.

ornament A decorative device in book design, such as an **initial, rule, border**, etc.

orphan In copy **layout** and **page makeup**, one or more lines of type left at the bottom of a **column** or page. Compare **widow**. *See also* **bad break**.

OS *See* **operating system**.

o.s. *See* **old style**.

oscilloscope (1906) A device that visually displays an electrical signal on the fluorescent screen of a **cathode-ray tube**.

other people's money A business term meaning to borrow capital elsewhere rather than using one's own. Abbreviated *OPM*.

out of print A book that is no longer available through the publisher. Abbreviated *OOP*. Compare **out of stock**.

out of register When printing **impressions** are not exactly aligned. *See also* **register**.

out of stock A book not available because its publisher's supply has been temporarily exhausted. Compare **out of print**. Abbreviated *OOS*.

outdent Text on the first line of a paragraph that prints to the left of the paragraph margin. Compare **indent**.

outer A package containing a number of smaller unit packages—a *display outer* if its main purpose is to be seen, a *shipping outer* if it is mainly for protection in transit.

outline (1790) *v.* To draw an outline. (1662) *n.* (1) The skeletal plan of an article, book, or other project. (2) The line marking the outer edges or limits of a shape or form.

outline font A printer **font** in which each character is stored as a mathematical formula, as distinguished from **bit-mapped** fonts that are stored as patterns of dots.

outline halftone A **halftone** engraving in which the background is cut away. Also

Text on the first line of this paragraph prints to the left of the paragraph margin.

Fig. O-3   An example of an outdent.

called *cut-out halftone*. Compare **highlight halftone**.

outline letter A letterform that is drawn in outline only with no solid parts.

output *v.* To transfer data from the **internal memory** of a computer to an **output device**. Examples include: **disk drives**; **display**; **floppy disk**; **hard disk**; **printers**. *n.* Whatever data comes out of a computer system, or any division of a system, as opposed to what goes in. *See also* **input**; **input/output**.

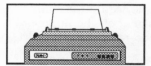

Fig. O-4   A printer is an output device.

output device A device that displays— draws, prints, photographs— the images that have been created and manipulated by using a computer. *See also* **impact printer**; **laser printer**; **monitor**; **nonimpact printer**.

output primitives The basic graphical entities, such as points, line segments, **characters**, **text strings**, and **polygons**.

output process The process that consists of the delivery of data from a computer system, or from any part of it.

outside The outer, vertical edge of a page, opposite the **binding edge**.

outside margin The **margin** at the unbound edge of a publication. Also called *fore edge margin*.

over the transom Unsolicited **manuscripts** sent to a publisher directly by the author rather than through an agent or at the request of an editor. *See also* **slush pile**.

overflow page *See* **A-page**.

overhang cover (1864) A **cover** larger than the page size of a book. Compare **flush cover**.

overhead (1) Extra space used by system files. (1914) (2) All the expenses of office, travel, time, research, and special equipment involved in any business.

overhead transparency (1951) An image printed on clear acetate and projected onto a screen for viewing by an audience.

overlay (1) An transparent plastic sheet or a piece of tissue paper placed over a **mechanical** or **keyline** to protect it, to indicate instructions to the printer or to show the breakdown for **color separation**. (2) An **overhead transparency**. (3) To place one image or text block on top of another, and be able to see both. *See also* **acetate overlay; correction overlay; tissue overlay**.

overmatter (1) Copy too long to fit the text area and must be cut. (2) Matter left over from one issue of a newspaper or periodical, which will either be used in a later issue or **killed**. Abbreviated *o/m.* Also called *overset*.

overprint *v.* (1863) To print one image over another impression. Particularly used in color work. If a tint or pattern is desired, a **second color** is printed over the primary color. (2) In word processing, to print one character over another. Used most often with foreign languages, for example, in accenting a word. (3) To create an **interrobang**. *n.* (1876) An item that is overprinted.

overrun (1) A printing of a quantity in excess of what is ordered or what is actually required. (2) An extra amount of finished copies of a book that the printer may produce above the stipulated order (should not exceed 10%). (3) An additional quantity of book covers a publisher may order for promotional purposes. Compare **underrun**.

overset *See overmatter.*

oversewn A method of **binding** or rebinding a book for extra strength, as for library use, in which each leaf is sewn individually into a book.

oversize Designating copy or line and halftone illustrations to be produced in a size larger than the size it will be after it has been reproduced. *See also* **paper size; tile**.

overstrike (1) Substituting one character for another on a **display**. (2) A character with a line through it, used in legal documents to show what was edited out.

overwrite To record into an area of storage so as to destroy the data that was previously stored there.

owner The person who creates a **file**.

Notes and New Words

Desktop Publisher's Dictionary

P

p *See* **page**.

packaging (1) The preparation and manufacture by an independent entrepreneur of a book that is to be distributed by an established publisher. (2) *See* **book packager**.

pad (1) To increase the length of an article either by adding more copy or by inserting **leading**. (2) To place spacing between art and its surrounding area.

padding (1) Plain paper, trimmed, that has cement applied to one edge to make into note pads. (2) Space placed between art and its surrounding area.

page (1589) *v.* (1) To divide **galley proofs** and **illustrations** into pages. (2) To advance text on a **screen** by one screen, or page, at a time. *n.* (1) One side of a **leaf**. It should not be called a page until it contains copy or is identified in some manner to show its sequential arrangement. (2) One **display screen** of text or illustration. Abbreviated *p* (singular), *pp* (plural).

Fig. P-1   Page
depth is the
length of the
text area on the
page.

page-and-turner Text running more than a
page.

page associated In **word processing**, **headers** and **footers** that remain with the page
number during **repagination**.

page-at-a-time printer *See* **page printer**.

page break In **Ventura**, an **attribute** or **tag**
that forces text to start a new page. Com-
pare **column break**, **line break**. *See also*
bad break.

page board A **board** to which **galleys** and
artwork have been attached.

page combine In **word processing**, a function that allows two pages of text to be
combined into one page.

page composition *See* **desktop publishing**.

page-content heading A heading that appears at the top of a page to identify its
contents. For example, the headings in
dictionaries and encyclopedias that give the
first and last entries on a page. The page-
content heading is **flush right** for
right-hand pages and **flush left** for left-
hand pages.

page depth The length of the text area on
the page.

page-description language Software that
tells a **laser printer**, and other **high-resolution** printers, how to format a page of text
or illustrations, including **typefaces** and
sizes, spacing, **margins**, etc. *See also* **Post-
Script**.

page display In word processing, shows
where page breaks will occur when the document is printed.

Page Down key A **keyboard** key that
moves the screen copy up.

page heading The description of a page context from a report, appearing on the top of
the page.

page height The physical height of the
paper on which text is printed.

page icon In **PageMaker**, an **icon** displayed in the bottom left corner of the **Publication window** that represents the **master page** and every regular page.

page layout *See* **layout**.

page makeup *See* **makeup**.

page number marker In **PageMaker**, a series of characters entered on a **master page** used to number pages automatically.

page numbering The method of assigning numbers to pages. **Roman numerals** are used on **front matter** pages. The **middle matter** is then numbered with the **Arabic numeral** 1, and subsequent pages are numbered in sequence.

page orientation Page position options: **portrait page** (also called *tall*), which runs horizontally across the narrower width of the page, and columns run down the longer length of the page, and **landscape page** (also called *wide*), in which text runs horizontally across the wider measure of the page.

page plate Paper or metal **printing plate** used to print a single page.

page printer A device that prints one page at a time, for example, a **xerographic printer**. Also called *page-at-a-time printer*. Compare **line printer**.

page proof A **proof** taken from each page and **proofread** as a final check. The galley corrections have been made, and illustrations, page numbers, and footnotes have been arranged in their proper places. Compare **galley proof**.

page rate Fixed rate of pay used by some periodicals, based on each page of material as it appears in print.

page size The dimensions of the pages of a publication. *See also* **margin**; **paper size**.

Page Up key A **keyboard** key that moves the screen copy down.

page width The physical width of the paper on which text is printed.

PageMaker (1985) A **desktop publishing** program, developed by Aldus, that uses computers to produce typeset-quality text and graphics. PageMaker is credited with starting the desktop publishing industry.

pages Plural of **page**, abbreviated *pp*.

pages per inch A term used to measure the thickness of **paper stock**. Abbreviated *ppi*.

paginate (1884) *v*. To number pages in consecutive order. *See also* **repagination**. *n*. In **word processing**, the automatic arrangement of text according to a preset number of page layout parameters. *See also* **makeup**.

paging terminal A **cathode-ray tube** terminal permitting the user to recover buffered information that has been rolled off the screen, both top and bottom, by pressing a button. *See also* **cursor arrow**.

paint In computer graphics, to shade an area of a **screen image**, for example, with **crosshatching**.

paint program Software that allows a computer user to design free-form art using **bit-mapped** images.

paintbrush icon Shape of the **pointer** when a **paint-type file** is being placed.

paint-type file A file that consists of **bit-mapped** patterns. Compare **object-oriented graphics**.

pamphlet (14c) (1) A publication consisting of several sheets of unbound printed matter, either stitched or stapled, or folded only, and having a **soft cover** or **self-cover**. (2) Denotes a treatise published in this format, usually on a controversial topic of interest. *See also* **booklet**.

pan To move the screen left or right, up or down to locate a particular part on the screen. *See also* **zoom**.

panel (1) In computer graphics, a predefined **screen image** that defines the locations and characteristics of **display fields** on a **display surface**. Also called *board, display panel*. (2) A square or rectangular design made up of **rules** or **borders**. (3) In cartoons, refers to the number of **boxed in** illustrations. *See also* **double-panel**; **multi-panel**; **single-panel**.

panel title page *See* **half-title page**.

Pantone Color Institute (1985) A research center that studies psychology of color and the societal and cultural trends pertaining to color and personality.

Pantone Matching System color Specially mixed colors used in printing.

paper (14c) (1) A product made from cellulose fibers derived mainly from wood and described in terms of **finish**, the process by which it is made, its relative weight, its thickness, whether cut into sheets of various standard or nonstandard sizes or delivered in the form of rolls, as well as its color. *See also* **basis weight**; **bulk**; **caliper**; **chemical pulp**; **sulfate process**; **sulfite process**; **web**. (2) Colloquial term for **newspaper**.

paper bail The part of a **printer** that holds the paper against the **platen**.

paper finish The surface characteristics of paper, for instance, whether it is **glossy** or matte. *See also* **antique**; **calendered finish**; **coated finish**; **cockle finish**; **crash finish**; **double-coated paper**; **dry finish**; **dull-coated paper**; **dull finish**; **eggshell finish**; **English finish**; **felt finish**; **friction-glazed finish**; **high finish**; **kid finish**; **laid**; **lawn finish**; **low finish**; **machine-finish paper**; **machine-glazed paper**; **marble finish**; **marking felt**; **matte finish**; **medieval laid finish**; **metallic finish**; **mica finish**; **mother-of-pearl finish**; **mottled finish**; **oiled paper**; **parchment finish**; **plater finish**; **rep finish**; **ripple finish**; **satin finish**; **single-coated paper**; **supercalendered finish**; **superfine**; **text finish**; **unglazed finish**; **vellum finish**; **water finish**; **wove finish**.

paper jam A condition in which paper forms have not fed properly during printing and have become wedged in the feeding or printing mechanism, thus preventing the correct forward movement of the forms.

paper size The size of the printer paper. Standard paper sizes are **letter** (8.5 in x 11 in), **legal** (8.5 in x 14 in), European **A4** (8.27 in x 11.69 in), and European **B5** (6.93 in x 9.84 in).

paper skip *See* **paper throw**.

paper stock The paper used for printing a book.

paper tape Strip of paper of specified dimensions on which data may be recorded, usually in the form of punched holes. Each character recorded on the tape is represented by a unique pattern of holes, called the *frame* or *row*.

paper tension unit The part of the printer that fits on top of the **platen** to assure proper paper-feed tension.

paper throw The movement of paper through a printer at a speed greater than that of single line spacing. Also called *paper skip*.

Paper Trade Journal (1872) A monthly magazine for the pulp and paper industry.

paper weights These have been traditionally defined as a "substance of...." Thus, a paper described as substance of 21-pound large post 500 is of the same weight as a hypothetical paper in sheets of large post size weighing 21 pounds per **ream** of 500 sheets. This system is being replaced by the metric method which gives the weight, in grams, of a 1 square-meter sheet of the paper in question, usually expressed as g/m^2 or *gsm*.

paperback (1899) A book bound with a flexible paper cover. Also called *paperbound*. Compare **hard cover**.

paperbound (1901) *See* **paperback**.

paper-out sensor In printer terminology, a small switch behind the **platen** that sends a signal when it is not in contact with paper.

papyrus (14c) Most important writing material used before the discovery of **paper** in about 150 B.C. It was made from thin strips of pith from the papyrus plant.

paragraph (1525) (1) A distinct section or subdivision of a letter, chapter, etc., that usually deals with a particular point and is always begun on a new line or is often indented. Common formats include:

- A *plain* paragraph has the first line indented and the other lines flush.
- A *hanging* paragraph has the first line set flush right and all others indented from the left.
- A *flush* paragraph has all lines set flush and extra space is used between paragraphs to separate them.

(1986) (2) In **Ventura**, any unique element, ended by pressing the **Enter key**, of the document that can be described with a **tag**.

paragraph indent A standard measurement of indentation used to mark paragraphs or other indented material. *See also* **indent**.

paragraph mark A typographic element (¶) used to direct the eye to the beginning of a paragraph. Often used when the paragraph is not indented.

paragraph mode (1986) In **Ventura**, an operational mode that includes paragraph styles, such as indents, character sizes and style, and line spacing. *See also* **frame mode; graphics mode; text mode**.

paragraph numbering Paragraphs numbered in technical manuals, proposals, reports, and instruction books that are useful for reference purposes and as aids to a logical presentation of subject matter.

paragraph symbol A character (¶) used as a **reference mark**. *See also* **paragraph mark**.

paragraph-style indent An **indent** wherein the first line is indented from the left-hand margin and the following lines are set **full measure**. *See also* **indent**.

parallel A computer connection scheme in which data elements are transmitted simultaneously, in parallel, over multiple conductors or signal paths.

Fig. P-2   A paragraph symbol.

parallel communications A communications technique that uses multiple interconnecting wires to send all **bits** comprising a character at once, in parallel.

parallel interface The connection between a computer and **peripheral equipment** that transmits all **bits** of a character at once, in parallel. Compare **serial interface**.

parallel port A channel for transferring information, in **parallel**, between a computer and **peripheral equipment** such as a **printer**. Compare **serial port**.

parallel printer A printer that receives all **bits** of a **byte** at once, in parallel. Compare **serial printer**.

parallel table A **table** that spreads across two pages. *See also* **broadside table; continued table; doubled table**.

parallel transmission The transmission of all **bits** of a **byte** at once, in **parallel**. The advantage over **serial transmission** is speed.

parameter (1) Variable that is given a constant value for a specific process. Commonly used in the printing industry to refer to the limits of any given system. (2) A qualifier included with a **command** to define more specifically what **DOS** is to do. Also called *argument, option.*

parchment (14c) A thin skin taken from a calf, sheep, goat, or other animal, and prepared to accept writing.

parchment finish Finish that makes paper resemble **parchment**.

parens *See* **parenthesis**.

parent directory The top level **directory** for a specified **directory pathname**. Also called *root directory.*

parenthesis (1568) Either or both of the curved lines ((or)) used to mark off an additional word or clause placed as an explanation or comment within an already completed sentence. Plural, *parentheses.* Abbreviated *parens. See also* **brace; bracket; close parenthesis; open parenthesis**.

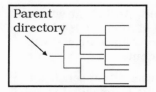

Fig. P-3   The parent directory is the root directory.

parity (1957) An error-detection technique used to check the reliability of data transmission.

parity bit A single **bit** within a **binary** word used to verify the accuracy of data transmissions. *See also* **American Standard Code for Information Interchange**.

parity check A test of a **parity bit** to see if information degradation has occurred during transmission.

parrot user A user at the lowest level of knowledge about a particular software product, who cannot yet generalize about his or her interactions with the computer. All he or she understands is that a key is pressed and the system responds. Compare **expert user**; **novice user**.

partition A portion of a **fixed disk** that is reserved for a group of **files** that operate under control of a common **operating system**.

passive graphics A mode of operation of a **display device** that does not allow an on-line user to alter or interact with a **display image**. Compare **interactive graphics**.

passive white space White space on a page that frames text and does not separate and differentiate various blocks of text. Compare **active white space**.

password A unique **string** of characters, chosen by the user, that a program or user must supply to meet security requirements before gaining access to data.

paste The act of moving text or artwork. from the **clipboard** to a **page**.

pasteboard The on-screen work area surrounding the page shown on the display.

pasted board Stiffening material used for the **covers** of most **hard cover** books. *See also* **case binding**.

paste-up (ca. 1930) Process of pasting an image or part of an image on a reproduction page or sheet that is to be photographed for **platemaking** and printing. It includes pasting blocks of text, art, preprints, or any other image in position. *See also* **board**; **camera-ready copy**; **mechanical**.

paste-up artist In the traditional publishing process, a person who pastes typeset **copy** and **artwork** onto paged boards to create **camera-ready copy**.

paste-up board Large pieces of paper with **nonreproducing blue** ink grids that are used to position a graphic, but whose line "disappears" when photocopied.

paste-up dummy Shows the printer which lines of type and which illustrations go on which pages and how they are to be arranged, spaced, etc.

patch A correction of copy or artwork made for **camera-ready copy** or film. *See also* **patching**.

patching Method of making corrections in **camera-ready copy** or film in which the corrected **patch** is set separately and pasted into position on the camera-ready copy or shot and stripped into film.

PAT file *See* **printer action table file**.

patent (14c) A grant of the exclusive right to make, use, and sell, for a limited period, the invention covered by the patent.

PATH A **PC/MS-DOS** command that specifies the **directories** that should be examined when the **operating system** is searching for a program or **batch** file to execute that was not found in the main directory.

path (1) The route the **disk operating system** takes to locate files. (2) The list of **directory** names that defines the location of a directory or a file in a directory.

pathname (1) The name of a **directory** path within a **tree-structured filing system**. (2) The portion of a file specification that defines the **path** to the file, which may include a **drive letter** followed by a colon such as *C:*.

pattern In graphics, the attributes used to **fill** a closed figure. Examples include **crosshatching** or horizontal or vertical lines. Colors may also be included. Also called *texture.*

payment on acceptance The author is paid for his or her work as soon as the buyer decides to use it.

payment on publication The author is paid for his or her work when it is published.

PC *See* **personal computer**.

PC-DOS (1981) The **disk operating system** developed for the original IBM PC. User interface is virtually identical with that of **MS-DOS**.

PC/MS-DOS *See* **MS-DOS**; **PC-DOS**.

PC Publishing (1986) A monthly magazine dedicated to desktop publishing and presentation graphics for IBM and IBM-compatible PC users.

PCB *See* **printed circuit board**.

PE *See* **printer's error**.

peak In **optical character recognition**, an extraneous mark extending outward from a character past the stroke edge of the character.

pearl An old type size, now equal to about 5 points.

pebbling A process of graining or crimping **glossy finish** paper after printing **halftones** to give an antique paper effect. Also called *ripple finish, roller embossing.*

pel A **picture element** of a **display**. Also called *pixel.*

pen control A **light pen** for communication between a processor and the operator.

penalty copy Copy difficult to compose because it is heavily corrected, faint, contains foreign language, etc., for which the **typesetter** charges a certain percentage over the regular rate.

pen name *See* **pseudonym**.

Fig. P-4   The front cover of the September 1988 issue of *PC Publishing.*

pencil icon In **PageMaker**, the shape of the **pointer** when a **draw-type graphic** is being placed.

pencil rough *See* **comprehensive**.

per inquiry ads Ads where the advertiser shares a percentage of revenues from all sales with the media carrying the ad, instead of buying ad space outright. Abbreviated *P.I. ads*.

perfect binding (1950) A **binding** process with a flat or squared spine. After folding and collating, the backs of the **signatures** are cut off. The cut edges are then roughened and an adhesive is applied. The books are usually finished with a paper **wraparound cover**. Also called *adhesive binding*. *See also* **binding**.

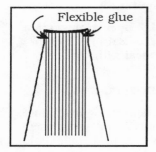

Flexible glue

Fig. P-5   Perfect bind-
ing has a flat or squared
spine achieved by gluing
sheet ends together.

perfect bound (1950) A book in which the pages and the cover are attached by glue.

perfecting press A press that prints both sides of a sheet of paper at one pass through the press. Also called *offset perfecting press, perfecter press*.

perfecter press *See* **perfecting press**.

perforate *v.* To cut minute holes in **stock** to facilitate separation of individual units, as in sheets of postage stamps. Compare **score**. (ca. 1538) *n.* A linear series of unconnected cuts in **continuous paper** that delineates a fold or page boundary. In *schoolbook perforating*, used extensively in school examination books from which students must tear answer sheets, perforation is made parallel to the **binding edge** of jaw-folded **signatures**. This process is also used in perforating checks in checkbooks.

performance-oriented writing A style of writing user **documentation** that focuses on the duties and tasks a particular user will perform rather than on the logical structure of the software being documented.

periodical (1798) A magazine issued on a regular schedule, such as monthly, annually, etc.

peripheral device *See* **peripheral input/output device**.

peripheral equipment (1966) An external item— such as a **printer, display unit, disk drive, graphics tablet**, or **modem**— added to a computer system to increase its usefulness and functions.

peripheral input/output device Any **input/output device**— such as a **terminal, printer**, or **tape drive**— attached to a computer.

periphery printer A special type of press for the **hot foil stamping** of cylindrical objects such as tubes and lipstick cases.

permanent file A **file** that is retained from one initial program load until the next. Compare **temporary file**.

permanent label A label assigned to a **fixed disk** that, when used, contains manufacturer and capacity information.

permanent memory Storage information remaining intact when power is turned off. Also called *nonvolatile memory*.

permission (1) The yes-or-no specification as to who has the ability to read, write, and execute a file. (2) Written approval to use quoted or **copyrighted** material, usually a note printed with the material indicating it is being used with the copyright owner's approval.

permutation index An **index** listing all words in a document's title in order that each word appears, in turn, as the first word, followed by remaining ones.

perpendicular-line tool Tool used to draw a straight line at any 90-degree increment.

personal computer (1977) Although any **microcomputer** may be called a *personal computer*, the term has evolved chiefly to refer to computers used for relatively small volumes of work in a business, as opposed to **home computers**, which are generally used at home to play games or do minor accounting, and **minicomputers** or **mainframes**, which are used for larger-volume work.

Fig. P-6   The August 1988 issue of *Personal Publishing.*

Personal Publishing (1985) A monthly **desktop publishing** magazine for **personal computer** users.

personalize To make a **form letter** seem like a personal letter.

pH (1909) A method of indicating acidity or alkalinity of **paper**. Scale is from 1 to 14, with 7 being neutral; below 7 is acid and above 7 is alkali. Paper with a pH value of 7 is desirable for any **artwork** or printed matter intended to have a long life.

phosphor dot Element of a **cathode-ray tube** that glows red, green, or blue.

phosphorescence Emitting light for a period of time following removal of a source of excitation. This phenomenon permits a trace to stay on a screen after the signal that has caused it is discontinued.

photo *See* **photograph**.

photo-offset (1926) Photographic method of **planographic printing** in which a negative print of the copy is used in the photochemical preparation of a metal plate. Also called *offset lithography, photolithography, planography, lithography. See also* **offset** **printing**; **printing method**.

photocomposing (1929) To photomechanically arrange **continuous-tone**, **line**, or **halftone** copy for reproduction. (2) The technique of exposing photosensitive materials onto film or **printing plates** using a photocomposing machine, also called a *step-and-repeat* machine.

photocomposition (1929) The setting of type directly on **film** or photosensitive paper for reproduction. Historically, the term has been used to include both **photomechanical composition** and **CRT composition**, but is now often considered to be synonymous with the former and to exclude the latter. Compare **hot metal composition**; **typewriter composition**. *See also* **photographic typesetter**; **phototypesetting**.

photocopy (ca. 1909) A photographic reproduction of graphic matter from the original. The correct generic term for **Photostat**.

photoengraving (1872) The process of making line and halftone **letterpress printing** plates by the action of light on a film. *See also* **engraving**.

photodisplay Display matter set on paper or film by photographic means.

photodisplay unit Machine that photographically sets **display type**.

photograph (1834) Picture of an object formed on sensitized paper, film, or other material by the action of light. Also called *photo*.

photographic proof Sample test print made from a negative. *See also* **proof**.

photographic typesetter (1) A machine whose type is output on film or negative. (2) A person who sets type that is output on film or negative.

photography (1839) An art and process whereby images are produced on sensitized surfaces, such as **film**, with light.

photogravure (1879) A type of **intaglio printing** in which photographic methods are used in the production of the **printing plate**. *See also* **lasergravure**; **printing method**.

photojournalism (ca. 1938) The practice of telling a story through a series of pictures, which may or may not accompany **manuscript copy** on the same subject.

photolithography (1856) *See* **offset-lithography**; **photo-offset**.

photomechanical (ca. 1889) Pertaining to any process of printing or duplicating images by mechanical means from a photographically prepared **printing plate**.

photomechanical composition **Photocomposition** performed by a typesetting machine employing film **matrices**. Compare **CRT composition**.

photomechanical printer A type of printer that uses light to create characters— either directly on paper or on a metal drum that transfers the image to the paper. **Laser**

printers and most typesetting equipment fall into this category.

Photomethods (1958) A monthly technical business magazine dedicated to the professional photographic and visual communication market.

photomontage (ca. 1935) A composite photograph that can be made in several ways by combining exposures, negatives, or prints. *See also* **montage**.

photoproof In **phototypesetting**, a rough **proof** for **proofreading**. Similar to a **galley proof** in metal typesetting.

photorepro Reproduction-quality **proof** of type produced by **phototypesetting** on photosensitive paper or by contact printing (through a film negative) of **phototypeset** materials. *See also* **diazo proof; film mechanical**.

photoset (1957) Copy set by means of a **phototypesetter**. Also called *filmset*.

Photostat Trade name for a photographic copy made on a photostat machine, which is of suitable quality for printing reproduction and used in **mechanicals** to indicate size, **cropping**, and position of **continuous-tone copy**. Also called *photocopy, stat*.

photostencil A screen-process stencil made on sensitized material.

phototypeset (1931) Keyboarding images of **typefaces** photographically on film, rather than in metal type forms.

phototypesetter (1) One of various machines used to photographically set, or compose, type images. Also called *photocomposition*. (2) A person who sets type on a phototypesetter. *See also* **typesetter**.

phototypesetting Cold-composition method of producing text matter by successively projecting the images of evenly spaced characters on light-sensitive film or on photographic paper. Also called *cold type, photocomposition*. Compare **hot metal composition**. *See also* **photographic typesetter**.

photounit Output, or **phototypesetting unit**, of a **photocomposition** system, which is responsible for the actual setting and exposing of the type onto photosensitive film or paper.

physical device Any hardware in a computer system.

physical input device cursor An **input device**— such as a **locator device**, **pick**, **keyboard**, or **button device**— that places data into a computer.

pi *v.* To mix up type accidentally. *n.* Mixed and jumbled handset type, slugs, and spacing material.

P.I. ads *See* **per inquiry ads**.

pi characters Special characters not usually included in a type font, such as **ligatures**, monetary symbols, decorative symbols, accented letters, mathematical signs, and **reference marks**. Also called *sorts*.

pic *See* **picture**.

pica (1588) (1) The standard unit of typographic measurement for column width and depth. 1 pica = 12 points = 0.166 in. *See also* Appendix 1; **em**; **line spacing**; **measure**; **measurement system**; **set**; **typographic measurement**; **unit system**; **wordspacing**. (2) Denotes a size of typewriter type measuring 6 lines to the vertical inch and 10 characters to the horizontal inch. Also called *10 pitch*. Compare **elite type**. (3) An old type size, now equal to about 12 points.

pica em *See* **pica**.

pica pole *See* **line gauge**.

pica rule *See* **line gauge**.

pica type *See* **pica**.

pick *v.* To lift particles of paper from **stock** during printing. *n.* Such particles collectively are called *pick*.

pick device A **physical input device** that identifies a **display element** or **display group**. Examples include a **puck** or **mouse**.

1 pica
⇓
12 points
⇓
0.166 in

Fig. P-7   The relationship between picas, points, and inches.

pick up *v.* To reuse an illustration or text for a new publication. Abbreviated *p.u. See also* **pickup**.

pickup *n.* Small rubberlike pad or sponge used to pick up excess rubber cement from a paste-up. Abbreviated *p.u.* Also called *mouse*.

pico Prefix meaning one million millionth, or one trillionth. For example, 1 *picosecond* is one trillionth of second.

pictorial drawing (1646) Any drawing that depicts a visual image of an object.

picture Any drawing or illustration, either **image** or **line art**. Abbreviated *pic* (singular), *pix* (plural).

picture element In computer graphics, the smallest element of a **display space** that can be independently assigned color and intensity. Abbreviated *pel, pixel.*

pie chart A circular chart divided into wedges resembling the cuts of a pie. Each wedge represents a percentage of the whole *pie.* Also called *circle chart. See also* **bar chart; column chart; curve chart; surface chart**.

piece A synonym for story.

piece fraction A small-sized fraction that is made up of two characters: the nominator and slash, or separating rule, as one character, and the denominator as the second character. For example, *3/* and *4* to make *3/4.* Compare **built-up fraction; case fraction**.

pigment The substance used for coloring in printing ink.

pin-feed platen A printer having sprocket-like pins for feeding **continuous forms** through a **printer**.

pin registration The use of highly accurate holes and special pins on copy, film, plates, and presses to ensure proper positioning, or alignment, of colors.

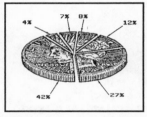

Fig. P-8   A pie chart is also called a circle graph.

pinks Pink **proofs** that are sometimes submitted by a printer for use in the **paste-up dummy**.

PIPE A **PC/MS-DOS** command that directs the output of one command to be used as the input of another command. Represented by a **vertical bar** (|).

pipe A process created by the **PIPE** command.

pipeline The program linkage established by performing one or more **pipes**.

pitch The number of characters printed per horizontal inch. For example, 12-pitch printing is 12 characters per horizontal inch.

pix *See* **picture**.

pixel (1969) The smallest unit of a computer graphics display that can be controlled through a program. It is the building block from which a graphics image is constructed. The size of a pixel relative to the complete video display of a computer is a function of the computer's graphics resolution. The higher the number of pixels, the higher the picture resolution. Also called *pel*. Acronym for *picture element*. *See also* **bit map**; **graphics resolution**; **plot**; **primitive**.

Pixel A bimonthly publication covering electronic imaging in science, technology, and medicine.

PLACE Command used to bring into **PageMaker** a text or graphics file created in a word processor or graphics program.

place mark In some programs a blinking **cursor** that shows the results of the program's action. For example, in a **spell check**, misspelled words may be flagged in this way.

plagiarism (1621) Copying or imitating another author's work and passing it off as one's own. *See also* **copyright**; **copyright infringement**; **fair use**.

Plan and Print (1928) A monthly magazine for reprographics designing and drafting and **computer-aided design**.

Fig. P-9   Planographic printing is a method of printing from a flat surface.

plane   A smooth-bottomed hardwood block used with a mallet to knock type to its **feet** on the **imposing table**.

planer   One who uses a **plane**.

planograph   *See* **multilith**; **offset lithography**; **photo-offset**.

planographic printing   (ca. 1909) Printing from a flat surface, e.g., **lithography**. *See also* **printing method**.

planography   The art or practice of **planographic printing**.

plasma panel   *See* **gas discharge display**.

plastic binding   A method of **mechanical binding** in which plastic teeth fit through notches in the pages. Also called *comb binding*.

plate, printing   *See* **printing plate**.

plate proof   A **proof** taken from a **printing plate**.

plate finish   *See* **plater finish**.

platemaking   The making of **printing plates**.

platen   (1541) (1) A round rubber cylinder that supports the paper and receives the impact when the keys are operated in a **dot-matrix printer**, **daisy-wheel printer**, or **typewriter**. (2) On a **printing press**, a flat surface that presses the paper against the inked type to produce the **impression**. *See also* **pin-feed platen**.

platen press   A style of **letterpress** in which an impression is taken by bringing together two flat surfaces, one holding the stock and the other the printing surface. *See also* **job press**.

plater   A plate **calender** in a papermaking machine.

plater finish   Glazed paper **finish** achieved by introducing sheets of paper between plates, or plate **calenders**.

play up   To emphasize.

playback   A type of **controlled field test** in which all user **keyboard** activities are digitally recorded and played back for later study and evaluation.

plot (1) To draw or diagram. (2) To establish reference points on a grid. The points so plotted are connected by lines.

plotter A printing device that prints data in a two-dimensional graphic representation.

plug-compatible (1) Two devices that may be plugged together without an **interface**. (2) A computer designed to use most software and hardware components built for the IBM PC.

ply Thickness of **blanks** and heavy **paper stock**. For example:

ply	inches
2	0.012
3	0.015
4	0.018
5	0.021
6	0.024
8	0.030
10	0.036

PMS color *See* **Pantone Matching System color**.

point *v.* To position a **pointer** using the **mouse** by pointing to that location, button, or character with the mouse arrow. *n.* (1) The standard unit of typographic measurement for **font** size, line **leading**, and **rule** thickness. 1 point = 1/12 pica = approximately 1/72 in = 0.1383 in. *See also* **Cicero**; **Didot**; **measurement system**; **pica**; **set solid**. (2) Any mark of punctuation, as the period, comma, etc. (3) Type is measured in terms of points, the standard sizes being 6, 7, 8, 9, 10, 11, 12, 14, 18, 24, 30, 36, 42, 48, 60, and 72. Type size is measured from the top of the **ascender** to the bottom of the **descender**. For example, 12-point type is approximately 1/6-in high. *See also* **leading**. (4) One-thousandth of an inch, a unit used in measuring paper products. *See also* **board**; **caliper**.

point constraint An **accuracy aid** in an interactive system that locks a newly entered point onto an existing point already defined. A **gravity field** around the existing point "attracts" the new one.

point-of-purchase *See* **point-of-sale**.

point-of-sale In advertising, a device or display of any kind installed near merchandise to aid sales. For example, display racks, animated and action pieces, posters, bookmarks, and banners. Abbreviated *p.o.s.* Also called *point-of-purchase*. *See also* **dump**; **slit-card**.

point size *See* **point**.

pointer (1) In computer graphics, a manually operated functional unit used to specify an **addressable point**. A pointer may be used to conduct interactive graphic operations such as the selection of one member of a predetermined set of **display elements**, or indication of a position on a display space while generating coordinate data. (2) The on-screen **icon** that moves when a **mouse** moves.

policy A publication's viewpoint. Also called *editorial policy, editorial slant*.

policy edit A **level of edit** in which the publication is checked to verify that the **style guide** of the publisher or company is followed.

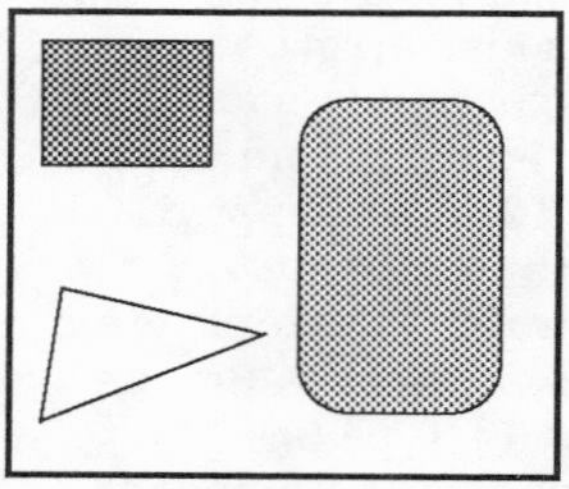

polygon (1571) A shape formed by three or more connected lines enclosing an area. It is one of the standard graphics **primitives**.

p.o.p. *See* **point-of-purchase**.

pop-down menu A type of **menu** that is pulled down, or displayed, by placing the **pointer** on the menu name. Also called *drop-down menu*. Compare *pull-down menu*.

port An electronic device that sends and receives electronic signals and is the connection point in the computer for **input/output peripherals** such as a **printer**, **modem**, or **mouse**.

portability The ability to use data sets or files with differing **operating systems**.

portable computer A computer designed to be transported easily from one location to another. Covers a range of computer sizes, from the extremely compact **laptop computers** to the larger **transportable computers**,

Fig. P-10   Examples of polygons.

which can be carried in much the same manner as luggage, but which must be set up on a desk or tabletop to be used.

portfolio (1722) Samples of a writer's or artist's work. *See also* **credits**.

portrait monitor A **monitor** whose height is greater than its width. Compare **landscape monitor**.

portrait page A page orientation in which the height is longer than the width. Also called *tall orientation*. Compare **landscape page**.

portrait printing The normal printing orientation for a page: horizontally across the shorter measurement of the page or paper. Compare **landscape printing**; **page orientation**.

portraiture (14c) (1) Process or art of depicting an individual by drawing, painting, or photographing from life, particularly an individual's face. (2) The depiction so produced.

p.o.s. *See* **point-of-sale**.

position (1) Where elements of a publication physically appear on the page. (2) Strategic placement of an ad where it will get maximum exposure. (3) The place within a list where a book falls in relation to other titles in the subject area.

positioning the caret In **PageMaker**, pointing at a location in the Edit window and **clicking** the left **mouse button**. *See also* **caret**.

positive **Artwork** or text that appears on the copy the same as it does on the positive film. Compare **negative**.

post binding A **mechanical binding** method in which screw posts are placed in the margin of a publication, used for publications that are subject to revision or for which it is desirable to add or remove sheets without difficulty. *See also* **comb binding**; **rivet binding**; **saddle-wired binding**; **side-stitched binding**; **spiral binding**.

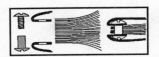

Fig. P-11   Post binding.

poster Large cardboard or thick-paper display sign.

PostScript (1985) A **page-description language** developed by Adobe Systems that defines the **typefaces** and sizes of the print and contains an outline of the typeface and a mathematical formula for determining the size. This description is completely independent of the printing device and is used by many high-resolution **printers** and **typesetters**.

pound sign (1) A character (#) that denotes a number or numeral. (2) A **proofreader's mark** to add space. *See also* Appendix 1.

pound symbol A character (£) that denotes the United Kingdom monetary unit. For example, "The cost is £75 per person."

powder ink *See* **dry ink**.

power supply A device that converts **alternating current** to low-voltage **direct current**.

pp *See* **page**.

ppi *See* **pages per inch**.

preface (14c) Statement forming part of the **front matter** of a book in which the author or editor states the purpose of the work and his expectations for it and sometimes expresses appreciation for assistance.

prelims (1891) *See* **preliminaries**.

preliminaries (1656) Pages preceding the text proper. Also called *front matter, prelims*. This is the order in which they appear:
- **half-title page**
- **frontispiece**
- **title page**
- **copyright**
- **dedication**
- **table of contents**
- **table of illustrations**
- **table of tables**
- **foreword**
- **preface**
- **acknowledgment**
- **introduction**

premium (1601) A publication given away free as part of a promotional campaign for a product or service.

prepack A **point-of-sale** temporary counter top or floor display unit, often made from cardboard, designed to hold and bring extra attention to merchandise.

prepress The process by which individual page negatives are transferred onto a **printing plate**, including **stripping**, **platemaking**, and **makeready**.

prepress proof A **proof** made using photographic techniques. Also called *bluelines*. *See also* **press proof**.

preprint (1) Any letter, number, symbol, design, **logotype**, **shading**, or line that is printed beforehand and subsequently **pasted** or **mortised** in place on a **board** or a **mechanical** for reproduction. (2) Part of a book printed and distributed before publication for promotional purposes.

prepublication copy A copy of a book that is circulated or sold prior to the **publication date**. Sometimes a discount is offered to stimulate early orders.

prepublication price A special lesser price offered on books bought before the official **publication date**.

Presentation Products Manager (1988) A magazine for corporate professionals and creative suppliers responsible for purchasing and creating presentations.

press *v.* To hold down a **key** or **mouse** button while an operation is completed. *n.* A machine for making printed impressions.

press book *See* **clipsheet**.

press feeder (1) One who hand-feeds a printing press with the sheets to be printed. (2) The automatic attachment that feeds sheets to a press.

press gripper The metal fingers that hold the sheet fast against the **impression cylinder**.

press kit (1968) A collection of publicity materials used to promote a book or an author to the media.

press proof A **proof** removed from the press to inspect line and color values, registration, quality, etc. It is the last proof taken before the complete run. *See also* **blueline**; **prepress proof**.

press release Information or announcement sent by a public relations firm or free-lance writer to newspapers and other outlets, designed to draw publicity. Also called *news release, publicity release.*

pressman (1598) One who operates a **printing press**.

pressrun (1945) Total number of copies of a publication produced during one printing. Also called *print run, run.*

pressure-sensitive Any material, such as adhesive- and wax-backed tapes, that will stick to another material when light pressure is applied.

presswork (1771) The operation of putting the ink on the paper. Most printing jobs consist of (1) **composition**, (2) presswork, (3) **binding**. Also called *machining.*

preventive maintenance Maintenance specifically intended to prevent faults from occurring. Corrective maintenance and preventive maintenance are both performed during maintenance time.

preview A feature of some **desktop publishing** programs that splits the screen so that the original text file is on one side and the resultant layout on the other side. Only the text file can be acted upon.

price estimate An educated guess of how much a job will cost. Also called *estimate.*

price quote A firm commitment on how much a job will cost.

primary colors (1612) Any set of colors from which all other colors may be derived. *See also* **secondary color**.

primary source (1) A person who has first-hand knowledge of the facts. (2) Documents directly bearing on the issue under consideration.

primitive A mathematical description of graphic entities, such as **points**, **line segments**, **characters**, **text strings**, or **polygons**.

PRINT A **PC/MS-DOS** command that **queues** from 1 to 10 **data files** for printing. The queued files print from a special **memory buffer**, allowing other tasks to be performed during printing. Also called *print spooler*.

Print (1940) A bimonthly graphic arts magazine.

print (1) Any mark made by a **printing press**. (2) Anything that is printed. (3) A publication. (4) A **printing**. (5) *See* **copy**. (6) *See* **PRINT**.

print-and-tumble *See* **work-and-tumble**.

print-and-turn *See* **work-and-turn**.

print area The area on a piece of paper—always smaller than the paper size—where the printer reproduces text and graphics. *See also* **margin**.

print, background *See* **background print**.

print buffer An area of **memory** that stores a document on its way to the printer to permit the user to work on something else while the document is printing. Compare **memory buffer**. *See also* **spooler**.

print density The relative amount of a page covered by type rather than by **white space**.

print echo *See* **Ctrl-Print Screen**.

print, foreground *See* **foreground print**

print format A representation of the manner by which data is printed, illustrating column width, position of page number, headings, and so on.

print head On a printer, the device that actually makes an image on the paper, whether a character from a **daisy wheel** or pins.

print queue The list of documents in line waiting to be printed in the order they were submitted by the operator. *See also* **PRINT**; **spooler**.

print quality In printer terminology, the quality of the printed page. A draft-quality printer is for high-speed, minimum dots per character jobs. A letter-quality printer is for final, polished correspondence.

print run *See* **pressrun**.

The Print Shop A program that allows a user to create cards, stationery, fliers, and banners.

print speed The speed at which a printer operates, expressed in a number of characters or pages per unit of time. *See also* **printer operating speed**.

print spooler *See* **PRINT**; **print queue**.

print to file Print the output to a **file** on a disk instead of to a printer.

print wheel An interchangeable printing element, used in some **impact printers**, that rotates to present fully-formed characters at a single print position that is struck with a hammer. *See also* **daisy wheel**; **daisy-wheel printer**.

printed circuit board (1946) A thin, usually rectangular board made of fiberglass or paper and impregnated with epoxy or phenolic. This is then laminated with copper on one or both sides. A wiring pattern is applied in special ink to the copper via a printing process and the excess copper is not protected by the ink. After the protective ink is removed, a copper version of the wiring pattern remains, taking the place of discreet wiring. Electronic devices, such as **integrated circuits**, are soldered to the board. Computer systems are made up of these boards. Also called *cards, printed wiring assembly, printed wiring board.* Abbreviated *PCB.*

printed wiring assembly *See* **printed circuit board**.

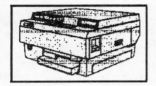

Fig. P-12   A laser printer.

printed wiring board *See* **printed circuit board**.

printer (1) In the traditional publishing process, one who creates **printing plates** from **camera-ready copy**, prints the publication, and binds it. (2) A computer output device for producing **hard copy**, i.e., paper printouts of computer files and programs. *See also* **daisy-wheel printer**; **dot-matrix printer**; **electrostatic process**; **impact printer**; **laser printer**; **line printer**; **nonimpact printer**; **page printer**; **thermal printer**. (3) Any machine that prints out a previously made original, operating either from opaque, translucent, or transparent copy or from a **microform** image.

printer action table file A file that enables the print routine to maximize the capabilities of a printer. Abbreviated *PAT file*.

printer font A **bit-mapped** or **outline font** installed in the printer or **downloaded** to the printer when a publication is printed. Usually distinguished from the **screen font**, which displays the text on the computer screen.

printer operating speed The rate at which printout occurs, expressed in **pages per minute, lines per minute,** or **characters per second**, or in words of five recorded characters including spaces, per minute.

printer speed *See* **printer operating speed**.

printer's devil (1763) The youngest apprentice in a printer's shop. Also called *devil.*

printer's error (1) An error in **typeset** copy that is the responsibility of the **typesetter**. (2) A correction of an error made by a printer, abbreviated and marked as *PE* on a **proof**. Compare **author's alterations**. *See also* **typographical error**.

printers' flowers *See* **fleurons**.

printer's proof *See* **master proof**.

printing (1) The art of causing a plate image to be transferred to a surface regardless of the method used. Printing consists of three parts: (a) type composition—**typesetting**, typing, **keyboarding**; (b)

printing— putting the image on paper; and
(c) **binding**— putting a cover on the publication. Also called *production.* (2) Denotes all
printed copies made in one **pressrun**. Also
called *impression.*

printing ink A nonfluid, pasty substance
used in **letterpress** and **offset-lithographic**
processes. **Newsprint ink** and **gravure ink**
are more fluid.

Printing Impressions (1958) A monthly
magazine for the printing industry.

printing method Any printing method used
for **printing**, including:
- **relief printing**
- **planographic printing**
- **intaglio printing**
- **letterpress printing**
- **offset printing**
- **stencil printing**

Printing News (1928) A weekly newspaper
of the graphic arts industry.

printing plate (1) The final printing master
that contains the image to be reproduced. It
may be metal, plastic, or other material. (2)
A **lithographic** plate, or **letterpress** block,
especially when unmounted. (3) Illustration
in a book printed on different paper from
the text pages.

printing press (1588) Any machine that
produces printed copies.

printing proof Impression of the type
image for use as a **proof**.

printing stock *See* **impression paper**.

printout (1953) Output of a **line printer** or
other printing device that produces normal-
reading copy from computer-stored data.

privacy (15c) The right of individuals and
organizations to control the collection and
use of their data or data about themselves.

privacy protection The establishment of
appropriate administrative, technical, or
physical safeguards to preserve a required
level of **privacy** for a computer system.

privately printed A book published by its
author. Also called *self-published. See also*

author-publisher; cooperative publishing; subsidy press.

prn (1) Short for *printer*. (2) Standard device name for the first **parallel port** (LPT1) in a **PC/MS-DOS** microcomputer system.

pro wheel *See* **proportional scale**.

process A particular computer activity. Also called *job*.

process-coated paper *See* **machine-coated paper**.

process color The method used to reproduce true-to-life, full-color originals. *See also* **flat color**.

process color printing Halftone reproduction of full-color art or photographs from a series of two or more plates, each printing a different color. *See also* **process colors**.

process colors Used in four-color printing: yellow, magenta, cyan, and black.

process letters A high-quality printed **form letter** made to be indistinguishable from a personally typed letter.

process status The current state of a **process**, or job: running, stopped, waiting, etc.

process work Four-color printing.

production The processes by which a publication is produced. These extend from the completion of the **manuscript** to the making of the **printing plates** from which the pages will be printed. Also called *printing*.

production manager (1935) In the traditional publishing process, one who manages the **production** process from receipt of complete **manuscript** to **camera-ready copy**.

program (1940) *v.* To design, write, and test programs. *n.* (1) A sequence of **instructions** telling a computer how to perform a task. A program can be in **machine language** or it can be a **high-level language** that is then translated into machine language. *See also* **central processing unit**. (2) In **phototypesetting**, the generic reference to a collection of **instructions** and operational routines, or the complete sequence of machine instructions and routine necessary to activate a **phototypesetting** machine, that is fed into and stored in the computer.

programmable function key A feature allowing a user to enter a program or key sequence and assign it to a **function key** and also display the program and edit it using normal **terminal** functions.

programming The act of writing a computer **program**: preparing a list of instructions for the computer to follow in performing a desired operation or task.

progressive proof A set of **proofs** of all color **printing plates** used separately for one operation and of the plates in combination, which give an indication of color quality and serve as a check against requirements. Also called *progs*.

progs *See* **progressive proof**.

promotional material Any printed matter— such as fliers, catalog sheets, letters, review excerpts, etc.—that is designed to publicize and sell a publication.

PROMPT A **PC/MS-DOS** command that modifies the form of the DOS prompt (C>).

prompt (1) **PC/MS-DOS** indicator on the display that is ready to accept the next command. (2) *See* **PROMPT**. (3) Any message presented to an **operator** by an **operating system** indicating that particular information is needed before a program can proceed.

proof A trial **impression** taken from type or **printing plates** at each stage of the printing process. Examples include:
- **galley proof** (of type)
- **revised proof**
- **engraver's proof** (of illustrations)
- **page proofs** (of type and illustrations)
- **foundry proofs** (if stereotypes or electrotypes are to be made)
- **stone proofs** (of all pages that are to be printed at once)
- **press proofs**

See also **blueline; folded and gathered pages; galley; photographic proof;**

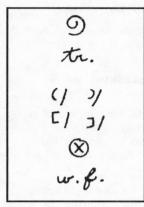

Fig. P-13   Proofreader's
marks signify corrections
and alterations in copy.

prepress proof; printing proof; progressive proof; pull a proof; reproduction proof.

proof press Hand-operated press for running off **proofs**.

proof sheet *See* **contact sheet**.

proofreader (1832) Person who reads the type that has been set against the original copy to make sure it is correct and who also may read for style, consistency, and fact. *See also* Appendix 3; **proofreader's marks**; **proofreading**.

proofreader's marks Standardized set of symbols used by **copy editors** and **proofreaders** to signify alterations and corrections in **copy** and **proofs**. *See also* Appendix 3.

proofreading (1920) Reading the original copy rather than the intermediate draft copy to detect and mark errors to be corrected. When two persons proofread copy, one is called the **copyholder** and the other the **proofreader**.

proportion Comparative relationship between the elements of a piece of printing.

proportional printing *See* **proportional spacing**.

proportional scale A two-part circular gauge used to determine proper percentages in **reduction** and **enlargement** of **artwork**. Also called *pro wheel, proportional scale wheel. See also* **scale**.

proportional spacing The function whereby characters are spaced according to their natural width. For example, an *M* is wider than an *i*. Also called *differential letterspacing*. Compare **monospace**.

proportional scale wheel *See* **proportional scale**.

proposal (1653) (1) A detailed plan of a proposed new enterprise that is used to sell that project. (2) A package consisting of an outline, sample chapters, author biography, and other supporting materials used by a writer to persuade a publisher to offer a contract for a book.

protection Safeguarding a file from accidental erasure or from the unwanted inspection
by others. *See also* **password**; **privacy**;
write-protect.

protective margin *See* **apron**.

protective slide A metal sleeve that slides
open when inserted into a **disk drive**. This
slide, used only on **microfloppy** diskettes,
protects the magnetic media surface.

protocol A computer communication specification defining software and hardware
configurations.

provisioning parts breakdown *See* **illustrated parts breakdown**.

pseudocode An artificial language that describes computer program algorithms
without using the syntax of any particular
programming language. Also called *structured programming*.

pseudonym (1833) (1) An assumed name
used to conceal an author's identity. (2) A
pen name.

p.u. *See* **pick up**; **pickup**.

public domain (1832) Previously printed
material whose property rights belong to the
public at large because of the loss or lack of
copyright protection. The source should be
acknowledged when used, but need not be
paid for. *See also* **fair use**.

publication (14c) *v.* The act or process of
publishing. *n.* (1) A published work. (2) In
Ventura, a combination of chapter files,
each of which may have its own set of text,
picture, and style sheet files. (3) In
PageMaker, a collection of pages created by
integrating text and graphics.

publication date A date, typically set about
three months after books are actually in
house, when a book is officially launched
and available for purchase.

Publication window A window that appears when **PageMaker** is started. Displays
a view of one or two pages, **menu bar**, **pasteboard**, **page icons**, **pointer**, **scroll bars**,
title bar, and **toolbox window**.

Fig. P-14   The August
1988 issue of *Publish!*

publicist (1792) One who prepares promotional materials or schedules media appearances either as an independent contractor or as part of the staff of a publisher, advertising agency, or public relations firm.

publicity release A news story written to obtain free publicity. Also called *news release.*

Publish! (1985) Monthly magazine dedicated to desktop publishing with emphasis on how to use **personal computers** to integrate text and graphics into printed communication.

Publish It! A **Ventura**-like **desktop publishing** program from Timeworks, Inc.

publisher (15c) Individual or firm that reproduces for sale to the public books, periodicals, pamphlets, sheet music, maps, and the like. The publisher prints or, more generally, causes to be printed, the copies of the work to be sold. In the traditional publishing process, the publisher manages the entire process.

Publishers' Library Promotion Group (1965) A group of staff members of publishing companies that are engaged in the promotion of **trade books** and **paperbacks** to schools and public libraries.

Publisher's PicturePak A **clip art** package—in **raster** and **vector** file formats—designed by professional illustrators.

Publishers' Weekly (1872) A weekly magazine devoted to book publishing and marketing.

Publishing Systems Group (1975) A group of newspaper publishers, commercial printers, in-house publishers, and other publishing groups seeking a better understanding of the publishing industry.

puck The hand-held **digitizer** portion of a **tablet** with which the user of a graphics system enters coordinate data. Also called *hand cursor.*

puff A praising **publicity release**.

pull a proof To make a print for **proofreading**.

pull-down menu A type of menu that is pulled down, or displayed, by placing the **pointer** on the menu name, then clicking a **mouse button**. Compare **pop-down menu**.

pull-out quote A quotation extracted from the text of an article and printed in larger type, often set off by ruled lines.

pull right To follow the arrow—usually while pressing a **mouse button**—on the right edge of a **menu** option to expose other menu choices.

pulling up a menu To expose menu choices by pressing a **mouse button** on the appropriate **button** or location.

pulp (1563) Material from which **paper** is made. It mainly consists of cellulose fibers and water, formerly obtained chiefly from rags, now from wood. *See also* **chemical pulp**; **mechanical wood pulp**; **rag paper**.

Pulp and Paper A monthly magazine serving the pulp and paper industry.

Pulp and Paper Canada A monthly magazine covering the pulp and paper industry in Canada.

pulps Magazines printed on coarse **paper stock**.

punch card (1921) *See* **Hollerith card**.

punched card *See* **Hollerith card**.

punctuation mark (1860) Any standardized mark or sign used in written matter to clarify meaning and to separate structural units.

purple prose Overblown language.

pyramid chart A **bar chart** in which the bottom bar represents the 100% quantity while bars above it become progressively smaller, indicating a reduction in the quantity. *See also* **pie chart**; **column chart**; **line chart**.

Notes and New Words

Notes and New Words

Q

QA *See* **query author.**

Q&A *See* **question and answer.**

quad (1879) *v.* In machine-set type, to fill out a line with spacing material, as when a heading has been set **flush left**, **centered**, or **flush right**. This and the analogous procedure in photocomposition are accomplished automatically. *n.* Piece of type metal less than the height of the **typeface**, used to insert spacing in lines of printed matter. It is measured in **ems** and **ens** of the point size of type used.

quaint character *see* **ligature.**

quality paperback *See* **trade paperback.**

quarter binding (1) Binding with a leather back only. (2) Any **cover material** used only on the **spine**. *See also* **full binding; three-quarter binding.**

quarto (1589) (1) A page a quarter the size of the basic sheet. (2) An old term for a book made from sheets which have been folded twice, each sheet forming four **leaves**

or eight pages. (3) A book measuring about 9 in x 12 in.

query (1) A one- or two-page letter created to interest an **editor** or **agent** in a book project or magazine article. It displays the author's writing ability and is meant to sell an idea. Abbreviated *qy*. Also called *query letter*. (2) On **manuscript** or **proof**, a question addressed to the author or editor. Also called **query author**. Abbreviated *QA*.

query author A **marginal note** to question an author regarding the meaning or accuracy of copy. It is the author's responsibility to check and revise the copy accordingly. Abbreviated *QA*.

query letter *See* **query**.

query-in-depth The ability to receive on command varying levels or amounts of information on a topic. The ability to have information presented on command, ranging from a general discussion of an item to a progressively more specific discussion of an item.

question and answer A form of interview in which the material is simply divided between the questions and the answers, preceded by an explanation of who the Q and A stand for. Abbreviated *Q&A*. *See also* **roundup**.

queue *v.* To place or arrange in a line. *n.* (1) A series of events waiting to be executed. (2) A line or list formed by items in a system waiting for service, for example, a **print queue**.

quire (15c) A collection of 24, or sometimes 25, sheets of paper of the same size and quality; one twentieth of a **ream**.

quoin (Rhymes with *coin*) Expandable and retractable blocklike or wedge-shaped devices operated by the use of a **quoin key** and used with **hot metal type** to **lock up** a type **form** in the **chase** prior to putting it on the press.

quoin key A tool used to expand or retract a **quoin**.

quote (1888) (1) A statement, often from a celebrity or key reviewer, used in advertising or for book cover copy. (2) An exact copy of original wording from another source, enclosed in quotation marks. (3) An offer to do work for a specific sum, a **price quote**.

quotes Marks that indicate speech. They can be a **single quote** (' ') or a **double quote** (" ").

qwerty keyboard The normal **typewriter** layout for **keyboards**, so named for the first six letters on the top row of the alphabetic section. Invented by Christopher L. Sholes in 1873. *See also* **azerty keyboard**; **Dvorak keyboard**.

qy *See* **query**.

R

rack A framework used to hold type **cases**.

rag paper High-quality paper made from cotton rags that are chopped, boiled, and beaten to pulp. The long, white fibers make a paper with excellent strength and folding endurance.

ragged Type that is not **justified** and that is allowed to run to various **line lengths**. **Ragged right** has a right margin that is not **justified**; **ragged left** has a left margin that is not justified.

ragged left A column or page of type set with the left side unjustified, or ragged. Compare **left-justified**. *See also* **alignment**.

ragged right A column or page of type set with the right side unjustified, or ragged. Compare **right-justified**. *See also* **alignment**.

raised printing Printing in which a raised designed is produced. *See also* **embossing**; **relief printing**; **thermography**.

RAM *See* **random access memory**.

> This paragraph is an example of a ragged right layout.
>
> This paragraph is an example of a ragged left layout.

Fig. R-1   The top box shows text aligned left; the lower box shows text aligned right.

RAM disk *See* **virtual disk**.

random access (ca. 1953) A method of providing or achieving **access** where the time to retrieve data is relatively constant and independent of the location of the item addressed earlier. Compare **sequential access**.

random access memory (ca. 1953) Internal computer memory that allows the direct access of any part of computer memory, regardless of physical location. *Random access memory* content changes often while the computer is used, and is lost when the computer is turned off. Abbreviated *RAM*. Also called *read-write memory*, or *RWM*.

random data file A file in which data is stored and retrieved without having to search sequentially through preceding data.

random scan A display device that allows the drawing of vectors in any direction. Compare **raster scan**.

range A *range right* and *range left* are equivalent to *flush right* and *flush left*. *See also* **alignment**.

range justified tape In photocomposition, a tape that indicates the ends of line only and does not include the widths of spaces required within each line **measure**. Compare **discrete justified tape**.

raster (ca. 1934) (1) In a video display, the pattern of horizontal lines traced by the electron beam from the top to the bottom of the screen. Compare **random scan**. *See also* **pixel**. (2) In computer graphics, a predetermined pattern of lines that provides uniform coverage of a display space.

raster-based graphics *See* **raster graphics**.

raster display A **display device** that uses the **raster scan** technique for assembling an electronic image on the screen by drawing a raster of horizontal lines.

raster graphics Computer images output to a **display device** that produces pictures through a **raster scan** technique, using **pixels** as building blocks. When viewed in detail, all lines except those that are horizontal and vertical have a stair-step appearance. Compare **vector graphics**.

raster grid On a **display device**, the grid of addressable coordinates on the **display surface**.

raster image *See* **raster graphics**.

raster printer A printer with expanded graphics capabilities that sprays ink rather than depending on the impact of an inked ribbon to create images.

raster scan The generation of a picture on a **raster display**.

raster scan device A **hardcopy** printer that prints an image line by line.

raster unit In computer graphics, the distance between adjacent **picture elements**.

rate card Card issued by a publisher showing the insertion rates of display and classified advertising and other pertinent information, such as information on mechanical requirements, contract and copy regulations, inserts, closing dates, special position of advertisements and cover rates, commissions and discounts, production charges, and circulation.

raw data (1) Statistical results not yet examined to eliminate incomplete, unresponsive, and other flawed data. *See also* **database**. (2) Information, usually in digital form, that has not yet been processed by a computer.

rb *See* **run back**.

RD A **PC/MS-DOS** command to remove a **directory**. Long form is **RMDIR**.

rd *See* **run down**.

read To gather data from a computer memory or other source, and to transfer it to a computer processor. Compare **write**.

read after write verify A function for determining that information currently being written is accurate as compared to the information source.

read-only A type of **access** to data that allows it to be read but not deleted or modified.

read-only file A **file** whose read-only attribute is set so that its contents can be displayed and read, but not changed or deleted.

read-only memory (ca. 1961) A type of computer memory—permanently recorded in hardware—that contains **instructions** that help a computer carry out routine tasks, such as starting itself up. The memory contents cannot be changed and are not lost when the computer is turned off. Because it cannot be changed, it is commonly used for systems programs, such as **operating systems** and language **interpreters**. Also called *firmware*, *fixed storage*, *read-only storage*. Abbreviated *ROM*. *See also* **boot**; **central processing unit**; **random access memory**.

read-write memory *See* **random access memory**.

readability (1570) The degree of difficulty reading **typeset** copy. Given legible type, the readability of a page will depend as much upon the **layout** as on the **typeface**.

reader's proof A **galley proof**, usually the specific proof read by the printer's **proofreader**, which will contain **queries** and corrections to be checked by the client. Also called *printer's proof*.

reading protocol A type of **controlled field test** in which readers are asked to think aloud while reading **documentation** during the performance of a simulated user task. The field test is tape-recorded for later study and examination.

reading to do A type of reading in which information is not retained or integrated in the reader's memory for later use, but is kept in memory only long enough to act on or use in a particular task.

reading to learn A type of reading in which information is retained and integrated in the reader's memory for later use.

reading type *See* **body type**.

readout Display of processed information on a terminal screen. Compare **printout**.

readout device A **video display unit**. Also called *character display device*.

ready print Inside sections of newspapers bought already printed with feature articles, advertisements, etc.

real time Performance of computer operations within the time span required to perform related physical processes, so that the computer operations do not limit or slow down a person working with the system.

ream (14c) Unit of quantity consisting of 500 sheets of fine writing or printing **paper** or 480 sheets of wrapping or tissue paper. The number unit is determined according to the grade and manufacturer; 500 is usual. *See also* **basis weight**; **quire**.

rebacked A publication repaired by replacing the old **spine** with a new one.

recess printing A printing method in which the ink is held in recesses below the surrounding surface, e.g., **gravure**, copperplate engraving, and **die-stamping**.

record *v.* To copy. *n.* A collection of related data or words, treated as a unit.

record separator In a **database** file, an indicator that shows where one **record** ends and the next begins.

recto (1824) A right-hand, or front, page. To *start recto* is to begin on a recto page, as a **preface** or index does. Compare **verso**. *See also* **folio**.

recto-verso Two-sided printing.

recursive (1934) (1) In reference to a **directory** system, the application to a directory, to all its offshoots, to all their offshoots, etc. (2) In reference to a computer **program**, the describing of a program that calls itself.

red-pencil (1946) (1) To censor. (2) To correct or revise.

red streak Streak of red ink appearing along the right margin of the front page of some newspapers to indicate a specific edition, such as the final edition, when more than one daily edition is published. Compare **blue streak**.

redact (15c) (1) To put in writing. (2) To select or adapt for publication, as in **edit**.

redactor (1816) One who redacts, especially an **editor**.

redboard *See* **board**.

redirection The process of causing a **command** or **program** to take its input from a file or device other than the **standard input**, or of causing the output of a command or program to be sent to a file or device other than the **standard output**. The **PC/MS-DOS** redirection symbols are the greater than (>) and less than (<) signs.

reduce To decrease the size of a photograph, artwork, or type for any reason. Compare **enlarge**.

reduced photo size The reduced size of a photograph to be reproduced in a publication.

reduction The photographic process of creating an image smaller than the original. A half-size image is expressed as a 50% reduction or **scale** 50%. Compare **enlargement**. *See also* **proportional scale**.

Fig. R-2   The picture above is full size. The picture below is reduced 75%.

reduction wheel *See* **proportional scale**.

reel-fed *See* **web-fed**.

reference card A short listing of major commands or ideas for a particular software product to be used by expert users who only need to be reminded of specific software features.

reference documentation A detailed comprehensive user document for experts or intermediate level users. It is organized for quick access and has few examples and little explanation.

reference library A special section maintained by most public libraries, filled with reference books— encyclopedias, almanacs, biographical dictionaries, books of statistics, etc.

reference mark (1856) A symbol used to key text or tabular matter to **footnotes**. They are used in this order: * † ‡ § ¶.

references Books, articles, or papers cited by the author of a published work and listed in the **back matter** or included in **footnotes**.

reflect To make a mirror image. Reflected settings of a page place a mirror image of those page settings on alternating pages.

refresh (1) The process of renewing the image on the **display surface**, typically 30 to 60 times a second. (2) In computer graphics, the process of repeatedly producing a display image on a **display space** so that the image remains visible. Also called *regenerate*.

refresh rate The number of times per second that a picture on a **video display unit** is renewed. In **raster displays**, the image is refreshed 30 to 60 times a second. In **vector displays**, the refresh rate is typically 10 to 60 times a second. A refresh rate must be fast enough to produce a flicker-free picture.

regenerate *See* **refresh**.

regional publication (1946) (1) A magazine devoted to the special interests or needs of people living in one part of the country. (2) An edition of a publication that carries advertisements related to that geographical entity in which it is sold.

register *v.* (1) The adjustment of **forms** or **printing plates** so they will print in correct position over another form or plate, as in color printing. (2) In printing, to align a type page so that it exactly backs the type page on the reverse side of the sheet. A printed page is in register when the impression is in the correct position on the paper. When such impressions are not exactly aligned, they are said to be *out of register*. *n.* A storage location within a digital computer device designed to store data, instruction, location, or status information.

register mark A symbol (⊠) used on **camera-ready copy** for positioning prior to photographing to ensure accurate **register**. *See also* **acetate overlay**; **crop mark**.

reglet A thin, wooden piece of **furniture**, about 6- to 12-point **slugs** used to fill out a **chase**.

rejection slip (1906) A printed form accompanying a **manuscript** returned to its author.

relational operator A mathematical sign indicating a relationship between to or more numbers, for example, >, >=, <, <=. *See also* **operator**.

release *v.* To let go of a **mouse button** after an operation is completed. *n.* A new **version** of a product.

relief printing (1875) One of the basic **printing methods** in which a raised surface receives a film of ink and then presses this ink onto paper. *See also* **flexography**; **letterpress**; **printing method**.

remainders Unsold copies of books marked down below original cost and sold in bookstores and by direct mail for a fraction of their cover price. *See also* **discount book**.

remaindering A publisher's selling of the remaining stock of unsuccessful books for a fraction of their list price.

remake To alter the **makeup** of a page or series of pages.

remarque (1882) (1) A drawn, etched, or incised scribble or sketch done on the margin of a **printing plate** and removed before the regular printing. (2) A **proof** taken before remarques have been removed.

remnant space Random advertising space, often in regional editions, which has not been sold when the magazine or newspaper is ready to go to press, usually available at a reduced rate.

remote device Any device not directly connected to a computer, but connected at another location to transmit or receive data. *See also* **CTTY**.

Fig. R-3   Relief printing uses a raised surface to receive ink and then presses the ink onto paper.

RENAME A **PC/MS-DOS** command that re-names an existing disk **file**.

rep finish *See* **ribbed finish**.

repaginate To adjust a multipage document as it is revised in order to ensure uniform page length and appearance. Compare **paginate**.

repeat-action key A key that, when held fully depressed, causes an action, such as typing a character, to be repeated until the key is released. Also called *automatic repeat key*, *live key*.

REPLACE A **PC/MS-DOS** command the replaces, or updates, all existing files on a target disk with matching files from a source disk.

replaceable parameter A symbolic reference, consisting of a percent sign followed by a one-digit number (such as %1), that can be included with commands in a **PC/MS-DOS batch file** to refer to the parameters entered in the **batch file**.

Report on Electronic Publishing A monthly market research report on **electronic publishing**.

reporting times (1) In a large project to be completed in stages, dates by which the author will give the editor a progress report. (2) The time it takes an editor to report acceptance or rejection of a **manuscript** or **query**.

reprint (1551) *v.* To print a story that has appeared in another publication. (1611) *n.* (1) Additional printing of all or part of a publication. (2) A general term to describe any new printing of a book. Compare **edition**; **limited edition**; **revised edition**.

reprint rights The rights to republish a book.

repro *See* **reproduction copy**.

repro proof *See* **reproduction proof**.

reproduce To make a copy from an original. Also called *duplicate*.

reproducibility Ability of line or **halftone** copy to be reproduced as acceptable and legible copy.

reproducible area Image area on reproducible copy or on a typeset **reproduction proof** that will appear in final form. **Crop** and **register marks**, title blocks, and file numbers are excluded.

reproduction copy *See* **camera-ready copy**.

reproduction master Any master used to make copies by any copying process. *See also* **reproduction proof**.

reproduction Photostat High-quality glossy **Photostat** used for reproduction. Abbreviated *reprostat*.

reproduction proof A proof from a **reproduction master** run off on a **proof press**. Also called *repro proof*. (2) Final, corrected photocomposed typography. Also called *black and white, etch proof, repro*. (3) **Camera-ready copy** on photosensitive paper to be pasted up on **mechanicals** to be photographed. *See also* **layout**.

reproduction typing Production by a typist of composition copy that is ultimately printed.

reprographics (1956) Branch of the graphic arts that is concerned with the reproduction of images and especially with copying machines and their methods and processes.

reprostat *See* **reproduction Photostat**.

required hyphen A grammatical hyphen that is not subject to **hyphen drop**.

resale number A number obtained from the state permitting the purchase of materials used to produce a book without paying sales tax, as tax will be collected when you sell the materials as a finished book. Also called *tax number*.

reserve-for-returns clause A paragraph in a publisher's contract that permits withholding payments to authors until **returns** from bookstores have been calculated or until return period has expired.

reset To return a computer or **peripheral equipment** to its **defaults** with either a **command** or by turning the computer or device off then on.

reset switch A switch or button on a computer that, when pressed, will cause the computer to go through its initialization sequence.

resolution A measure of the ability to discriminate between the smallest separate parts of an object or image. In **vector displays**, screen resolution is measured as lines per inch. In **raster displays**, resolution is expressed as the number of horizontal and vertical **pixels** that can be displayed. *See also* **addressable point**. *High-resolution* images have more dots per inch and look smoother than *low-resolution* images. The resolution of images displayed on the screen is usually lower than that of the final **laser** printout. **Laser printers** print 300 dots per inch or more; **typesetters** print 1,200 dots per inch or more.

resolution, graphics *See* **graphics resolution**.

RESTORE A **PC/MS-DOS** command that reads **BACKUP** files from **flexible disks** and writes them to a **fixed disk**.

retouching Corrective treatment of a negative, positive, or copy to correct flaws or to improve appearance.

returns Books that have not been sold by bookstores and wholesalers and are sent back to a publisher for credit or a cash refund. *See also* **on consignment**.

Return key A **keyboard** key that is pressed to confirm a selected option or to initiate a command. Also called *carriage return, Enter key*.

reverse Text or a graphic on the printed page that appears opposite of normal. Usually, text and graphics are black on a white background; when reversed, they are white on black.

reverse indexing In word processing, the feature that causes the typing position or

Reverse Type

Fig. R-4   Reverse type is usually white text on a black background.

display pointer to be moved to the corresponding character position of the preceding typing line.

reverse leading *See* **leading**.

reverse type In printing, refers to type that drops out of the background and assumes the color of the paper.

reverse video A form of **highlighting** a character, field, or **cursor** by reversing the color of the **character**, **field**, or cursor with its background.

reversing out Printing a white image on a solid background or tint panel. When an image of type or of a drawing appears in white surrounded by a solid block of color or black, it is said to be *reversed out*.

review (1651) *v*. To critically evaluate a work, citing its strengths and weaknesses. *n*. A magazine carrying literary stories, critical articles, and commentary.

review copy A complimentary copy of a book sent to reviewers or potential wholesale purchasers. Also called *advance copy*.

revise (1591) *v*. To look over again in order to correct or improve; to make a new, amended, improved, or up-to-date version of a work. *n*. (1) A printing **proof** that incorporates changes marked in a previous proof. (2) *See* **revised proof**.

revised edition A new **edition** of a previously published book containing updated or supplementary material. *See also* **edition; first edition; limited edition; new edition**.

revised galley A **galley** having the corrections and alterations marked on a previous galley. Usually requested when the revisions have been extensive.

revised proof A second, or subsequent, **proof** in which earlier corrections have been incorporated.

revision A revised version.

revision cycle Path of a typed document from initial **keyboarding** to final output.

rewrite (1914) *See* **copy editing**.

rewrite man (1914) A person who **rewrites** copy.

rewrite rule (1961) A grammar rule that specifies the constituents of a single symbol.

RGB color monitor A graphics monitor which is driven directly by an RGB (red, green, blue) color input signal. Compare **composite**.

rhetorical features Extra-linguistic features of a document that frame its presentation and that make the document effective.

ribbed finish A paper finish with a slotted, ribbed, or rippled surface. Abbreviated *rep finish*.

ribbon copy Copy made with a **typewriter**, **dot-matrix printer**, or other machine in which keys are struck against a ribbon to form the impression.

rider Provision added to and made part of a document such as an insurance policy.

right-hand page A recto page, usually numbered with an odd number. *See* **page numbering**.

right-justify To align characters horizontally so that the rightmost characters are aligned. Also called *flush right, right-justified*.

right-reading A photographic image in which the right-to-left orientation appears as in the original subject. Compare **wrong-reading**. *See also* **flop**.

right runaround *See* **runaround**.

rights The legal ability to reproduce or publish a work in any form, in whole or in part, which its author may sell or retain. *See also* **all rights; copyright; first serial rights; foreign rights; second serial rights; subsidiary rights; Universal Copyright Convention**.

Right justified type is type that is aligned on the rightmost margin.

Fig. R-5   An example of text that is right justified.

Rightwriter A writing aid that points out possible errors of grammar, style, usage, and punctuation.

ring-binder (1929) A loose-leaf binder in which split metal rings attached to a metal back hold perforated sheets of paper.

ripple finish Paper finish with a wavy appearance. It is produced by **embossing** or by using a **plater**, a calender in the paper-making machine. Also called *pebbling, roller embossing.*

river In a body of text, the appearance of irregular white space between words that accidentally line up vertically or diagonally. Caused by ineffective software **justification** and **proportional spacing**.

rivet binding The use of rivets to bind a book. *See also* **binding**. Also called *velo binding.*

RMDIR A **PC/MS-DOS** command that removes a **directory** from a **disk**. The short form is *RD.*

roan An inexpensive binding leather, made of sheepskin.

roll In computer graphics, to **scroll** in an upward or downward direction.

roll-coated paper *See* **machine-coated paper**.

roll-fed press *See* **web press**.

roll-leaf stamping A process of stamping gold, silver, or other colors on covers of books, stationery, and like work.

rolled paper *See* **impression paper**.

roller embossing *See* **pebbling**.

rom The **proofreader's mark** for **roman**.

ROM *See* **read-only memory**.

roman Of or relating to a type style with upright characters, the regular style of type used commonly for books and newspapers. Abbreviated *rom.* Compare **italic**.

Roman figure *See* **Roman numeral**.

Roman numeral (1735) A numeral in a system of notation based on the ancient Roman system and used until the tenth century A.D. It is still used in certain formal contexts, as in numbering acts and scenes in a play. Compare **Arabic numeral**. The more prevalent Roman numerals:

I	1
V	5
X	10
L	50
C	100
D	500
M	1,000

roman type *See* **roman**.

root directory The top-level, or main, **directory** within a **multiple-level filing system**; it is the base directory from which all other directories stem, directly or indirectly. Also called *parent directory*.

ROP *See* **run-of-press**.

rotary press A printing press in which the printing material is locked on a rotating cylinder. The paper passes between two cylinders, one of which serves to support the paper while the other prints it. The material must, therefore, be on a curved plate, either an **electrotype** or a **stereotype**. *See also* **flexography**. Compare **flatbed press**.

rotogravure (1913) The process of **intaglio printing** on a **rotary press**. *See also* **printing method**.

photogravure paper Book paper manufactured especially for **intaglio printing**. It has an **English finish**, a smooth, even surface on both sides of the sheet.

rough The first, unfinished sketch of a **layout** made to give the general effect rather than the exact details, usually done on tracing paper, giving a general idea of the size and position of the various elements of the design. *See also* **thumbnail sketch**.

rough draft The first versions of any written material, to be revised and polished before publication. Compare **final draft**.

rough proof *See* **galley proof**.

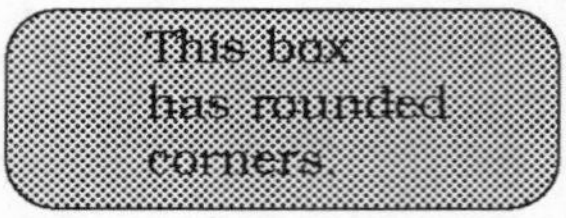

Fig. R-6   Boxed text
surrounded by a
rounded-corner box.

roundup Article form in which several persons' answers to the same question are given. *See also* **question and answer**.

rounded corner Squares and rectangles with rounded corners. Compare **mitered corner**; **squared corner**.

rounded-corner tool The shape the cursor assumes when in the mode for making rounded-corner squares and rectangles.

rounding In bookbinding, imparting a convex curve to the **spine**.

rout To cut away or deepen the blank, or nonprinting, areas in a metal **printing plate** with a special engraver's tool, so that they will not become inked and make a mark on the paper.

routine In computer technology, a set of **instructions** to be followed in a particular order, such as a **hyphenation routine** in **computer-assisted composition**.

row Information or data lined up horizontally, as in a **chart** or matrix. *See also* **column**; **stub**.

royal paper Paper size measuring 19 in x 24 in.

royalty Percentage of money from sales of a book paid to the author as specified in the book contract. Compare **advance**; **net receipts**. *See also* **author's alterations**.

RS-232C A data communication industry standard for a serial interface that connects computers and various forms of **peripheral equipment**, such as **modems** and **printers**.

rub-on type A transfer type in which letters, attached to a sheet of plastic, are pressed onto a sheet of paper with a blunt instrument to transfer the type from the plastic sheet to the paper.

rub-out character *See* **delete character**.

rubber blanket *See* **blanket**.

rubber rectangle A rectangle that can be expanded and contracted by moving the **pointer** with a **mouse**.

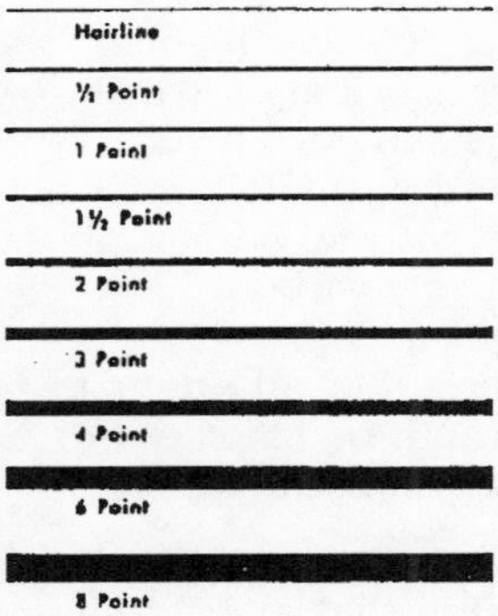

rubberbanding In computer graphics, moving the ends of a set of straight lines while the other ends remain fixed.

rubric The heading of a chapter or other division of a book, printed in red ink, with the remainder of the book printed in black ink.

rubylith Red-colored **acetate overlay** used to make a **window** on the **page board** for the printing of **halftones**. The coating is designed to be "peeled off" in unwanted areas.

rule (ca. 1862) (1) A line. (2) A metal strip with a **type-high** face that prints a linear design. (3) A line or linear design produced by or as if by such a strip. (4) A **pica** ruler. (5) Black lines added to a page— for example, between columns— to improve the design or increase readability of a publication.

ruled glass screen *See* **crossline screen**.

ruler Electronic rulers displayed, one across the top of a window and one down the left side, showing measures in inches, picas, or millimeters. Increments (**tick marks**) on the rulers depend on the size and resolution of the screen, as well as on the view. *See also* **measurement system**; **ruler zero point**.

ruler guides Nonprinting extensions of the **tick marks** on the rulers, which form horizontal and vertical dotted, dashed, or blue lines on the screen and are used to align text and graphics on the page.

ruler zero point In **PageMaker** and **Ventura**, the intersection of the two screen **rulers** is at 0. The default zero point is at the intersection of the left and top margins, but can be altered by the user. Also called *zero point*.

ruling line Any horizontal or vertical line used to separate text or frames from the surrounding layout.

run *v.* To process a given body of data by a computer. *n.* (1) The number of copies to be printed in a **pressrun**. (2) Material produced at the same time by a paper or cloth mill.

run around *See* **runaround**.

Hairline

½ Point

1 Point

1½ Point

2 Point

3 Point

4 Point

6 Point

8 Point

Fig. R-7   Examples of rules.

run back (1) To transfer text from the beginning of one line to the end of the preceding line. (2) In **proofreading**, to move material from beginning of one line to the end of the one above it. Abbreviated *rb*.

run down (1) To transfer text from the end of one line to the beginning of the following line. (2) In **proofreading**, to move material from the end of one line to the beginning of the next. Abbreviated *rd*.

run-in (ca. 1878) *v.* (1) To merge a paragraph with the preceding or following one. The **proofreader's mark** is a line drawn from the last word of the sentence before the break to the first word of the following sentence. (2) To set type with no paragraph breaks or to insert new copy without making a new paragraph. *n.* A **proofreader's** notation directing that an existing break, such as a paragraph, be ignored and the text continued without a break as one paragraph.

run-in heading A **heading** that appears on the same line with the text that follows it.

run-of-paper (ca. 1923) To place an advertisement or copy anywhere in a newspaper at the option of the editor.

run of press Designating color work offered by a publisher, such as one who publishes a trade journal. The color work is regularly offered and printed as stock-in-trade. (2) Multicolored printing in newspapers during high-speed **pressruns**. Abbreviated *ROP*.

run on *v.* To continue without starting a new line or a new paragraph. *n.* (1) In **printing**, extra copies printed at the same time as the original run. (2) In **typesetting**, text continuing on the same line. (3) In grammar, a sentence that contains a **comma fault**.

run out To make a **hanging indent**.

run over (1) In **flush-and-hang** material, all lines after the first of a particular entry. (2) The continuation of a **heading** on a second line; (3) Typeset material that exceeds the space estimated or allotted.

run ragged Copy set flush to the left or right **margin**, but not justified.

runaround (ca. 1915) Type set in lines shorter than **full measure** in order to fit around an illustration. *See also* **text wrap**. A *right runaround* places the text copy to the right of the illustration; a *left runaround*, to the left.

running Continuing. For instance, **running headers** and **running footers** appear on every page.

running copy Continuing *text*, as opposed to **headlines**.

running foot Any symbol, number, or term that is repeated at the bottom of each page of a publication. Also called *footer*. *See also* **folio**.

running head (1) A title line or headline that is repeated across the top of each page in a magazine or book. (2) The title of a book, chapter, or section of a book printed across the top of each page. Also called *folio line, header, running title*. *See also* **folio**; **page-content heading**.

running heading *See* **running head**.

running text The text of an article or advertisement as opposed to **display type**. Also called *straight matter, body copy*.

running title *See* **running head**.

RWM *See* **read-write memory**.

Desktop Publisher's Dictionary

S

s&c *See* **sized and calendered**.

s&sc *See* **sized and supercalendered**.

saddle In **binding**, the middle part of a book's **spine**.

saddle-stitched binding *See* **saddle-wired binding**.

saddle-wired binding A method of **mechanical binding** that permits a book or magazine to be secured by a stitch made by driving wire staples through the **center fold**. Also called *side-stitched binding*. *See also* **binding**; **comb binding**; **post binding**; **saddle-stitched binding**; **rivet-binding**; **spiral binding**.

sales representative (1901) An individual who represents a publisher's books to retailers, wholesalers, etc., in exchange for a commission. Also called *traveler*.

salvage fee *See* **kill fee**.

same size Indicating that the copy is not to be enlarged or reduced. Abbreviated *S/S, ss*.

Fig. S-1   In saddle-stitched binding a wire staple is driven through the center fold of a publication.

sample page Typeset sample of a book's intended design.

SAN *See* **standard account number**.

sans serif Without **serifs**, said of a letter that does not have a finishing stroke or line projecting from the end of the main stroke. Usually this is found in a **modern** typeface such as Helvetica. *See also* **type style**.

SASE *See* **self-addressed, stamped envelope**.

SAT file *See* **sheet feeder action table**.

satin finish Smooth paper **finish** that resembles satin.

satin white Coating mixture for quality coated and enameled papers.

saturation One of the three perceived color dimensions, which indicates the degree of difference from the light-source color of the same **brightness**. *See also* **hue**.

save A computer command that transfers a program from the **internal memory** of a computer to an **external memory** device, usually a disk, so that it can be preserved after the computer is turned off or while the computer is executing another program, then be loaded into the computer's memory again at a later time.

s.c. *See* **small capital letter**.

scale (1931) *v.* To calculate how much a (**cropped**) drawing or photograph must be reduced or enlarged in order to fit the **layout**, and to mark this information on the **artwork** for the guidance of the printer. Selective scaling can be made to one of the dimensions while the others remain the same; keeping the height and width of a picture proportional as the scale is changed prevents distortion. Also called *dimensioning, sizing. n.* A device used in copyfitting, typesetting, and layout. Also called *proportional scale.*

scale factor A quantity used in scaling by which the quantity to be altered is multiplied or divided.

scan *v.* (1) To examine each item in a list, especially in an information retrieval system. (2) To perceive whether, for example, a communications link or **input/output** channels are in use. (3) To analyze images on a line-by-line basis, for example, the raster lines of a **CRT** screen. *n.* (1) In word processing, a rapid view of displayed text by vertical **scrolling**. (2) A reading strategy in which the reader's eyes quickly move through a text, ignoring all but specific, predetermined items of interest.

scanned-image file A **bit-mapped file** created with **hardware** that **digitizes** images.

scanned-image icon Shape of the **pointer** when a **scanned-image file** is being placed.

scanner An imaging device that captures the contents of a drawing or photograph, converting the image into a series of dots, a raster-scanned image.

scanning rate The resolution at which an image is scanned. For example, 300 dots per inch or 400 dots per inch.

scatter graph A graph that represents separate values or quantities. Also called *dot chart*.

scattering An **index** problem in which information on one topic is placed under several index terms, thus falsely suggesting to a reader that information is missing.

scenario writing principle A reader-based writing technique in which writing is organized around actions, reader's questions, and headings with a human focus.

schedule (1862) A written scheme that details the planned dates involved in the production of any piece of print, with copies to all concerned. *See also* **production**; **production manager**.

schema (1796) An unconscious set of expectations that informs during the reading process and allows readers to anticipate various aspects of a document.

schematic (1701) Drawing that shows the layout of a system.

schoolbook perforating *See* **perforate**.

scientific impersonal writing style The use of third-person pronouns, passive voice, and nominalizations in order to erase human agency in a text. The style is not recommended for use in user documentation.

scissoring In computer graphics, removing parts of a **screen image** that lies outside a window. Also called *clipping*.

scissors editing Cutting out unwanted copy.

scope The range over which an action or definition applies.

score To crease or incise paper or card stock with a blunt blade along the line of a fold to prevent cracking and to facilitate folding. Compare **perforate**.

scored card A special card that contains one or more scored lines to facilitate precise folding or separation of certain parts of the card.

scratch disk A working disk normally used for experimentation or practice.

scratch pad (1) A memory area in computers used as a temporary working section for intermediate results. (2) A notepad.

screamer Journalistic jargon for an exclamation mark. Also called *bang*.

screen (1) Plate glass with cross-ruled opaque lines used in cameras to break **continuous-tone** illustrations and **artwork** into **halftone screens**. (2) A **halftone screen**. (3) The dot pattern in the printed image produced by such a screen. (4) The face of a **cathode-ray tube**. (5) A **shading pattern** made up of dots with a certain level of gray. Usually measured as a percentage of pure black: a 100% screen is solid black while a 10% screen is light gray.

screen of text What is actually visible on the **screen**. Because there are 22–23 lines of text per screen, one screen of text is not necessarily equivalent to one page of text.

screen cursor An indicating symbol, usually an underline, generated by the display hardware or by the graphics program and displayed on the **screen**. The screen cursor indicates the current position of an **input device**, such as a **stylus**, and is an essential visual link between the **operator** and the display. Also called *aiming symbol*.

screen dumping Copying the contents of a **video display unit** screen to a printer or to disk.

screen font *See* **font**.

screen image In computer graphics, a pattern of points, lines, and characters displayed on an illuminated display surface of a display device. Also called *display image*.

screen-oriented programs In word processing, programs that display a page or part of a page on a video screen exactly as it will appear on the printed page. Also called *WYSIWYG (what-you-see-is-what-you-get)*.

screen process A more accurate term for what is commonly called **silk screen printing**.

screen ruling While the dots in a **halftone** vary in size, their frequency, measured in **lines per inch** (lpi), is constant. Newspapers use a screen ruling of about 85 lpi while high-quality publications use 133 to 150 lpi. Also called *linescreen*.

screen size The measure of the amount of information that a **cathode-ray tube** screen displays.

screen symbol A symbol that appears on the screen but not appear in the printed document.

screened print Print made from **continuous-tone copy** and screened during photographic exposure. *See also* **Velox**.

script (15c) (1) Type characters that resemble handwritten copy. *See also* **type style**. (2) Abbreviation for *manuscript, typescript*.

script font Any type designed to look like handwriting or calligraphy, such as Zapf Chancery. *See also* **font**.

scroll (1973) (1) In computer graphics, to move a **screen image** vertically or horizontally in a manner such that new data appears at one edge as old data disappears at the opposite edge. (2) To move through **online documentation** that occurs as if it were a continuous roll of information that can be moved forward or backward by the user.

scroll arrow An arrow at the top and bottom of the **scroll bar**. Click on a scroll arrow to scroll the window's contents in the direction the arrow is pointing. Also called *cursor arrow, directional arrow. See also* **slider**.

scroll bar Gray bars on a window on which the user can move horizontally or vertically to change the view in the window or to select from choices presented in a list. *See also* **scroll arrow**; **slider**.

scroll button A button located at the top and bottom of the **scroll bar** that allows the user to scroll by line or by page through a document.

SDP *See* **standard documentation process**.

search In word processing, a feature that enables **strings** of recorded text to be located. Also called *seek*.

search and replace In word processing, an operation that finds one or more occurrences of a word or **string** pattern and replaces it with another.

search capability The method employed by the system to search for an editing point.

search path The **path** the **disk operating system** searches to find a particular **file**.

seasons The time of year when most publishers release their books. While books are published throughout the year, they are generally grouped in two seasons, spring and fall.

Fig. S-2   Scroll bar locations on Ventura's screen.

second color A printing color other than the first, which is usually black.

second cover Inside surface of the front cover of a publication, usually identified as such for advertising purposes. *See also* **back cover**; **third cover**.

second serial rights The rights for a magazine excerpt or serial that appears after the **publication date**. *See also* **first rights**; **rights**.

secondary color (1831) A color formed by combining equal quantities of **primary colors**.

secondary mouse button On a multiple-button mouse, the button that is not the main button. *See also* **mouse buttons**.

secondary source (1) A person who has opinions or hearsay evidence on the subject under consideration. (2) Critical articles or opinions, as distinct from firsthand knowledge. *See also* **primary source**.

section *v.* In computer graphics, to construct the bounded or unbounded intersecting plane with respect to one or more displayed objects and then to display the intersection. *n.* (1) A **signature** or group of signatures. (2) A printed sheet folded to page size. (3) Usually, part of a chapter of a publication. Sometimes, however, sections may replace chapters as the highest divisions of a publication.

sectional view View obtained by cutting away part of an object in an **illustration** or engineering drawing in order to show the shape and construction of the interior.

sectionalizing Arranging a technical publication in **sections**.

sector That part of a track or band on a **magnetic drum**, a **magnetic disk**, or a **disk pack** that can be accessed by the magnetic heads in the course of a predetermined rotational displacement of the particular device.

sector chart *See* **pie chart**.

see-through *See* **show through**.

seek To selectively position the access mechanism of a direct-access device. Also called *search.*

seek time The time needed to position the access mechanism of a **direct-access** storage device at a specified position. *See also* **access time**.

SELECT A **PC/MS-DOS** command used to set date, time, currency, and decimal format for different countries.

select (1) To designate an **icon** as the one that will be affected by the next action taken. (2) To click on an icon or **menu** choice. *See also* **Return key**.

selection In word processing, choosing and assembling blocks of recorded text for the purpose of constructing a new document.

selection area Area of a text block or graphic defined by the **handles** displayed when that text block or graphic is selected.

selection box A box drawn by dragging the **pointer** to enclose and select more than one graphic or text block at a time. *See also* **drag**.

Selectric Trade name for a popular office **typewriter** system using a simple, ball-shaped type element, manufactured by IBM. Compare **typebar**.

self-addressed, stamped envelope An **envelope** enclosed is an envelope sent to someone. The enclosed envelope contains the sender's address and a stamp. It is usually sent with unsolicited matter— such as manuscripts and questionnaires— to facilitate replies. Abbreviated *SASE.*

self-cover Cover of the same stock as the inside pages of a publication and printed at the same time as the inside pages.

self-ends The first and last pages of a document used to attach it to the binding. Also called *endleaf, endpaper.*

self-mailer (ca. 1942) A printed piece on which the address is printed directly without use of an envelope.

self-publish To publish one's own work. Also called *privately printed*. Compare **cooperative publishing; subsidy press**.

self-test (1) A method of checking the operation of a **computer** or **peripheral equipment**. (2) In printer terminology, when the self-test is turned on, the printer prints the characters that are stored in its **read-only memory**.

semi-bold A weight of a **typeface** a little heavier than the normal text version but not as heavy as a **boldface**.

semiannual Once every six months.

semimonthly Once every two weeks.

semiweekly Twice a week.

sentence complexity A measure of the complexity of a sentence's structure. Sentence structures containing embedded words, phrases, or clauses between the beginning of a sentence and the subject, between the subject and the verb, and between a modifier and the item it modifies are considered to be more complex.

separation negative *See* **color separation**.

sequential access (1) A mode of data retrieval where data is recovered in the order in which is was written to the storage medium. Compare **random access**. (2) A means of finding information in a document based on its sequential position, such as by its page number or its physical position in a document. *See also* **access**.

sequential data file A file from which data is read or to which data is written— one after the other.

sequential thematic organization of proposals A writing style that uses rigid format specifications to make text easier to read. Abbreviated *STOP*.

serial A computer connection scheme in which data is transmitted in a sequential or serial stream over an electrical conductor. *See also* **serial interface**.

serial access Entering or retrieving **data** from a **storage device** in such a way that the process depends on a reference to data previously accessed. Compare **direct access**.

serial communications A communications technique that uses as few as two interconnecting wires to transmit data **bits** one at a time in each direction.

serial interface The connection between a computer and **peripheral equipment** that transmits data one **bit** at a time. Compare **parallel interface**.

serial port The communications connection (labeled as COM1, COM2, COM3, or COM4 in **PC/MS-DOS** microcomputer systems) to which devices such as a **modem** or a **serial printer** can be attached. Compare **parallel port**.

serial printer A printer that receives data one **bit** at a time. Also called *character printer*. Compare **parallel printer**.

serial transmission In data transfer, transmission of information between a **computer** and **peripheral equipment** one **bit** at a time. Compare **parallel transmission**.

serialization (1892) Printing a piece in consecutive installments, usually in **periodicals**.

series (1611) A list of items in a sentence connected by commas, numbers, letters, or bullets.

serif (1841) (1) The short horizontal stroke that projects at the tops and bottoms of characters which is used to increase the horizontal emphasis in a line of type and to increase the distinctiveness of each letter. Compare **sans serif**. (2) Originally, in handwritten letters, a beginning or finishing stroke of the pen.

serrated edges (1668) Roughly cut edges of paper, as in newspapers.

service bureau An outside company that provides keyboarding, training, printing, and operating support for companies for a fee. *See also* **computer bureau**.

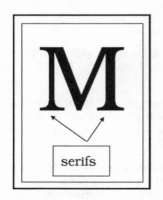

serifs

service mark (1947) A mark or device used to identify a service, such as insurance or transportation, offered to customers. Compare **trademark**.

SET A set environment **PC/MS-DOS** command that displays the computer's environment and permits changes to the setting from the **keyboard**.

set *v.* To assemble letters into words and lines. *n.* In **typography**, the width of a piece of type, generally spoken of as *condensed, extended, thin, fat.*

set solid To set type without **leading**.

setoff *See* **offset**.

setting a stick Adjusting a **composing stick** to a **pica** measure or half-pica **measure**.

setup The combination of **software** and **hardware** attached to a computer.

sewing *see* **binding**.

Seybold Report on Desktop Publishing A monthly newsletter that analyzes desktop publishing software and applications.

Seybold Report on Publishing Systems (1971) A monthly newsletter devoted to publishing systems.

shade pattern A pattern that fills a drawn object. *See also* **screen**.

shading *v.* (1) In computer graphics, emphasizing a given **display group** by changing the attitudes of all the other display groups in the same **display field**. (1663) (2) In drawings, a patterned screen added to enhance the artwork and to **highlight** specific areas. *n.* A device used for layout variation and emphasis and to improve the appearance of copy.

shadow (1) A letter form with extra weight down one side giving a shadow effect. (2) Shaded or darker portions of a **halftone**.

shadow box (ca. 1909) Frame drawn around copy to give the illusion of a shadow.

Shadow box

Fig. S-3   A shadow box is a frame around copy to give the illusion of a shadow.

shape A spatial form, such as a square, rectangle, circle, or oval.

SHARE A **PC/MS-DOS** command that reserves disk space for multiuser control information.

shared logic Where several computers simultaneously use the memory and processing powers of a single **central processing unit** controller.

shared resource A **hardware** device, such as a printer, that is shared by several computers simultaneously.

shareware Software passed from user to user, especially through **user groups**.

sheet Piece of paper with or without copy. Also called *leaf. See also* **page**.

sheet-fed press (1888) A press that prints on individual sheets of paper. Compare **web press**.

sheet-fed scanner A **scanner** into which single pages are fed. Compare **flatbed scanner**.

sheet feeder A device attached to a **printer** to automatically feed out sheets of paper or forms from one or more input drawers and to remove the finished printed sheets to an output drawer.

sheet feeder action table A **file** that instructs the sheet feeder so that it operates properly. Abbreviated *SAT file*.

sheetwise A method of printing in which a different **form** is used for each side of a sheet. Compare **work-and-turn**.

shelf life (1927) The length of time a document will remain serviceable to users.

shelfback *See* **spine**.

SHELL A **PC/MS-DOS** command used by system programmers to specify the name and location of a command processor to be used in place of the standard DOS command processor, COMMAND.COM.

shelter book A magazine that focuses on housing or related subjects.

shift (1) To move data to the left or right. (2) To activate the **Shift key**.

Shift-click To hold down the **Shift key** while clicking on **icons** or lines of text to be selected.

Shift key (1904) A **keyboard** key that lowers or raises the type case to print in **uppercase** or **lowercase**. *See also* **beating the Shift**.

shilling mark *See* **virgule**.

shingle To vary slightly the placement of the type image from page to page, so that, after **binding** and **trimming**, the outside margins will be equal in width.

shingling A method of making a column or page of type out of many separate cards or slips of paper, each containing one or more lines of type. The type must be positioned near the edge of each card, and the cards are then overlapped like shingles on a roof.

shipping outer A package, used mainly for protection in transit, that contains a number of smaller unit packages. *See also* **display outer; outer**.

Sholes, Christopher L. Inventor of the **qwerty keyboard** typewriter.

short and The ampersand (&).

short dash *See* **en dash**.

short page In **makeup**, a page that runs shorter than provided for in the design, usually to improve page makeup.

short rate discount Any discount less than the usual 40%. Schools often buy on a 20% short rate.

short rated When advertising contract obligations are not met and the advertiser is rebilled at the higher actual usage rates.

short run (1948) Small printing jobs of a few hundred (for neighborhood printing) or a few thousand (for book manufacturers) books or booklets.

short tear-off In printers, a feature that automatically feeds the **perforation** of

continuous paper to the tear-off position and then feeds the paper back to the loading position.

short-term memory (1) A term given to that part of human memory in which information is initially processed. (2) A metaphor for human memory taken from a computer model.

short title page *See* **half-title page**.

shoulder That part of **hot metal type** not covered by the **face**.

show card A large, hand-lettered poster or advertising placard.

show through Visibility of printed matter on the opposite side of a sheet due to poor paper quality, excessive ink penetration, or too heavy an impression on press. Also called *see-through.*

shrink wrap (1966) A clear plastic covering heat shrunk to fit tightly and used in shipping from the manufacturer to avoid damaging the contents.

shutdown (1888) The suspension or cessation of any operation. *See also* **crash**.

side head *See* **sidehead**.

side-sewn *See* **side-stitched binding**.

side stab *See* **side-stitched binding**.

side-stitched binding A method of mechanical binding in which a booklet or a **signature** is stitched at the sides in the closed position; the pages cannot be opened to their full width as a result. Also called *side-sewn binding, side stab, side-wired binding, singer-sewn. See also* **case binding**; **comb binding**; **mechanical binding**; **post binding**; **rivet-binding**; **saddle-wired binding**; **Smythe sewn**; **spiral binding**.

side-wired binding *See* **side-stitched binding**.

sidebar (1945) (1) In a publication, a short, related feature that accompanies a longer piece and is set off by means of a box, and often by special type treatment or tinted paper. (1986) (2) In **Ventura**, a panel to the

Fig. S-4 In a side-stitched binding a signature is stitched at the sides in a closed position.

left of the working area that contains the
mode selections, **assignment list**, **addition button**, **scroll bars**, and **current selection box**.

sidehead A caption, heading, or title that appears at the side of a page or column.

signature A folded printed sheet of paper ready for sewing into a book. It usually consists of 16 pages, but may have 8, 12, 24, 32, 48, or 64 pages. *See also* **imposition**; **unbound signature**.

signature press A machine used to press **signatures** together to expel air from between the sheets.

silhouette (1783) Outline of an object, especially a portrait profile, filled in with black or another solid color. *See also* **cutout halftone**.

silicon (1817) An element, widely found in sand and clay, that is mixed with many other elements to provide magnetic properties. It is used for transistors and many other semiconductors.

silicon chip (1904) A wafer of **silicon** providing a semiconductor base for a number of electrical circuits. *See also* **chip**.

silk-screen printing (1942) A printing method whereby ink is forced through the pores of a fabric screen stencil bearing a reverse image of the design to be printed. A more expensive process used for imprinting heavy stock paper.

silver print *See* **proof**.

Simply Stated (1977) An irregularly published newsletter that helps writers improve documentation.

simulation The representation of a system and the way it works.

simultaneous editions The printing of **hard cover** and **paperback** editions of a book at the same time. *See also* **split runs**.

Simultaneous Peripheral Operations On-line *See* **spool; spooler**.

simultaneous submission Submitting the same **manuscript** to more than one publisher at the same time.

singer-sewn *See* **side-stitched binding**.

single-coated paper Coated or enameled paper to which only one coat has been applied.

single-color press Printing press capable of printing only one color at a time.

single copy order A book order of only one copy. Many publishers do not give discounts on single copy orders.

single-density A system of recording to a lower density in order to put less data on a given size of medium. For example, a single-density diskette stores one-half as much information as a **double-density** diskette.

single-panel A cartoon with only one **boxed in** illustration. *See also* **double-panel**.

single printing Printing first on one side of a sheet and then on the reverse side by either the **work-and-turn** or the **work-and-tumble** method. Compare **perfecting press**.

single quote A single quotation mark (' or ') that indicates a quote within a quote.

single-sided page An option in **desktop publishing** programs for creating publications to be reproduced on one side of a sheet of paper. *See also* **double-sided page**.

single-sided publication A publication with pages reproduced on one side only of each sheet of paper. *See also* **double-sided publication**.

sinkage The distance from the top of the top line on a text page to the first line of text at which chapter openings and similar material are set.

size *v.* To treat paper chemically in order to modify its surface qualities. *n.* (1) Gelatinous materials used for glazing or coating papers during paper making process. (2) A sticky yellow ink used in bronzing and flock-ing. The metallic gold and silver dust adheres to the sticky ink when dusted. (3) Gluelike material added to paper to make it stiffer and more resistant to moisture. (4) *See* **scale**.

size box (1) In **PageMaker** and **Windows**, a box in the upper right corner of the screen that is used to alternately change the win-dow's size from small to full. (2) In **Ventura**, a small square box in the lower right corner of the screen that is used to make the screen window smaller. *See also* **full box**.

sized and calendered A smooth-finished paper stock. Abbreviated *s&c*.

sized and supercalendered A glossy paper stock. Abbreviated *s&sc*.

sketching Freehand drawing of lines with an interactive display. *See also* **brush**; **con-straint**; **fill**; **rubberbanding**; **shading**.

skid A unit of paper, usually delivered on movable wooden platforms and weighing about 3,000 pounds.

skim A reading strategy in which the reader's eyes move quickly through a text with the purpose of ascertaining the general drift of a publication.

slab serif A more descriptive phrase that is an alternative for **Egyptian** typefaces. *See also* **typeface nomenclature**.

slant (1) *See* **virgule**. (2) The device, in pho-totypesetting, which enables the characters to be set at an angle, thus producing a sloped roman. *See also* **oblique**. (1655) (3) The **angle** of a specific approach to any given material that appeals to special inter-ests of the intended readers.

slash *See* **virgule**.

slash mark *See* **virgule**.

slave In computer terminology, a device operated wholly by data input and pro-grammed from another part of the system.

sleeve An **envelope** used to store **diskettes** to prevent accidental contact with the exposed recording surface.

slick A magazine printed on glossy paper and having a large circulation.

slide A protective device on 3.5-inch diskettes that slides open when inserted into a disk drive. It protects the magnetic media surface.

slider Rectangle that moves inside the **scroll bar**. Drag the slider up or down to move to different parts of the screen. *See also* **scroll arrow**.

slip-sheet (ca. 1909) *v.* (1) To insert blank leaves between printed sheets to avoid **offsetting** an image on one sheet onto the back of the next sheet. Also called *interleave*. (2) In the preparation of copy, to insert pages in proper sequence to designate the placement of illustrations that are still being prepared. *n.* The sheet of paper inserted to avoid an offsetting image.

slipcase (ca. 1925) A protective box in which a book or set of volumes fits. When shelved, the **spines** of the books are visible.

slit-card A display poster designed to fit into or around a book. *See also* **point-of-sale**.

slit on press To cut printed sheets or web longitudinally before they reach the **folder**.

slitter Device used to cut paper as it passes from the printing press.

slug (1) A lead greater than 6 points. (2) A line of type or spacing material cast by a **linecasting machine**. (3) An identifying word or phrase at the top of each **manuscript** page. Also called *slugline*.

slugline *See* **slug**.

slush pile The accumulation of unsolicited **manuscripts** in a publishing company's office. It is scanned by **junior editors** when time allows. *See also* **over the transom**.

small In **Ventura**, **small capital letters**.

small capital letter (1770) (1) A
proofreader's direction—a double underline—to set copy in **uppercase** letters the
same size as the lowercase letters being
used. (2) An uppercase letter specially
drawn to range with the lowercase **x-height**.
Abbreviated *s.c., sm caps. See also* **caps
and small caps.** Recommended uses:

- professional qualifications, e.g., MD, ASAE
- for BC and AD in dates
- for a periodical's title when mentioned in its
  own text

small caps *See* **small capital letter.**

small pica Old type size, now equal to
about 11 points.

Small Press (1983) A bimonthly magazine
addressing the needs of the independent
publisher.

smart terminal A terminal possessing
some computing power of its own.

smashing (1833) Pressing **signatures** together so that they will lie flat in binding.

sm caps *See* **small capital letter.**

Smythe sewn A form of binding used for
many **hard cover** books. The signatures are
first sewn together by passing the thread
through the fold of each **signature** and lock-
ing it at the back, then glued into the hard
cover. It's a sturdy, but costly, form of binding. *See also* **binding; case binding; casing
in; perfect binding; side-wired binding.**

snap-to *See* **grid snap.**

snap-to-guides Margin guides, column
guides, and ruler guides that exert a magnetic pull on the pointer or any text or
graphic near the guides.

Society for Technical Communication
(1960) A national association for technical writers.

Society of American Graphic Artists
(1915) A society of American of graphic artists who work in the print media.

Society of National Association Publications A national association of voluntary associations and societies who own, operate, or control publications.

Society of Publication Designers (1964) A society of art directors, designers, editors, and graphic artists with responsibility for the layout and design of consumer, business, and professional publications and newspapers.

soft carriage return A **return** that results from an automatic word wrap. Also called *carriage return.*

soft character set A **character set** that can be modified through **software** to meet the needs of the programmer. Such user-defined character sets can be used to create the impression of **high-resolution graphics** but do not require the amount of computer memory necessary for **bit-mapped** high resolution. *See also* **American Standard Code for Information Interchange**.

soft copy *See* **softcopy**.

soft cover (1952) Any book cover other than a **hard cover** or a **self-cover**.

softcopy (1) Computer output that is delivered to disks, tapes, and cassettes. Compare **hardcopy**. (2) Text copy typed on paper, as opposed to **camera-ready copy**. Softcopy is not final copy.

software (1962) The "soft" or programming components of a computer system, including the **programs**, languages, procedures, and any associated **documentation** pertaining to the operation of a computer system. Compare **hardware**. *See also* **firmware**.

software documentation Program listings or documentation consisting of technical manuals describing the operation and use of programs.

software orientation Organizing a document based on the organization of the software.

software package A computer program supplied **off-the-shelf** on disks, complete with reference manual, application notes, and often including special circuit cards, starter files, and other accessories for the user who has a specific computing application. *See also* **turnkey system**.

software psychology The application of psychology to the development of software and to its various human interface elements.

solid (1) 100% tint panel unbroken by dots or lines. (2) Type composition not leaded. Also called *set solid.*

solid matter (1) Extensive areas of small type unbroken by **headings** or **illustrations**. Also called *straight matter.* (2) Type that has been **set solid**.

solid modeling The creation of visual models of three-dimensional objects that simulate the physical characteristics of the original—its height, weight, what it is made of, etc.

solidus *See* **virgule**.

solidus fraction A fraction whose numbers are separated by a **solidus**.

SORT A **PC/MS-DOS** filter **utility** that alphabetizes data from the **standard input device** en route to the **standard output device**. Input and output devices can be redirected as needed.

sort *v.* (1) To alphabetize. (2) To rearrange blocks of text in groups according to specific instructions. *n.* (1) Symbols, designs, braces, stars, and the like, that are not included in a regular **font** of type characters. Also called *pi characters. See also* **dingbat**. (2) Body of metal with a character in relief cast at one end. The nonprinting area (less than **type high**) of the sort above and below the character is called the *shoulder.* That

Fig. S-5   A solid panel is a 100% tint unbroken by dots or lines.

part of the character extending beyond the body of the sort is called the *kern*.

source note A note set below or sometimes above a table that gives the source of the information in the table.

sp A **proofreader's mark** meaning to spell out rather than abbreviate or use initials.

space Metal blank used in spacing between words in type composition.

space advertising Advertising requiring **artwork**.

space character A graphic character that is usually represented by a blank site in a series of graphics.

spaceband (1904) A device used to provide equal spacing between words on **linecasting machines**. *See also* **justify**.

spacing (1703) The lateral spacing between words, sentences, columns, and paragraph indentions. Compare **leading**. *See also* **em**; **en**; **figure space**; **hair space**; **quad**; **thin space**.

spacing guide In **PageMaker**, an object used to help measure and standardize the spaces between text and graphics, between headings and body copy, or between any of the elements on a page.

spanner head In tables, a **decked head** that is set on top of a column and spans the width of two or more subordinate **column heads** beneath it.

special character A graphic character in a **character set** that is not a letter, digit, or space character. *See also* **metacharacter**.

special order On the retail level, an order by a consumer for a book not in stock; on the wholesale level, an order received from a bookseller that requires special handling, such as a rush order.

specification tree *See* **check-out chart**.

specifications The physical details of a publishing project, such as type **font** and size, binding, trim size, number of pages, etc. Abbreviated *specs*.

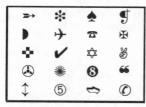

Fig. S-6   Some special characters from the Zapf Dingbat character set.

specs *See* **specifications**.

speculation Writing a piece with no insurance that the publisher or editor will purchase it or reimburse expenses in any way. Compare **assignment**.

spell check To use a spell check program to verify spellings in a document.

spelling (12c) The act of forming words or putting letters together. *See also* **spell check**.

sph *See* **sheets per hour**.

spin-off (1950) Article formed from research and writing leftovers.

spine The back of a bound book that connects the front and back covers. The part of a book binding visible when the book is shelved. Also called *backbone, shelfback*.

spine out Books placed on shelves so that only the spine shows. Most libraries show books in this manner; some bookstores do to save space.

Fig. S-7   Spiral binding.

spiral binding A **mechanical binding** in which a continuous spiral wire or plastic strip is passed through holes at the **gutter margin**, usually on paperback books. *See also* **binding**; **comb binding**; **mechanical binding**; **post binding**; **rivet-binding**; **saddle-stitched binding**; **side-stitched binding**.

split fountain A device that permits two or more colors of ink to be run on the same printing press at the same time.

split runs (1) Different ads run in regional editions of the same magazine issue, an ideal tool for mail order testing. (2) An edition of a book printed simultaneously in **paperback** and **hard cover**. *See also* **simultaneous editions**.

split screens The facility for dividing a **display** into two or more independent areas, each of which can contain different information or information from different software elements.

sponsored book *see* **premium**.

spool The reading of input data streams and the writing of output data streams on **auxiliary storage devices**, concurrently with job execution, in a format convenient for later processing or output operations. Acronym for *Simultaneous Peripheral Operations Online*. *See also* **spooler**.

spooler A computer **program** that can store data to be outputted to a low-speed **peripheral input/output device**, such as a **printer**, and parcel that data out byte by byte while the computer performs other tasks and executes other programs, thus allowing computer output to be performed simultaneously with other processing tasks. *See also* **print queue**.

spot In technical illustrating, an object that forms part of an assembly and is drawn in solid black in a small drawing adjacent to the drawing of the complete assembly. The spot indicates origin only and is used as a reference point. Also called *locator*.

spot art A type of art work in which small figures or symbols function primarily as headings or section labels or to decorate and enhance **layout**.

spot letter *See* **earmark character**.

spread (1) Two facing pages in a publication, with or without a **gutter**. (2) A long story, often with many illustrations. *See also* **center spread**.

spreadsheet Software used primarily for mathematical applications, such as budgets, inventories, and financial modeling.

square backed A binding technique where folded sheets are stacked one on another. Not usually considered suitable for less than 48 pages. *See also* **binding**.

square bracket (ca. 1883) *See* **bracket**.

squared corner Squares and rectangles with square corners. *See also* **mitered corner; rounded corner**.

squared-corner tool The shape the cursor takes when in the mode to make square-cornered boxes.

square four Four pages imposed so that when printed on both sides and cut, two sections of four pages each are made.

square grid Grid ruled in squares and designated by the number of lines per inch. A 4-by-4 grid, for example, has four lines per inch in both directions. Also called *cross-section grid*.

square serif A family of type styles sometimes called *Egyptian*. *See also* **slab serif**.

square up To specify an illustration as a rectangle. Compare **contour**.

SRAM *See* **static random access memory**.

SRDS *See* ***Standard Rate and Data Services, Inc.***

S/S *See* **same size**.

ss *See* **same size**.

stacker Device attached to a delivery conveyor that collects, compresses, and bundles **signatures**.

stacking In technical illustrating, placing nomenclature on an illustration so that a vertical line drawn through it shows balanced copy.

stacking order Order in which overlapping text and graphics are arranged on the page and on the screen.

staff writer A writer on the regular payroll of a periodical or newspaper.

staining The coloring of the edges of book pages for decorative effect. *See also* **gilding**.

stamp In **case binding**, to imprint the **spine** of the case and, sometimes, the front cover, with hard metal dies. Stamping may be done **blind**, with **foil**, or with ink.

stamping Die stamping or embossing. Imprinting lettering or a design on a book cover. *See also* **blocking**.

standalone (1969) (1) A self-contained computer that is not linked to a central computer. (2) The use of a program element, document, or piece of hardware independent from other program elements, documents, or pieces of hardware.

standalone modem A modem that is separate from the unit with which it operates. Compare **internal modem**.

Standard Account Number A code, assigned by **R.R. Bowker**, for identification of **book dealers**, **libraries**, **schools**, and **school systems**, and used in book order **fulfillment**. Abbreviated *SAN*.

standard development methodology A process used to develop computer systems, such as SDM 70, on an industry-wide basis.

standard device One of several standard **interfaces** with a microcomputer which are addressable by **PC/MS-DOS**. For example, **console** (standard input and standard output), **input/output ports** (serial and parallel), and **disk files**.

standard documentation process A series of widely applicable techniques to be used in the development of software documentation. Abbreviated *SDP*.

standard input The device from which a program reads its input unless the input is **redirected**. In **PC/MS-DOS** the **keyboard** is one-half of the **console**. Short for *standard input device*.

standard input device *See* **standard input**.

standard output The device to which a program sends its output unless the output is **redirected**. In **PC/MS-DOS** the **display** is one-half of the **console**. Short for *standard output device*.

standard output device *See* **standard output**.

Standard Rate and Data Services, Inc. A group of reference books designed especially for ad agencies, but useful in other marketing efforts, as well, containing advertising rates and data for publications.

standard trim size Any of a variety of page measurements standards to a particular kind of book. For example, mass market paperbacks are 4.25 in x 7 in; trade books are 5.5 in x 8.5 in, 6 in x 9 in, 6.5 in x 9.25 in; and illustrated books and workbooks are 8.5 in x 11 in.

standing form Printing form that will be used repeatedly and, therefore, will not be disassembled or melted down.

standing head A **title** regularly used.

standing matter Type composition, photo-engravings, and other plates held over for another printing.

standing type Metal type that has been set and is ready for printing. "Keep type stand-ing" (KTS) is an order to the printer to hold the made-up pages for a possible sub-sequent printing. Compare **kill**. *See also* **standing form**.

stapling (14c) A publication fastened or stitched by stapling. *See also* **saddle-wired binding**; **side-stitched binding**.

starting point The current **cursor** location position in a CRT **display device**.

stat *See* **Photostat**.

stat down To *stat down* is to **reduce** a piece of copy photographically. *See also* **Pho-tostat**.

stat up To *stat up* is to **enlarge** a piece of copy photographically. *See also* **Photostat**.

statement (1) A chronological listing of all charges and credits to date for a specific ac-count. (2) An **instruction** that causes a computer to perform a particular operation or task.

static RAM *See* **static random access memory**.

static random access memory Fast, semi-conductor memory that retains its contents without periodic, time-consuming refresh cy-cles from the **central processing unit**. The trickle of electricity from a battery is enough to maintain this type of memory. Abbre-viated *SRAM, static RAM.* Compare **dynamic random access memory**.

status line In display-based word pro-cessing equipment, a line reserved for the display of information to the operator concerning the processing of the text.

step and repeat Of, relating to, or employing a method in which successive exposures of a single image are made on a printing surface. For example, a camera or projector that advances one step (frame, page, etc.) horizontally or vertically for every exposure, according to a preset sequence.

stereotype (1817) A letterpress **printing plate** cast from a papier-mâché matrix made by forcing the latter into the face of type matter and drying it by baking.

stet (1821) Latin word meaning "let it stand," a **proofreader's mark** used to indicate that words crossed out in copy or proof are to remain as they were originally written. *Stet* is written in the margin and heavy dots are placed under the affected words.

stick *See* **composing stick**.

stickup initial *See* **initial up**.

stipple (1760) *v.* (1) To produce a **gradation** of light and shade in graphic arts by stippling small points, larger dots, or longer strokes. (2) To make small short marks, that together produce an even or softly graded shadow. (3) To speckle or fleck. *n.* (1) An area in a drawing composed of many fine dots in a random pattern. (2) Illustration board with a pattern of raised dots on its surface.

stock Paper, paperboard, or other paper product on which an image is printed, copied, or duplicated. *See also* **paper**.

stone proof In **lithography**, a proof of a type **form** taken after it is locked up and ready to go on the press.

STOP *See* **sequential thematic organization of proposals**.

stop bit A signal used in **serial communications** that marks the end of a **character**.

stop key A **keyboard** key that terminates or interrupts an operation. Also called *Break key, cancel key, Esc key.*

A stickup initial is aligned at the bottom with the first ine of text but sticks up into the white space above.

Fig. S-8   A stickup initial, also called an initial up.

storage device A mechanical device— either inside or outside the computer— for recording data in digital form on a magnetic medium, such as tape, disks, or drums.

storage capacity The amount of data that can be contained in a **storage device**, measured in binary digits, bytes, characters, words, or other units of data.

story All the text typed or compiled— one text block or several text blocks threaded together— at an insertion point outside existing **text blocks**.

storyboard (ca. 1946) A method of planning a publication in which the design is horizontally depicted on a series of separate forms or sheets of paper, rather than vertically as one piece of paper behind the other. This planning method emphasizes movement through a document rather than the document's organizational hierarchy.

straight edge (1812) Instrument with one or more straight long edges, particularly a ruler having measured increments. *See also* **ruler guides**.

straight matter Body matter or plain paragraph type composition, text that is not interrupted by **headings**, **tables**, **illustrations**, or displayed equations. Also called *running text, solid matter, straight copy.*

stress (1) In **typography**, the apparent direction of the weight of a letter from the vertical to the oblique. (2) *See also* **diacritical marks**.

stretch Rubber plates stretch on the press in the direction of rotation of the cylinder. The amount of stretch depends on the diameter of the cylinder.

strike-on composition *See* **typewriter composition**.

string A unique sequence of characters.

stringer Writer who does occasional work for a publication often as a correspondent from a certain location. The term came into being because such writers were paid by the column inch and the editor would "string" their copy together to measure it to determine their pay.

strip The process of preparing a negative or series of negatives for **platemaking**. To *strip in* is to combine a photographic negative with one or more others in preparation for making a printing plate. *Stripping into flats* is the taping of negatives to plastic sheets before burning plates. *See also* **imposition**. (2) In reproduction copy, to remove all or part of text copy or an illustration by mortising and replacing material with something else.

stripper One who makes **flats**— arranging and affixing the negatives or positives on the **goldenrod** paper or acetate sheet— in a printing plant.

stripping table A glass-topped table with a light source beneath the glass, on which a **stripper** works. Also called *light table*.

stroke (1597) (1) One of the lines of a letter of the alphabet. (2) In character recognition, a straight line or arc used as a segment of a **graphics character**. (3) In computer graphics, a straight line or arc used as a segment of **display element**.

stroke counter A device that counts every key depression that is made. Sometimes used to monitor **operator** production.

structured programming An artificial language that describes computer program algorithms without using the syntax of any particular programming language. Also called *pseudocode*.

structured writing A writing style based on **STOP** and **playscript** that seeks to discipline the writing of text on a page by requiring it to conform to rigid physical specifications. The purpose of this style is to make text easier to read. It is characterized by the horizontal lines above and below paragraphs that separate them out from the rest of the information on a page in defined blocks.

stub A vertical column at the extreme left side of a **table**.

stubhead A heading over a **stub**.

stuffer Printed circular enclosed in an envelope with regularly mailed material, such as an invoice.

style (1) One of the variations within a **typeface**, such as roman, bold, or italic. *See also* **font**. (2) Rules of uniformity in matters of spelling, punctuation, abbreviation, capitalization, rulings, headings, typography, and the like used throughout a publication. *See also* **house style**.

style guide Instructions on punctuation, capitalization, and other typographical matters, provided to writers by some major publishers to ensure correctness and uniformity throughout a **manuscript**.

style sheet In **Ventura**, a file that contains page layout settings, margin and column settings, and a series of typographic **tags** for each document. *See also* **style guide**.

stylus A pencil-shaped graphic **input device**, used in conjunction with a digitizing tablet to enter instructions and data into an interactive graphics systems. The stylus can be used for picking, locating, or sketching. (1807) (2) An instrument for engraving or etching. *See also* **light pen**; **mouse**.

stylus printer *See* **dot-matrix printer**.

subdirectory A **directory** branching off from another directory.

subhead (1673) (1) A heading of a subdivision, as in an outline or **index**. (2) A secondary title or heading, usually printed in a contrasting **typeface**. (3) A small **headline** in text copy used for spacing article out on page or to break solid copy. *See also* **bank head**; **crosshead**; **headline**.

subroutine A subsidiary **routine** executed when called by some other program. Initial execution never starts in a subroutine.

subscript A distinguishing letter or number written immediately below the **baseline** and to the right or left of another character. Also called *inferior*. Compare **superscript**.

$$H_2O$$

Fig. S-9   The "2" is a subscript.

subsidiary rights All **rights** not sold to the publisher in the initial contract, including movie, television, and paperback for books, and second serial and world rights for magazine articles.

substrate In printing, the surface that is to be printed.

subsidy press A company that charges writers to publish their work, then usually retains ownership of the books and does little, if any, promotion. Also called *vanity press, cooperative publisher*.

substance Same as **basis weight**.

substantive edit An editing activity in which the editor examines the content of a document for completeness and organization. *See also* **levels of edit**.

SUBST A **disk operating system** command that substitutes a disk drive designator in place of a subdirectory **pathname**.

substitution table A layout chart for **keyboard** that shows which standard character keys can be used as special character keys.

subtitle (1878) A second or additional title further explaining a book's content and scope. *See also* **alternative title**.

suction feed Method of feeding sheet paper into a printing press or other device in which suction devices are used to transport the paper in its initial progress through the press. Compare **friction feed, hand feed**.

sulfate process A process of papermaking in which wood chips from both deciduous and coniferous trees are cooked in a solution of caustic soda and sodium sulfide to produce the pulp from which the paper is made.

sulfite process A process of papermaking in which wood chips from coniferous trees are cooked in a solution of lime and sulfurous acid to produce the pulp from which the paper is made. Paper made from sulfite pulp generally has fewer impurities and is more permanent than paper from sulfate pulp.

summary (1509) Supplement to the abstract of a publication, usually consisting of technical data. It precedes the body of the text.

super Heavy gauze used to form the **hinge** in a **case bound** book.

supercalender A machine, similar to a **calender** but separate from the papermaking machine, used to give additional smoothness and hardness to paper.

supercalendered finish Glossy finish applied to paper by passing it repeatedly through the calender rolls of a papermaking machine. Compare **calendered finish**.

superfine (1575) Designating high-grade writing paper.

superior character A character or figure that is a **superscript**.

superior figure See **superior character**.

superscript (1909) A distinguishing letter or number written immediately above and to the right or left of another character, usually in a type size smaller than normal, such as ^{123}. Also called *superior*. Compare **subscript**.

supplement (14c) Addition to a book or a newspaper or other periodical, intended to supply deficiencies or add special interest to a subject. It can be a separate publication printed to augment or change an original publication.

surface chart Graphical representation with plotted points moving across it from left to right in a logical sequence. The pattern thus reflected is extended to the base of the chart by shading or **crosshatching**. See also **bar chart**; **column chart**; **curve chart**; **pie chart**.

surface sizing A sealant applied to paper by spraying it on both sides before it has run over the last series of dryer rollers in the papermaking machine.

surprinting (ca. 1917) Imposing unscreened line art on a plate on which **halftone** art has already been printed. (2)

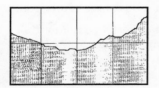

Fig. S-10   A surface chart.

Printing over copy that has already been printed.

swash initial A large initial letter with flourishes that begins a chapter or section. They are a florid version of the standard italic capital letters. Also called *swash letter*.

swash letter *See* **swash initial**.

swatch (1647) In printing, a color sample.

swim In computer graphics, undesired movement of **display elements** about their normal positions.

syllable hyphen *See* **discretionary hyphen**.

symbol (15c) Any character, letter, or drawn configuration that is identified with or serves to explain the meaning of something. Unless a symbol is universally understood, a **key** or **legend** should be furnished to explain its intent.

symmetrical layout The arrangement of type mass elements over a given axis, so that a division through that axis will divide it into halves and the parts are in balanced proportions on either side of a dividing line.

synchronous communication *See* **synchronous data transmission**.

synchronous data transmission Data transmission in which the nominal signal element spacing is fixed, in which the receive–transmit clock rates match and little or no buffering or rate matching is required. Also called *synchronous communication*. Compare **asynchronous data transmission**.

syndicate (1624) An editorial company that sells the work of **columnists** and other regular contributors to numerous outlets in this country and abroad.

syndication (1882) The multiple distribution of an author's work through various publishing channels.

syntax (1574) The rules governing the way in which words are put together to form phrases, clauses, or sentences.

syntax checker A program that tests documents for violations of the **syntax** of that language.

SYS A **PC/MS-DOS** command that transfers a copy of the **operating system** to the system tracks of the designated disk.

system Often used as a short form of a particular operating system, for example, **PC/MS-DOS**, Xenix, or CP/M-86.

system, computer *See* **computer system**.

system manager The individual responsible for maintaining a **computer system**. Also ensures that system problems are corrected and that users are managed efficiently.

system, operating *See* **operating system**.

system prompt The characters **disk operating system** displays when it is at the command level and ready to accept a command. Unless specified otherwise, the system prompt consists of the letter of the current drive followed by a greater than sign, for example, C:>.

systems documentation Documents such as internal code comments or pseudocode that are examples of communication between system developers and system maintenance programmers.

systems program A program whose purpose is to control the operation of all or part of the computer system, such as managing the printer or interpreting commands.

Notes and New Words

T

tab *v.* To set up in rows or columns. *n.* (1) *See* **index guide**. (2) *See* **indent**. (3) *See* **bleeding edge**.

Tab key A **keyboard** key that allows a user to move to another tab or field.

table A collection of data in which each item is uniquely identified by a label, by its position relative to the other items, or by some other means.

table of contents Portion of the **front matter** of a publication that lists the parts, chapters, sections, and the numbers and titles of paragraphs. A **table of illustrations** and a **table of tables** may also be included and follow in that order. Also called *contents*.

table of illustrations A list noting illustrations used in the text. It is part of a book's **front matter**. Also called *list of illustrations*.

table of tables A list noting tables used in the text. It is part of a book's **front matter**. Also called *list of tables*.

table spanner *See* **cut-in head**.

tablet In computer graphics, a locator device with a flat surface and a mechanism that converts indicated positions on the surface into coordinate data. Used with a **stylus** or **puck**. Also called *digitizing tablet*.

tablet menu A selection of user commands that are implemented on a **digitizing tablet** for easy access. It may be either fixed (permanently engraved on the tablet) or laid out on a removable sheet that can be exchanged for another menu sheet.

tabloid (1906) Newspaper about half the size of a regular newspaper. Text matter is compressed, and emphasis is placed on photographs.

tabular matter List of words or figures in columns, usually separated by blank space or rules. *See also* **tab**.

tacking Mounting a **cut** on a wooden block with tacks. This method requires a larger wood margin around the cut than **flush blocking**.

tactile keyboard A keyboard display laid out on a flat surface and gives a physical indication that a key has been struck. Also called *elastomer keyboard, membrane keyboard*.

tag (1) In **Ventura**, an element of a **style sheet** that contains a consistent set of type and format specifications. (2) One or more characters, attached to a set of data, that contains information about the set, including identification.

tag ends Partial line at extreme top or bottom of page. *See also* **orphan**; **widow**.

tag image file format An image document format that can be imported into some **desktop publishing** applications. Abbreviated *TIFF*.

tail *See* **descender**.

tail margin Bottom **margin** of a page. Also called *bottom margin, foot margin*.

tailpiece Decorative design employed at the end of a chapter or section to mark the conclusion of the chapter or section.

Copyright	©
Trademark	™
Dagger	†
Pound	£

Fig. T-1   Tabular matter.

tall orientation *See* **portrait page**.

tape (1) In photocomposition, a *range justified tape* indicates the ends of lines only; a *discrete justified tape* indicates also the widths of space required within each line. An *idiot tape* is a preliminary to these. (2) *See* **magnetic tape**.

tape drive A mechanism for controlling the movement of magnetic tape, commonly used to move **magnetic tape** past a read head or write head, or to allow automatic rewinding. Also called *tape deck, tape unit.*

tape library A repository for dismountable **magnetic tapes**. *See also* **disk library**.

target date (1945) Date set for completing a task that presumably will allow ample time for quality control before the **deadline**.

target printer The printer on which the user intends to print the final version of a publication.

task (1) The business or organizational activity that requires the use of a computer, for example, publishing a newsletter for a client using a desktop publishing program. (2) Task-oriented documentation emphasizes the tool-like quality of software and the idea that the best tool is the tool that best fits the tool-user's way of doing things. Task-orientation is a viewpoint rather than an actual description of specific steps.

tax number *See* **resale number**.

teacher's key *See* **teacher's manual**.

teacher's manual Guide for use by teachers in classroom instruction. Such a manual supplements a specific textbook, but is printed and bound separately. Also called *teacher's key.*

tear sheet (ca. 1924) Literally, a page torn from a periodical or newspaper that contains reviews, ads, or stories cut from the periodicals in which they appear. Some publications reprint individual articles separately and will supply these "tear sheets" to the author or its readers.

Technical Association of the Graphic Arts (1948) A professional society of scientists and technicians in research or in control of graphic arts processes or related industries.

Technical Association of the Pulp and Paper Industry (1915) A group of executives, managers, engineers, scientists, supervisors, and technologists in pulp, packaging, paper, and allied industries.

technical illustration Graphic art profession that embraces the art of making drawings for technical reports, proposals, manuals, and catalogs, as well as visual aids such as briefing charts, slides, posters, and the like. Technical illustrations include **wiring diagrams**, cutaways, **schematics, organization charts, graphs, flow diagrams, assembled views**, and **exploded views**.

Technical Illustrators Management Association (1980) An association of professional, technical illustrators employed by industrial plants or self-employed.

technical writer One who practices the art of **technical writing**.

technical writing The process of writing in which the writer acts as an intermediary between a particular piece of equipment and its users. It is best when it serves to ease interactions between the user and the piece of equipment. It is best accomplished by translating the technical knowledge of a particular field into clear and interesting language that a lay person can understand. Manuals on how to build a computer, operate a tank, or use specialized medical equipment are all products of technical writing.

telecommunications (ca. 1933) Electronic communications of data, documents, or messages between one computer and another using a telephone and a **modem**.

telecommuting A worker who performs his or her job at home and telecommunicates with the office via a **modem**.

telephone coupler A device for putting a regular telephone handset into service as a

modem. Usually, it works acoustically, but it may also work inductively.

teletext (ca. 1975) A form of **videotex** that is noninteractive and usually consists of textual information only, such as stock market listings, movie reviews, and airline schedules.

template (1) Guide made of highly polished transparent or translucent plastic material, containing patterns for use in pencil and ink work. (2) The first page of a **data file**, which defines the following records. (3) The concept of writing in which standard pieces of text are used in a sort of fill-in-the-blank way regardless of audience, purpose, or occasion. (4) A previously setup, but empty, file that contains specific page setup and formatting for a publication so it can be renamed and text poured into it.

temporary file (1) A file that can be erased or overwritten when it is no longer needed. Compare **permanent file**. (2) A file that **PC/MS-DOS** may create when told to **redirect** command input or output; deleted by DOS when the command is completed.

temporary label An adhesive-backed label allowing the contents of a disk to be identified.

10-key pad A separate set of keys numbered 0 through 9 on a **keyboard** that allows easy entry of numbers. Similar to a calculator keypad. Also called *keypad*.

10-pitch type *See* **pica**; **pitch**.

terminal (1) A set of input and output devices, typically a **video display unit** or **printer** and a **keyboard**, used for transmitting information to and from a computer system. (2) Individual **workstations** in a **time-sharing** system.

Texas Instruments graphics architecture (1988) A graphics processor that shows text and graphics at very high resolution, greater than 1,024 x 768 pixels. Abbreviated *TIGA*.

text (14c) (1) Information for human comprehension that is intended for presentation in a two-dimensional form. It consists of

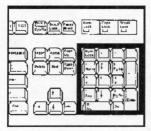

Fig. T-2   A 10-key pad on a keyboard.

symbols, phrases, or sentences in natural or artificial language, pictures, diagrams, and tables. (2) Straight type matter in a book. (3) The words, characters, numbers, and information that constitute a **desktop publishing** document. (4) Printed matter forming the main body of a work, as opposed to **front matter** and **back matter**, illustrative material, **tables**, extracts, etc.

text block A variable amount of text.

text area height The height occupied by text on the page, including **headers** and **footers**.

text area width The width occupied by text on the page.

text associated Part of a document that remains with the text during repagination, for example, a **header**.

text box A box in which text is typed.

text cursor A **cursor** that indicates where characters that are typed will appear.

text editing The process of making additions, deletions, and changes to a document.

text editor A computer program that allows the user to create and modify textual material, then output it to a printer. Also called *editor, word processor.*

text file A **file** that contains ordinary letters, numbers, and punctuation marks.

text finish Paper finish that is smoother than **antique finish** but not so smooth as **machine-finish paper**.

text function In a graphics system, a function that permits text to be entered into a drawing.

text grammar knowledge An unconscious knowledge of the formatting and organization conventions used in a particular type of document. This knowledge directs the process of reading for any new example of the document type. For example, experienced software application designers know that the first item they will find in any feasibility study is the summary or abstract.

They expect such an item in each and every new feasibility study they read, and any variation from this expected order causes confusion.

text icon An icon indicating the **text mode**.

text mode In **Ventura**, an operational mode that permits entering and editing text and setting text **attributes**.

text-only file Text created with another application and saved without **type specifications** or other **formatting**. *See also* **American Standard Code for Information Interchange**.

text page *See* **type page**.

text paper High-quality uncoated paper of good appearance used for books, booklets, brochures, programs, and the like.

text processing (1965) *See* **text editor; word processing**.

text revision The process of stopping, reading, printing, or skipping a character, word, line, sentence, or paragraph for the purpose of inserting, replacing, or deleting text when editing.

text tool In **Ventura**, a tool used to select text for editing. When selected, the **pointer** looks like an **I-beam**.

text type In typography, type that is smaller than 14 points. Also called *body type*.

text wrap (1) Automatic line breaks at the right edge of a column or at the right margin of a page. (2) The ability to wrap text around a graphic on a page layout.

texture *See* **pattern**.

thermal printer A type of **dot-matrix printer** that forms printed characters by applying heat to chemically treated paper. *See also* **impact printer; laser printer; nonimpact printer; printer**.

thermography (1840) The process of dusting freshly printed sheets with resinous powder; when heated, the powder fuses, forming a raised surface of the print, usually used on business cards and wedding announcements.

thesaurus (1823) A dictionary of synonyms and antonyms.

thick space A space that is one-third of an **em**. Also called *three-em space, three-to-the-em space.*

thin space A space that is one-fourth of an **em** space. Also called *four-em space, four-to-the-em space.* Compare **em space, en space, figure space; hair space; thick space.**

third cover Inside back cover of a periodical. *See also* **back cover; second cover; fourth cover.**

-30- Signifies the end of the **manuscript** or text. Also written *#30#.*

threaded text In **PageMaker,** blocks of text that are connected across the columns on a page and across pages from the beginning to end of the article.

3.5-inch disk A **floppy disk** that can be read from or written to on both sides, holding 1.44 million characters. Also called *microfloppy.*

three-dimensional alphabets For display and architectural use these are available as standard designs in a wide range of sizes and a variety of materials (cork, plastics, metal, etc.).

three-em space *See* **thick space.**

three-knife trimmer A machine that trims the top, bottom, and one-side (the *fore edge*) of pages in a single operation.

three-quarter binding (1) Binding with a leather back and leather corners, with the leather back and that of the corners almost meeting. (2) Any **cover material** used to bind the back and the corners of a book. *See also* **full binding; quarter binding.**

three-to-the-em space *See* **thick space.**

three-up *see* **two-up.**

throughput (1922) (1) The complicated cycle from thought origination until it is typed and ready for distribution. (2) The overall rate at which a computer system can do a task or process jobs.

thumb index (1903) A notch or semicircle cut in the fore edge of a book to make referencing easier. Also called *thumb tab*. *See also* **bleeding edge**; **index guide**.

thumb tab *See* **thumb index**.

thumbnail sketch A small, concise sketch used particularly as an initial miniature version of a page presentation. *See also* **rough**.

tick marks (1) Short, fine lines imposed on a **chart** or **graph** to represent evenly spaced points on a scale between the vertical or horizontal division lines. (2) Marks on the rulers showing increments of measure. *See also* **measurement system**; **ruler guides**.

tickler file A reminder file, to tickle the memory, calibrated to days of the week or month.

TIFF *See* **tag image file format**.

TIGA *See* **Texas Instruments graphics architecture**.

tight (1) An issue with little space left for additional material. Compare **wide open**. (2) An article that has covered all angles. (3) Copy that is well-written.

tilde (1864) A **diacritical** mark (~) that indicates a sound value. For example, the ñ in *mañana*.

tile A part of a page printed on a single sheet of paper. For a complete page, the tiles are assembled and pasted together. *See also* **oversize**.

TIME A **PC/MS-DOS** command that displays and sets the system time.

time in progress sheet A record of days and hours spent on an assignment, useful in computing hourly rates to be charged to a publication. Abbreviated *TIP sheet*. Also called *time log*.

time log *See* **time in progress sheet**.

time-out error Printer stops because it has not received information for a while. Occurs when printing complex pages and the printer takes a long time to image a large **bit-mapped** image.

time sharing (1967) The allocation of computer resources among several users.

tint (1) A very light color, usually used for backgrounds for type matter and illustrations. (2) An area made up of dots or lines.

tint block (1) A solid or screened background for printing tints. (2) A cut processed to print a panel of color.

tip-in The insertion of an additional page or material, by pasting, into a publication. *See also* **insert**; **wrap**; **wraparound**.

TIP sheet *See* **time in progress sheet**.

tissue (ca. 1777) A very thin paper, usually .001-in thick.

tissue overlay Thin, translucent paper placed over **artwork** for protection and correction. *See also* **mounting and flapping**; **register mark**.

tissue proof Additional proof printed on tissue by some typesetters and furnished to a customer as an act of courtesy with a regular order for **reproduction proofs**.

titanium dioxide (ca. 1924) Used as a "white loading" in papermaking to increase the paper's whiteness and **opacity**.

title (14c) (1) Any one of the books a publisher currently has in print. (2) The name of a particular publication. (3) Synonym for a book. (4) A **caption** that appears at the center of a page or column. Also called *center head*. (5) A **headline**.

title bar Bar across the top of a **window**, listing **disk drives** or **files**.

title page (1613) The page in a book's **front matter**, on the right, which usually gives the title, author(s) or editor(s), publisher, and place and date of publication. *See also* **half-title page**.

TK *See* **to come**.

Fig. T-3　A tint is an area made up of dots or lines.

to come Designates written or photo-graphic material not available at the time of **manuscript** submission, to be supplied later by the author. Abbreviated *TK*.

toggle switch (ca. 1924) An on/off switch, command, or option, used to describe cases in which the same command is invoked to turn a feature on and off.

tonality (1838) The tonal **gradation** of a photograph.

tone (1) The strength of a color from solid to light. (2) The shades of a photograph or il-lustration that is printed as a series of dots.

tone art *See* **halftone art**.

toner Very fine powder used to form the image in some copying processes and in **electrostatic screen printing**. In all cases, the ink must be fused by heat or chemical means to fix the image. Also called *dry ink, powder ink*.

toolbox window In **PageMaker**, the window overlapping the **Publication window** and containing **icons** for the tools used to work with text and graphics.

tooling Decoration of **bookbinding** by means of finishing tools.

tool (1) A compact, well-designed program designed to do a specific task. (2) A **screen symbol** used by **desktop publishing** pro-grams to allow the user to manipulate text and graphics.

tooth Ability of paper to take printing ink, drawing ink, pencil, and the like. If paper readily accepts these materials, it is said to have *tooth*.

top margin *See* **head margin**.

touch screen A device attached to the **screen** of a video monitor that allows the user to input positional information to a computer by pointing at the screen. Often used for selecting options from a **menu**.

touch typing (1888) Typewriting without looking at the keys.

tower A computer housing unit designed to stand and operate on its side.

track The portion of a moving magnetic data medium, such as a drum, tape, or **disk**, that is accessible to a given reading head position.

track ball An input device especially useful in computer graphics that is essentially a **mouse** turned upside-down; rather than moving the mouse along the surface to send information to the computer, the base stays stationary and the user moves his or her hand over the top of the ball causing it to rotate, moving the **cursor** one direction or another proportionally. Also called *control ball.*

tractor That part of the **printer** that moves **continuous paper** through the printer.

tractor feed A means for accurately positioning and transporting **fanfold paper** in printers.

tractor feeder A device attached to a **printer** to automatically feed edge-perforated roll paper or forms.

tractor holes *See* **carrier holes**.

trade books (ca. 1945) General fiction and nonfiction, as opposed to textbooks and reference works, sold to the general public, primarily through bookstores.

trade journals Magazines for the book trade, such as *Library Journal*, **Publisher's Weekly**, or **desktop publishing**, such as *PC Publishing*, *Personal Publishing*, or *Ventura Professional!*

trade name (1861) *See* **brand name**.

trade paperback Paperbacks (5 in x 8 in to 7 in x 10 in) sold in bookstores only, often the **signatures** of the **hard cover** edition in a **soft cover** binding. Also called *quality paperback.*

trade publisher A conventional publishing house, publishing books for a mass audience, which typically pays authors **advances** and **royalties**. Compare **self-publish**; **subsidy press**.

Fig. T-4   Trademark for CONVEX Computer Corporation.

trade reviews Reviews in **trade journals**.

trademark (1906) Any word, name, symbol, or device, or any combination thereof, adopted and used by a manufacturer or merchant to identify his goods and to distinguish them from those manufactured or sold by others. Compare **service mark**.

trailer (1) A line of type below the body copy used to identify the copy. (2) *See* **footer**.

trailing edge Last portion of a moving object that follows the remaining portion. Compare **leading edge**.

transfer To send data from one place and to receive the data at another place. Also called *move*.

transfer sheet Sheet of translucent **acetate** or paper containing preprinted characters and symbols, used in preparing **cold-composition**, **camera-ready copy**. Books of plasticized letters, numbers, and symbols that can be transferred from the purchased book to the documenter-produced manuscript.

transfer time The amount of time it takes to send data from one place and to receive the data at another place. *See also* **access time; latent period**.

transmission The sending of data from one place for reception elsewhere. Also called *data transmission*. *See also* **American Standard Code for Information Interchange**.

transmit To send data from one place for reception elsewhere.

transparency Artwork for a color print, resembling a color slide. *See also* **overhead transparency; overlay**.

transportable computer A **portable computer** that is about suitcase size and can be carried like luggage, but must be set on a table or desk and connected to a source of **AC** power to be used. Compare **laptop computer**.

transpose (ca. 1947) (1) To change a word, letter, or group of words from one place to another. (2) In **proofreading** and **editing**, to switch the positions of two words, sentences, paragraphs, etc. *See also* Appendix 4. (3) To move copy from one position to another.

transposition sign A **proofreader's mark** that is a line curving over one element and under another to indicate transposition of characters, words, phrases, or sentences. *See also* Appendix 4.

traveler *See* **jobber**; **sales representative**.

TREE A **PC/MS-DOS** command that displays a hierarchy of disk directories.

tree-structured filing system *See* **multi-level filing system**.

trim *v.* (1) To shorten an article. Compare **pad**. (2) To cut the edges of a folded sheet to page size. *n.* The cut edges themselves.

trim height The intended height of the final page.

trim marks Marks placed on a **page proof** or page negative to show where the edge of the page will be after the printed **signatures** have been **trimmed** to their final size. *See also* **crop mark**.

trim size (ca. 1929) The actual size, as of a book page, after excess material required in production has been cut off. (2) The finished size of a book after the **signatures** have been **trimmed** and folded. *See also* **standard trim size**.

trim width The intended width of the final page.

triple-click To press and release the main **mouse button** quickly three times in succession.

Trojan horse A more common **virus** that differs in that it is unable to replicate itself.

troubleshoot (1931) To detect, locate, and eliminate errors in computer **programs** or faults in **hardware**.

TRS DOS (Pronounced *triss doss*) The **disk operating system** designed for Tandy Radio Shack computers.

tub sizing In the manufacture of paper, immersing the paper in a solution of glue. Better grades of rag-content **bond paper** are tub sized.

tumble *See* **work-and-tumble**.

turnaround time The elapsed time between the acceptance or beginning of a job until the completed job is delivered.

turned page layout A page format in which the top and bottom of a typical page are turned 90 degrees and become the left and right.

turnkey system A totally integrated system, including hardware, software, installation, training, and maintenance, supplied in a ready-to-run condition by a single vendor who takes responsibility for its technical success.

tutorial (1923) Information conveyed in a step-by-step breakdown with many examples and graphics. Tutorials usually contain overviews and summaries for each step and are designed to be the first material read by a user. This type of material should, therefore, contain simple language and an abundance of metaphors.

tv screen A **shadow box** used to frame an illustration. The corners are rounded, as in a tv screen.

12-pitch type *See* **elite**; **pitch**.

two-line letter An **initial letter** covering two lines of the text matter.

two-scale chart A **column chart** in which two values are compared. The vertical columns usually represent quantity, and the horizontal dimension represents time. *See also* **bar chart**; **curve chart**; **pie chart**; **surface chart**.

two-thirder An advanced apprentice printer.

two-up In **offset lithography**, to duplicate the printing image on the plate so that two

Fig. T-5   A tv screen used to surround an illustration.

copies of the piece are printed at the same time, side-by-side. Compare **four-up**.

tympan The paper that covers the **platen** or **impression cylinder** of a **letterpress**.

TYPE A **PC/MS-DOS** command that displays the contents of a designated **file** on the screen.

type case *See* **case**.

type face *See* **typeface**.

type family All the **fonts** associated with a particular **typeface**, including **italic**, **boldface**, and **bold italic** versions.

type font Type of a given size and style. *See also* **font**.

type founder (1797) One who designs and produces metal printing type for **hand composition**. Also is applied to those individuals designing type for **computer-assisted composition**.

type gauge *See* **line gauge**.

type height The height-to-paper of type in the **Anglo-American point system** is 0.918 in, in the **Didot** system, 0.928 in.

type high Designating the measurement from the base of the type to the top of the **typeface**: 0.918 in.

type list A list of all the words, numbers, and mathematical symbols that form the labels on the figures and that are going to be **typeset** rather than hand-lettered or applied.

type louse A mythical bug, for which naïve novices search and never find, to their chagrin, in print shops.

type master In **phototypesetting**, the glass plate that contains the film font negative. Also called *type matrix*.

type matrix *See* **image master**.

type page The area of a page that includes all copy, measured from the ascender of the top line to the **descender** of the bottom line, usually including the **running head** and

folio (but not a **drop folio**). Also called *text page, type area.*

type size The size of a particular type. The designation of type sizes by **points** refers to the vertical size of the **sort** and has no definite reference to the size of the **typeface** itself. All the different styles of 12-point faces, for instance, are approximately the same size, but there is considerable variation.

type size finder *See* **loupe**.

type spec *See* **type specifications**.

type specifications A summary of typographic requirements such as the following example:

- TEXT TYPE— Univers light (685) 8D/9pt + 1pt lead.
- COLUMN WIDTH— 13 picas, justified.
- PARAGRAPHS— No extra space between paragraphs. First lines of paragraphs to be indented one em, except in the first paragraph of a chapter or article, under a **head** or **crosshead**.
- CROSSHEADS— Univers bold (693) 8D/9pt u/lc with 6 pt space above, 2pt below. Flush left.
- MAIN HEADS— 28D/30 pt Univers bold condensed (694) except where otherwise noted.
- CAPTIONS— Univers bold italic (693) 7D/8pt flush left, ragged right.

type specimen (ca. 1891) Sample of type showing the various names, sizes, faces, and other information, offered for sale or available to the customer as a printing service.

type style In typography, versions of different **typefaces** which, together with the range of alternative sizes, **character set**, symbol set, pitch, or spacing, and point size of the type, comprise a **family** of type. The name of the typestyle describes the version of the typeface, as in **condensed**, **light condensed**, **bold extended**, or **italic**. There are five general classes, known as *roman, italic, script, gothic,* and *text*:

- ROMAN— The type commonly used in books and all classes of ordinary reading matter.
- ITALIC— The slanting letter is mainly used for emphasis and display. This is an imitation handwriting and is used in the printing of announcements, invitations, and stationary.

- GOTHIC—Also called *sans serif*, these are plain type styles with lines of uniform thickness and without serifs.
- TEXT—This is a survivor of the first types cast and is an imitation of the hand lettering which prevailed before movable types were invented and is also called *black letter, Fraktur*.

type wheel *See* **print wheel**.

typebar Original **typewriter** mechanism in which each character is cast into its own separate type bar which is then caused to strike the ribbon by the operation of the appropriate key.

typeface (1904) (1) The printing surface of a piece of type which bears the character about to be printed. (2) Denotes the style of any particular set of types. There are four basic forms of typefaces: text, roman, italic, and script. Also called *face*.

typeface nomenclature Apart from the fact that every typeface has a name of its own, there are various systems of nomenclature for different kinds of type design. The following are generally acceptable names for kinds differentiated by their serif formation:

- roman—with curved or bracketed serifs.
- modern (roman)—with contrasting thick and think strokes; serifs of hairline thinness; vertical stress.
- Egyptian—with thick squarish serifs.
- Gothic—the earliest style of type design, derived from medieval handwriting. Note, however, that some sans serif faces are named Gothic; and that Gothic is more often referred to as black letter or Old English in Britain and as **Fraktur** on the Continent.
- sans serif—without serifs. Most sans serif typefaces, except Gill Sans, can also be called *grotesque*, which is also called *grot*. In the Vox classification, they are *Lineales*.
- script—type imitating handwriting of a flowing nature, done with pen or brush.

typeface family *See* **type family**.

typemark To specify on the **manuscript** how type is to be set.

typeover In word processing, the ability to replace text simply and quickly by typing new information over the old.

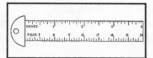

Fig. T-6   A typescale.

typescale A ruler marked in **point**, **em**, and **en** increments. *See also* **line gauge**.

typescript (1893) A typewritten **manuscript** and especially one that is intended for use as printer's copy. Abbreviated *script*.

typeset (1867) To produce text using high-quality typefaces, proportional character design, and principles of graphic design.

typesetter (1) A person, firm, or facility that sets type. (2) A device that produces the type from keyboarded instructions. (3) In **photocomposition**, a typesetting machine in which text is output on photographic film or paper.

typesetting Composing and setting type by hand, with hot metal typecasting machines, or with photographic typesetters. Also called *character assembly*.

TypeWorld (1977) A biweekly publication for the electronic publishing industry, typesetting, and automated publishing, with a special emphasis on **hardware**.

typewriter (1868) A keyboard-operated mechanical device that produces writing in characters similar to those produced by **typesetting**. The characters are activated by striking a key, which strikes a ribbon that transfers ink to paper. *See also* **platen**.

typewriter composition (1868) Text matter produced by typewriter. Also called *strike-on composition*.

typo (1922) A **typographical error**. A misprint.

typographer (1643) (1) One who sets type, also called *compositor*. (2) One skilled in **typography** as a designer or as a printer. (3) A type designer.

typographic measurement *See* **ascender**; **descender**; **display type**; **linespacing**; **pica**; **point**; **set**; **unit system**; **wordspacing**; **x-height**.

typographical error (1593) An error made by the **compositor** or **operator**. Abbreviated *typo*. *See also* **author's alteration**; **printer's error**.

typography (1697) The art and technique of working with type, with reference to the style, format, and general appearance of the printed page.

Notes and New Words

U

U&lc A monthly magazine providing detailed treatment of the latest technical aspects of **typography**.

u.c. *See* **uppercase**.

ultra An exaggerated heavy weight of a particular **typeface**.

unavailable command A **menu** command that cannot be chosen at the present time because it has no meaning in the context of what is being done. Unavailable commands appear in **ghost** letters. Compare **available command**.

unbound signature (12c) In **case binding**, sewn **signatures** plus **endpapers**, but not enclosed in a rigid cover. *See also* **case binding**; **casing in**; **side-wired binding**; **Smythe sewn**.

uncoated paper Paper used for the **letterpress printing** of catalogs, books, direct-mail pieces, folders, etc. Manufactured in four finishes: **machine**, **antique**, **English**, and **supercalendered**.

uncoated offset paper *See* **offset paper**.

uncommon word list A list of words that the average reader may not understand, including misspellings, slang, and jargon.

uncorrected proof **Proof** of a book, minus corrections, used as advance reading copy for **review** in **trade journals**.

under-the-cover modem *See* **integrated modem**.

underline (1721) A line drawn under a word or line especially for emphasis or to indicate intent to italicize. For example: <u>This sentence is underlined</u>.

underlying page A special frame automatically created whenever a new document is started in **Ventura**. This frame, defined by Page Layout option, contains the physical size of the page, printing orientation, and selection of either single or double sided formatting. Additional frames are placed on top of the underlying page. Called **master page** in **PageMaker**.

underrun When a printer manufactures fewer copies than were ordered. Compare **overrun**.

underscore (1901) *See* **underline**.

unglazed finish Paper finish without luster.

union shop *See* **closed shop**.

unit (1510) A variable measure usually ranging from one-tenth to one-eighteenth of an **em** that is used by composition equipment for measuring the width of letters and spaces.

unit cost The production cost to print one book or publication.

unit system In machine typesetting, the method of relating character widths to **unit** measurements. The units are not standard dimensions but vary according to the proportions of the **typeface** design. *See also* **set**.

Universal Copyright Convention An agreement, ratified by more than 90 nations, to offer the **copyrighted** works of citizens of other nations the same protections extended to those of their own citizens. *See also* **copyright infringement**; **plagiarism**.

universal discount schedule A system that gives everyone the same discount, whether wholesaler, bookstore, individual, or library.

unjustified Text set flush left with the right-hand edge uneven. Also called *ragged right*.

unselected The normal state of an **icon** before being **selected**. *See also* **deselect**.

up In computing, a system that is operating. Compare **down**.

up-charge An additional fee incurred over and above a stated price.

update (1965) To change a file, creating a new or updated version.

update checklist A list to be used during updating. It is a comprehensive list of all information that appears in more than one place in a piece of documentation, since change in one place would result in a change elsewhere in the document. It is developed by the original documenter for the maintenance documenter and is developed immediately after the drafting phase.

upload To transfer information from a user's system to a remote computer system. Compare **download**.

upper case *See* **uppercase**.

uppercase (ca. 1738) The capital letters of a **font**. Abbreviated *u.c.* Also called *caps*. Compare **small caps**. Compare **lowercase**.

user The person who makes use of computer **hardware** and **software**, as opposed to the systems designer (an engineer) or programmer, who create the hardware or software.

user-defined characters Characters defined and stored temporarily in the printer by the user. Also called *downloaded characters*.

user-defined graphics characters Graphics characters that are designed by the user or programmer of a computer, rather than by the designers of the computer system itself.

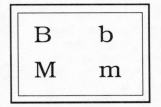

Fig. U-1   Uppercase letters (left) and lowercase letters (right).

See also **American Standard Code for Information Interchange; bit-mapping; character set; high-resolution graphics.**

user-friendly Systems that are easy to learn and use so that relatively untrained users can interact with the computer. Typically, offers clear **prompts** or **menus** to guide the user and use an easily manipulated **input device** such as a **mouse** or a **joystick.** *See also* **joystick; mouse; prompt.**

user group (1955) A group of persons who own and use a specific **microcomputer** or **software**, to discuss problems, exchange information, share programs, trade equipment, engage in projects relating to that microcomputer, and exchange **freeware.**

user interface The means by which information is passed back and forth between the user and the software, for example, system messages and commands. Computer-user interfaces may be command line or graphics oriented.

user prompt Message, either visual or audible, intended to assist in carrying out the next operation needed to execute a computing or **telecommunications** function.

user role orientation A way of organizing **documentation** based on the titles of users using the **software.**

utility A program that performs a commonly-used task, made up of functions or small tasks which the computer performs, that can be used to aid a programmer in performing a specific task, such as cross-referencing variables in a program, dumping the contents of memory to the video display, testing for bad RAM chips, and so on.

Notes and New Words

Notes and New Words

V

vacuum forming A method of shaping a thermoplastic sheet to the shape of a tool. In no sense a printing process. Often used in conjunction with silk-screen printing or foil blocking, e.g., in the production of plaques, showcards, display material, and leaflet racks.

values Relative lightness and darkness of different areas of a picture as represented in **tones, shading, line balance, layout,** and the like. *See also* **density.**

vandyke *See* **blueprint.**

vanity press (1950) *See* **subsidy press.**

variable (1816) A symbol that may have an infinite number of values.

variant spelling (1848) A secondary way to spell a word, usually less accepted. Example: *wooly* is a variant of *woolly.* Compare **alternate spelling.**

varnish (14c) *v.* To apply fixative to reproduction copy or to a completed printed sheet for protection or appearance. *n.* (1) A substance used in making printing ink. (2) A shiny protective coating applied to printed matter, such as a paperback cover, that results in a hard, glossy surface to protect it. (3) A vehicle.

VDISK A **PC/MS-DOS utility** program that establishes a memory disk. Added to DOS at system turn-on.

VDT *See* **video display terminal**.

VDU *See* **video display unit**.

vector (1865) (1) In mathematics, a quantity having direction in space and magnitude, or the line representing it. (2) In computer graphics, a directed line segment that plots the contour of a letterform.

vector-based graphics *See* **curve-linear graphics**.

vector graphics The most common class of graphics, where all vector output consists of smooth lines and curves drawn point-to-point by the output unit as ordered by the computer. *See also* **computer graphics**; **object-oriented files**. Compare **raster graphics**.

vector display A line-drawing display that creates images by drawing **vectors** on the phosphor surface of the **cathode-ray tube display**. It is a **random scan** device and its electron beam can connect any two points anywhere on a display surface.

vehicle *See* **varnish**.

vellum (15c) Kind of fine paper resembling **parchment**. It has a high-quality finish and the content is 100% rag.

vellum finish (1565) Paper finish similar to **text finish**: smooth and dull.

velo binding An inexpensive fused plastic binding. Also called *rivet binding. See also* **binding**.

Velox A **photoprint** of a **continuous-tone** subject that has been transferred into line art by means of a **halftone screen**.

vendor (1594) (1) Any supplier who sells goods or services. (2) A company that sells

Fig. V-1   An example of a vector graphic.

computers, peripheral devices, time-sharing service, or computer services. Compare **service bureau**.

Ventura *See* **Ventura Publisher**.

Ventura Letter (1985) A semimonthly publication dedicated to North American users of **Ventura Publisher**.

Ventura Publisher (1986) A page layout program that permits users to create typeset documents by combining text and pictures. Also called *Ventura, Xerox Ventura Publisher*.

Ventura Publisher User's Group A user group for **Ventura Publisher**.

Ventura Professional! (1986) Official monthly newsletter of the Ventura Publisher User's Group.

VER A **PC/MS-DOS** command that displays the version of DOS currently loaded.

VERIFY A **PC/MS-DOS** command that verifies the integrity of copied data.

version A separate program product, based on an existing program product, that usually has significant new codes or new functions. Each version has its own license, terms, conditions, product type number, monthly charge, documentation, and programming support category. Also called *release, modification level.*

verso (1839) The back side of a **leaf**. In a book, a left-hand page. Compare **recto**.

vertical Often refers to a vertical platen press, or **job press**.

vertical bar A symbol (|) used in some **commands**, such as indicating a **PIPE**.

vertical column chart *See* **column chart**.

vertical dimension Distance between the top and bottom of an image when the image is held in an upright, or reading, position. Also known as the **height**, regardless of its length with respect to the horizontal.

vertical justification Justification running the length of a page. Pages of a document can be the same length or ragged bottom. *See also* **leading**.

vertical line pattern In Publish Pac, a half-tone pattern used to emphasize horizontal lines or smooth contours.

vertical page Page that contains right-reading copy when it is held in a normal reading position. Also called *portrait page*. Compare **broadside, landscape page**.

vertical scrolling The ability to move vertically, a line at a time, up and down through a display page or more of text.

VGA *See* **video graphics adapter**.

video display terminal A terminal device with **keyboard**, logic system, and **CRT display**, connected to a main computer. If previously keyboarded material can be retrieved and altered, it is often called an *editing terminal* or *VDT*.

video display unit A **cathode-ray tube** that may be part of either a **video display terminal** or of a **standalone** computer.

video graphics adapter (1987) A printed-circuit adapter board in an IBM or IBM-compatible computer system that controls the display. Shows both text and graphics at high resolution (640 x 480 **pixels**) in up to 256,000 colors. Used in IBM PS/2 and other computers. Abbreviated *VGA*.

video interface A piece of hardware that enables the video display screen on a computer to generate colors. The interface scans the computer's memory to determine what colors should be displayed and what position they should assume on the screen.

video terminal A **terminal** having a **keyboard** for sending information to the computer and a picture tube like a TV for displaying information. The video terminal is fast, silent, and has no moving parts. Its chief drawback is that it does not make a permanent record of the information displayed.

videotex (1979) Generic term for the transmission of text or graphics information over telephone lines, for receipt by computers

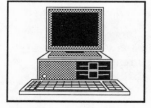

Fig. V-2 A video terminal sitting on top of a computer cabinet.

and terminals. Videotex is usually a noninteractive service. *See also* **teletext**.

view A function of a **desktop publishing** or other program that presents different views of the screen: a normal view (which presents text and graphics at their actual size), a reduced view (which presents text and graphics at a smaller than actual size), or an enlarged or zoom view (which presents text and graphics at a larger than actual size).

view point In computer graphics, the origin from which angles and scales are used to map virtual space into display space.

vignette (ca. 1611) (1) A very short sketch or story. (2) To make a photograph, regulating the light so the edges of the photographed subject fade into the background, leaving no clear boundaries. (3) **Halftone** copy in which the background fades from heavier to lighter tones until it is completely absorbed by the color of the paper.

virgule (1837) A slanted line (/) used chiefly to represent a word (as *or* or *per*) that is not written out, to separate lines of poetry when quoted in **run-in** fashion, to separate or set off certain adjacent elements of text, and to set off phonemic transcription. Also called *oblique, shilling mark, slant, slash mark, solidus.*

virtual disk A portion of the computer's **random access memory** reserved for use as a simulated disk drive. Also called *electronic disk, RAM disk.* Unless saved on a physical disk, the contents of a virtual disk are lost when the computer is turned off.

virus (1987) A software equivalent of an infection intruder. This programmer-induced disease may infect a computer, causing it to loose data, make computers act abnormally, and replicate itself to be passed on to others. *See also* **Trojan horse**.

visual (1938) *See* **artwork**.

visual display terminal *See* **video display terminal**.

visual display unit *See* **video display unit**.

visual editor An editor that shows a screen full of text at a time and allows the user to move a **cursor** to any part of the screen and effect changes there.

visual space The amount of space that "appears" between lines.

visualization (1883) A graphic metaphor used repeatedly in a text as its primary organizing device. Its purpose is to increase the ease by which one can read, understand, and remember information.

visuals (1938) *See* **artwork**.

VOL A **PC/MS-DOS** command that displays the **volume label** of the designated disk.

volatile Becoming lost or erased when power is removed.

volatile memory Computer memory that loses its contents when computer power is turned off. The most common form of volatile memory is **random access memory**. Also called *dynamic random access memory, read-write memory*. Compare **nonvolatile memory**. *See also* **volatile storage**.

volatile storage A storage device whose contents are lost when power is removed. Compare **nonvolatile storage**.

volume label An 11-character identifying name assigned to a **disk** when it is formatted. With the **PC/MS-DOS** command **LABEL**, it is possible to change or delete a volume label. Also called *volume name*. *See also* **VOL**.

volume name *See* **volume label**.

Notes and New Words

Notes and New Words

W

wait state Short periods of processor inactivity that allows slower computer components, such as memory, to catch up.

warm boot Re-initialization of the computer and **disk operating system** without turning the power off. With **PC/MS-DOS**, this is achieved by simultaneously pressing the Ctrl, Alt, and Del keys.

water finish High-quality glossy paper **finish** obtained by applying water to one or more calender rolls in the papermaking process.

watermark (1678) Design, trademark, name, logotype, or the like impressed on paper by the **dandy roll** or other rollers during the paper manufacturing process, produced by thinning the paper slightly so that the design shows when the paper is held up to the light.

web The paper being fed to a press from a roll rather than in sheet sizes.

web-fed (1947) Applied to printing presses using paper in reel form rather than in sheets. Also called *reel-fed*.

web offset printing (1967) Lithographic printing from rolled stock. *See also* **offset lithography**.

web press (1875) A fast, sophisticated printing press that uses roll-fed paper rather than sheets. Compare **sheet-fed press**.

wetware (1) Information and instructions stored in the human brain. (2) Human effort, measured in hours. (3) People.

wf *See* **wrong font**.

What You See Is What You Get (1982) Its acronym, *WYSIWYG*, is pronounced "wizzy-wig," and it refers to the ability to display on the computer screen a close representation of the printed copy.

wheel graph *See* **pie chart**.

when room Copy or art that can be used at any time when there is room.

white space (1849) That part of a blank page not covered by type and **artwork**.

wholesaler (1857) A person or company who buys from a publisher, then sells to a bookstore or library. Also called *jobber*, *distributor*.

wide menu A single menu in which both general and specific, or initial and subsequent program choices are all presented simultaneously. Compare **deep menu**.

wide open A publication with plenty of room for additional material. Compare **tight**.

wide orientation *See* **landscape**.

widow (1) Short last line of a paragraph that is carried over to the top of the next column or page, where it stands alone. Compare **orphan**. (2) A single word on the last line of a paragraph.

width (1629) (1) In the graphic arts, the distance between two points along the horizontal dimension. *See also* **height**. (2) In

Fig. W-1   The width of a letter is its hozirontal dimension.

typography, the horizontal dimension of a particular size of type.

width table A file that contains font metric information for proportional spacing of characters.

wild card A character that allows the user to search for text **strings** in which certain parts of the string do not matter. **PC/MS-DOS** recognizes two wild card characters: the question mark (?), which can represent any single character, and the asterisk (*), which can represent more that one character. Also called *metacharacter. See also* **filename; literal**.

wild copy Text copy that has been typed or printed to be cut and pasted as **callouts** for **illustrations** or for use in the composition of **graphs, charts,** or **mechanicals**.

window (1) In computer graphics, a prede-fined part of the virtual space. (2) A hardware and software system that allows a computer user to run two or more programs simultaneously on the same computer, with each program assigned its portion of the video display, called a *window,* which may be expanded, contracted, moved, or over-lapped. (3) A rectangle (of red acetate or black paper or any other material that has a smooth edge when cut and photographs as black) pasted on **camera-ready copy** in the blank space left for a **halftone** illustration. When a negative is made of the page, the rectangle becomes a clear opening, or *win-dow,* in the film, into which the halftone negative is **stripped,** thus combining the type and halftone components onto one **flat**. Also called *black patch.* (4) Die-cut opening on the front cover of a publication that re-veals the title or other information printed on the **title page**.

window envelope (1919) An envelope with a transparent panel in it through which the name and address typed on the enclosure can be read.

windowing The ability to simultaneously display a collage of material, that is, graphics or different parts of text from the same document, on a computer screen.

Fig. W-2   A window en-velope.

windowshade In **PageMaker**, horizontal lines, each with a loop, that span the top and bottom of a text block. *See also* **handle**.

wire binding *See* **side-wire binding**; **spiral binding**.

wire service (1944) A news-gathering organization that sells information to its subscribers. For example, UPI, Reuters, and AP.

wire side In the manufacture of paper, the side of the paper next to the wire, the underside, as it is conveyed along a belt. It is slightly less smooth than the other side (the **felt side**).

wiring diagram Diagram of an electrical or electronic system in which wire numbers, colors, and sizes are shown together with an orthographic pictorial drawing representing the parts of the system.

WithStyle A program that allows a user to manage and edit **Ventura** style sheets.

woodcut (1662) Engraving cut in a block of wood. *See also* **cut**.

wood pulp (1866) Most paper is made from wood pulp, either **groundwood pulp** or the more expensive, but better, **chemical pulp**.

wood-pulp bond *See* **bond paper**.

word In computer terminology, a sequence of **binary digits** conveying meaning in combination, often processed as a whole by the computer. Always a specific size or number of digits, depending on the computer.

word division Dividing words at the end of a line. *See also* **hyphenation**.

word frequency list A list of all the words in the document and the number of times they occur.

word-of-mouth (1553) An informal, but important, kind of advertising in which a product is praised by one person to another.

word processing (1973) (1) The production of typewritten documents (as business letters) with automated and usually computerized typing and text-editing equipment. (2) The use of editors and other computer programs to prepare, alter, check, and format text.

word processor (1977) (1) A keyboard-operated terminal usually with a video display and a magnetic storage device for use in **word processing**, capable of performing many functions and operations, this automated system is used to create, edit, store, and print text. (2) Computers that have been specifically designed for and are pretty much dedicated to the task of word processing.

word publishing (1988) A word processing package that approaches the results of the full-fledged **desktop publishing** packages.

word spacing In typesetting, the spacing between words, a critical factor in the **readability** of text. Influenced by such factors as **type size, typestyle, kerning, x-height, letterspacing**, and **justification**.

word wrap A feature that automatically moves a word to the beginning of the next line if it will not fit at the end of the original line. Occurs when a word is entered that is too long to fit on the current line. *See also* **carriage return; hard carriage return; soft carriage return; text wrap**.

wordspacing *See* **word spacing**.

work-and-tumble To print one side of a sheet of paper and then turn the sheet over from **gripper** to back while using the same side guide. The sheet is turned end for end. Also called *print-and-tumble*. Compare **work-and-turn**.

work-and-turn To print one side of a sheet of paper and then turn the sheet over from left to right and print on the opposite side. The same **gripper edge** is used for both sides of the sheet. Also called *print-and-turn*. Compare **sheetwise, work-and-tumble**.

work for hire Work done for a fee in which the author has no **copyright** or ownership. *See also* **ghost writer**.

work station *See* **workstation**.

An example of word spacing.

An example of word spacing.

Fig. W-3   Normal wordspacing is at the top. The bottom example is double the amount of word spacing.

---

work-up (1903) Defect appearing on a printed impression because of **leading**, **furniture**, or a **slug** that has worked up to a surface of the printing form.

working directory The **directory** in which a user's commands take place, given that no other directory is specified.

working title A preliminary title used while a book is in preparation.

workstation (1931) (1) An area equipped for a single worker. (2) A computer connected to a larger system via a **network**. (3) A computer system designed for use by one person at a time, and may have a **terminal** connected to a computer, or it may be a **standalone** system with local processing capability.

wove finish An uncoated paper **finish** that has no visible laid lines.

wove paper (1815) Paper having the appearance of a piece of cloth, having fine lines running each way of the sheet. The effect is produced by the metal screening of the **dandy roll** as it passes over the wet web of paper during manufacture.

wrap A wrap in a book or magazine is an insert that has not been **tipped in**, but has been wrapped around one of the **signatures**, so that it is stitched into the binding as securely as any other page.

wraparound (1) Wraparound occurs when a line of text reaches the right-hand side of the screen and the operator does not press **Return**. If the operator keeps typing, the cursor and text will travel "around" the back of the screen and continue at the left side of the next line. Also called *word wrap*. (2) A folded sheet of paper bearing printed illustrations, slipped around the outside of a signature before sewing as a means of adding such illustrations to a book without the necessity of tipping in single leaves.

wraparound cover Soft cover used to bind or hold a booklet, brochure, etc. It consists of one sheet of stock that forms both front and back covers. Any type of **mechanical binding** may be used.

write (1) To make a permanent or transient recording of data in a storage device or on a data medium. (2) To alter the memory of the computer in a specific way. (3) Writing to computer memory refers to the act of placing and storing data in that memory. Compare **read**.

write-protect Means that the data can be *read from* but not *written to* a magnetic storage medium. This guarantees that the disk, diskette, or tape won't be written on, accidentally destroying data already on the diskette.

write-protect notch A notch cut in the jacket of a diskette that authorizes or denies writing to the diskette depending on whether the notch is covered or uncovered.

write protection Restriction of writing into a data set, file, or storage area by a user or program not authorized to do so.

writer *see* **author**.

Writer (1887) A monthly magazine for free-lance writers that offers practical information and advice on how to write publishable material and where to sell it.

writer's conference A seminar attended by students of writing as well as established writers and featuring workshops, lectures, and discussions conducted by specialists in their field.

Writer's Digest (1920) Monthly magazine for writers.

Writer's Market A comprehensive annual compilation of publisher's names, addresses, current needs, and general policies and contract terms. *See also* **Literary Market Place**.

writing (13c) The action of making a permanent or transient recording of data in a storage device or on a data medium.

writing paper (ca. 1548) Any paper suitable for writing with pen and ink.

wrong font (1) A wrong face of type in a piece of type composition. (2) A **proofreader's mark** indicating that in one or

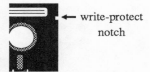

← write-protect
notch

Fig. W-4   The write-protect notch.

more words, the printer has used the wrong font (face) of type. Abbreviated *wf*.

wrong-reading Having a reversed right-to-left orientation. Compare **right-reading**.

WYSIWYG (1982) *See* **What You See Is What You Get**.

Notes and New Words

Notes and New Words

X

x Twenty-fourth letter of the alphabet used in the graphic arts to denote magnification of an image.

x-height In typography, the mean height of lowercase characters, excluding **ascenders** and **descenders**. It is strictly a dimension rather than a unit of measurement. It is the x-height rather than the point size that determines the visual size of type. *See also* **baseline**.

x-line The line that marks the tops of the **lowercase** letters, without ascenders. Also called *mean line*.

XCOPY A **PC/MS-DOS** command that copies files from one directory to another.

xerographic printer (1948) A device for printing an optical image on paper in which light and dark areas are represented by electrostatically charged areas on the paper. A powdered ink dusted on the paper adheres to the charged areas and is melted into the paper by heat. *See also* **xerography**.

xerography (1948) A copying process that uses electrostatic forces to form an image, which does not require contact between the printing surface and the printed surface; the ink, in powder form, electrostatically jumps the gap between the two.

Xerox Pipeline (1988) A quarterly newsletter produced to provide **Ventura** users with technical, applications, and operational information to keep their systems running at the highest level possible.

Xerox Ventura Publisher *See* **Ventura Publisher**.

Fig. X-1   The first issue of *Xerox Pipeline*, a newsletter for Ventura users.

Notes and New Words

Notes and New Words

Y

yearbook (1710) (1) A book published yearly as a report. (2) A school publication that is compiled to record that year's happenings.

yearly (12c) A publication issued annually.

yellow journal (1896) A cheaply sensational newspaper or periodical.

yellow journalism (1899) **Journalism** that takes an emotional, sensational, and trashy approach to its writing.

yellow pages (1954) A listing of products or services that is independently published.

Notes and New Words

Z

zap To damage a hardware device by a static discharge or faulty power.

zero point In **PageMaker** and **Ventura**, the intersection of the two screen rulers is at 0. The default zero point is at the intersection of the left and top margins, but can be altered by the user. Also called *ruler zero point*.

zoom (1886) To enlarge an area of the screen. *See also* **view**.

zooming (1) *Zooming in* produces an **enlargement** of individual **primitives**, while *zooming out* enables the entire scene to be viewed. (2) In computer graphics, progressively scaling to give the visual impression of movement of all or part of a display group toward or away from an observer.

Zapf Dingbats An International Typeface Corporation font that contains **dingbats**.

Notes and New Words

Appendix 1

Inch-Pica-Point Conversion Chart

Inches	Picas (approx.)	Points (approx.)
0.0625	0.375	4.5
0.125	0.75	9
0.25	1.5	18
0.5	3	36
0.75	4.5	54
1	6	72
1.25	7.5	90
1.5	9	108
1.75	10.5	126
2	12	144
2.25	13.5	162
2.5	15	180
2.75	16.5	198
3	18	216
3.25	19.5	234
3.5	21	252
3.75	22.5	270
4	24	288
4.25	25.5	306
4.5	27	324
4.75	28.5	342
5	30	360
5.25	31.5	378
5.5	33	396
5.75	34.5	414
6	36	432
6.25	37.5	450
6.5	39	468
6.75	40.5	486
7	42	504
7.25	43.5	522
7.5	45	540
7.75	46.5	558
8	48	576
8.25	49.5	594
8.50	51	612
8.75	52.5	630
9	54	648

Inches	Picas (approx.)	Points (approx.)
9.25	55.5	666
9.5	57	684
9.75	58.5	702
10	60	720
10.25	61.5	738
10.5	63	756
10.75	64.5	774
11	66	792
11.25	67.5	810
11.5	69	828
11.75	70.5	846
12	72	864

Appendix 2

Point-Inch-Pica Conversion Chart[1]

Points	Inches	Picas
1	0.01384	
2	0.0277	
3	0.0415	
4	0.0553	
5	0.0692	
6	0.0830	
7	0.9690	
8	0.1107	
9	0.1245	
10	0.1384	
11	0.1522	
12	0.166	1
	0.332	2
	0.498	3
	0.664	4
	0.830	5
	0.996	6
	1.162	7
	1.328	8
	1.494	9
	1.660	10
	1.826	11
	1.993	12

[1]   NOTE: 12 points = 1 pica; 6 picas = 1 in (approx.)

Appendix 3

ASCII Codes

ASCII Code	ASCII Definition
0	Null
1	Start heading
2	Start text
3	End text
4	End transmit
5	Enquiry
6	Acknowledge
7	Bell (signal)
8	Backspace
9	Horizontal tab
10	Line feed
11	Vertical tab
12	Form feed
13	Carriage return
14	Shift out
15	Shift in
16	Data link escape
17	Dev control 1
18	Dev control 2
19	Dev control 3
20	Dev control 4
21	Negative acknowledge
22	Synchronous idle
23	End transmission block
24	Cancel
25	End of medium
26	Substitute
27	Escape
28	File separate
29	Group separate
30	Record separate
31	Unit separate
32	Space
33	!
34	"
35	#
36	$

ASCII Code	Definition
37	%
38	&
39	'
40	(
41	)
42	*
43	+
44	,
45	-
46	.
47	/
48	0
49	1
50	2
51	3
52	4
53	5
54	6
55	7
56	8
57	9
58	:
59	;
60	<
61	=
62	
63	?
64	@
65	A
66	B
67	C
68	D
69	E
70	F
71	G
72	H
73	I
74	J
75	K
76	L
77	M
78	N
79	O

ASCII Code	Definition
80	P
81	Q
82	R
83	S
84	T
85	U
86	V
87	W
88	X
89	Y
90	Z
91	[
92	\
93	]
94	^
95	_
96	(space)
97	a
98	b
99	c
100	d
101	e
102	f
103	g
104	h
105	i
106	j
107	k
108	l
109	m
110	n
111	o
112	p
113	q
114	r
115	s
116	t
117	u
118	v
119	w
120	x
121	y
122	z

ASCII Code	Definition
123	{
124	|
125	}
126	~
127	Delete

Appendix 4

Proofreader's Marks

Mark	Explanation
$\wedge$	Insert the copy written in margin at this place
℘	Delete or take out
#	Insert a space
$\wedge$	Insert a letter
l.c.	Set in lowercase letters
w.f.	Wrong font
ital	Set in italic
rom.	Set in roman
bf	Set in boldface
⊙	Insert a period
tr.	Transpose letters or words
stet ⋯	Let it stand as is and disregard all marks above the dots
=/	Insert a hyphen
eq #	Equalize the spacing
⌞⌟	Lower to the point indicated
⌜⌝	Raise to the point indicated
⌃	Insert a comma
⌄	Insert an apostrophe
⌄⌄	Enclose in quotation marks

Mark	Explanation
(/)/	Enclose in parentheses
[/]/	Enclose in brackets
≡	Replace with a capital letter
⁀‿	Draw the word together
a‸ 1‸	Insert inferior figure
²⌄ ᵃ⌄	Insert superior figure
out— see copy	Words have been left out, set from copy
æ	Use the diphthong
fi lig.	Use the ligature of these two letters
⑤	Spell out the words marked with a circle
(five)	Use figures
¶	Start a new paragraph
no ¶	Should not be a paragraph; run in
(?)	Query to author, encircled
?/	Set a question mark
1/M	Em dash
1/N	En dash
□	Indent 1 em
□□	Indent 2 ems
;/	Insert a semicolon
(:)	Insert a colon
!/	Insert an exclamation point

Appendix 5

Bibliography

American National Standards Committee, X3, Information Processing Systems. *American National Dictionary for Information Processing Systems.* 1984. Homewood, Ill.: Dow Jones-Irwin.

Apple Computer, Inc. *HyperCard User's Guide.* 1987. Cupertino, Calif.: Apple Computer, Inc.

Apple Computer, Inc. *Macintosh SE.* 1987. Cupertino, Calif.: Apple Computer, Inc.

Apple Computer, Inc. *Macintosh Utilities User's Guide.* 1987. Cupertino, Calif.: Apple Computer, Inc.

Arts and Letters. *Arts and Letters User's Guide.* 1988. Dallas, Tex.: Computer Support Corporation.

Ashton-Tate. *MultiMate Advantage Reference Manual.* Second printing. April 1986. Torrance, Calif.: Ashton-Tate.

Baldwin, Margaret; and Pack, Gary. *Computer Graphics.* 1984. New York, N.Y.: Franklin Watts.

Bann, David. *The Print Production Handbook.* 1985. Cincinnati, Ohio: North Light.

Barnes, Kate. *Using MultiMate Advantage.* 2nd ed. 1987. Indianapolis, Ind.: Que.

Bly, Robert W.; and Blake, Gary. *Technical Writing: Structure, Standards, and Style.* 1982. New York, N.Y.: McGraw-Hill.

Bonura, Larry S. *Desktop Publisher's Bibliography.* 1988. Richardson, Tex.: Word Workers.

Boswell, John. *The Awful Truth About Publishing: Why They Always Reject Your Manuscript—And What You Can Do About It.* 1986. New York, N.Y.: Warner Books.

Bove, Tony; Rhodes, Cheryl; and Thomas, Wes. *The Art of Desktop Publishing: Using Personal Computers to Publish It Yourself.* 1987. New York, N.Y.: Bantam Books.

Brockmann, R. John. *Writing Better Computer User Documentation: From Paper to Online.* 1986. New York, N.Y.: John Wiley & Sons.

Burns, Diane; and Venit, S. *Using PageMaker on the IBM.* 1987. Indianapolis, Ind.: Que Corporation.

Burns, Diane; Venit, S.; and Mercer, Linda J. *Using Ventura Publisher.* 1988. Carmel, Ind.: Que Corporation.

Cane, Mike. *The Computer Phone Book.* 1983. New York, N.Y.: Plume.

Cassill, Kay. *The Complete Handbook for Free-lance Writers.* 1981. Cincinnati, Ohio: Writer's Digest Books.

Cavuoto, James; and Berst, Jesse. *Inside Xerox Ventura Publisher: A Guide to Professional-Quality Desktop Publishing on the IBM PC.* 1987. Torrance, Calif.: Micro Publishing.

The Chicago Manual of Style. 1984. 13th ed. Chicago, Ill.: University of Chicago Press.

Craig, James. *Designing With Type: A Basic Course in Typography.* Rev. ed. 1980. New York, N.Y.: Watson-Guptill Publications.

Davis, Alec. *Graphics: Design Into Production.* 1973. New York, N.Y.: Pitman Publishing Corporation.

David, Carol. *Ventura Publisher: A Training Guide.* 1988. Dallas, Tex.: Micro Ventures.

Ditlea, Steve, editor. *Digital Deli: The Comprehensive, User-Lovable Menu of Computer Lore, Culture, Lifestyles, and Fancy.* 1984. New York, N.Y.: Workman Publishing.

Elfenbein, Julien. *Business Journalism: Its Function and Future.* 2nd ed. 1945. New York, N.Y.: Harper & Brothers Publishers.

Epson LQ-850/1050 User's Guide. 1987. Nagano, Japan: Seiko Epson Corporation.

Felici, James; and Nace, Ted. *Desktop Publishing Skills: A Primer for Typesetting with Computers and Laser Printers.* 1987. Reading, Mass.: Addison-Wesley Publishing Company.

French, Christopher W., editor. *The Associated Press Stylebook and Libel Manual.* Rev. ed. 1987. Reading, Mass.: Addison-Wesley Publishing Company.

Grout, Bill; Athanasopoulos, Irene; and Kutlin, Rebecca. *Desktop Publishing From A to Z.* 1986. Berkeley, Calif.: Osborne McGraw-Hill.

Harvey, Greg; and Nelson, Kay Yarborough. *WordPerfect Desktop Companion.* 1987. San Francisco, Calif.: Sybex.

Holmes, Nigel. *Designer's Guide to Creating Charts and Diagrams.* 1984. New York, N.Y.: Watson-Guptill.

Holt, Robert Lawrence. *How to Publish, Promote, and Sell Your Own Book: The Insider's Guide to Everything You Need to Know About Self-Publishing, From Pasteup to Publicity.* 1985. New York, N.Y.: St. Martin's Press.

Holtz, Matthew. *Mastering Ventura.* 1988. San Francisco, Calif.: Sybex.

Hutchings, Ernest A.D. *A Survey of Printing Processes.* 2nd ed. 1980. London, England: Heinemann.

The Idea Factory. *Xerox Ventura Publisher: A User's Guide to Basic Design.* 1987. Rochester, N.Y.: The Idea Factory.

Jantz, Richard J. *Ventura Publisher for the IBM PC: Mastering Desktop Publishing.* 1987. New York, N.Y.: John Wiley & Sons.

Kaehler, Carol. *MacProject.* 1984. Cupertino, Calif.: Apple Computer, Inc.

Karch, R. Randolph. *Graphic Arts Procedures.* 4th ed. 1970. Chicago, Ill.: American Technical Society.

Kerstetter, Robert W. *Illustrated Ventura.* 1988. Plano, Tex.: Wordware Publishing.

Kleper, Michael L. *The Illustrated Handbook of Desktop Publishing and Typesetting.* 1987. Blue Ridge Summit, Penn.: TAB Professional and Reference Books.

Kremer, John. *101 Ways to Market Your Books: For Publishers and Authors*. 1986. Fairfield, Iowa: Ad-Lib Publications.

Krumm, Rob. *Ventura: Desktop Publishing, Style Sheets, Fonts, Layout, Multiple-Frame Documents, and Graphic Design*. 1988. Portland, Ore.: MIS: Press.

Lampton, Christopher. *The Micro Dictionary*. 1984. New York, N.Y.: Franklin Watts.

Lippi, Robert. *How to Buy Good Printing and Save Money: A Printing Buyer's Guide*. 1987. New York, N.Y.: Art Direction Book Company.

Lowell, John. *A–Z Guide to Computer Graphics*. 1985. New York, N.Y.: McGraw-Hill.

Lubow, Martha, and Berst, Jesse. *Publishing Power With Ventura: The Complete Teaching Guide to Xerox Ventura Publisher*. 1988. Thousand Oaks, Calif.: New Riders Publishing.

Makuta, Daniel J., and Lawrence, William F. *The Complete Desktop Publisher*. Greensboro, N.C.: Compute! Publications.

Martin-Hoffman, Diana, editor. *1986 Artist's Market*. 1985. Cincinnati, Ohio: Writer's Digest Books.

Matthews, Martin S., and Matthews, Carole Boggs. *Using PageMaker for the PC*. 1987. Berkeley, Calif.: Osborne McGraw-Hill.

McClelland, Deke, and Danuloff, Craig. *Desktop Publishing Type and Graphics: A Comprehensive Handbook*. 1987. Boston, Mass.: Harcourt Brace Jovanovich.

The McGraw-Hill Author's Book. 1968. New York, N.Y.: McGraw-Hill.

Melcher, Daniel; and Larrick, Nancy. *Printing and Promotion Handbook: How to Plan, Produce, and Use Printing, Advertising, and Direct Mail*. 1966. New York, N.Y.: McGraw-Hill.

Meyer, John. *Xerox Ventura Publisher Reference Guide*. 1987. Lewisville, Tex.: Xerox Corporation.

Micro Training and Development Corporation. *Ventura: Beginner's Course*. 1988. Atlanta, Ga.: Micro Training and Development Corporation.

Miles, John. *Design for Desktop Publishing: A Guide to Layout and Typography on the Personal Computer.* 1987. San Francisco, Calif.: Chronicle Books.

Mitchell, Joan P. *The New Writer: Techniques for Writing Well With a Computer.* 1987. Redmond, Wash.: Microsoft Press.

Moore, Phyllis. *Illustrated PageMaker.* 1988. Plano, Tex.: Wordware Publishing, Inc.

Morgan, Roberta. *How to Break Into Publishing.* 1980. New York, N.Y.: Barnes and Noble Books.

Nace, Ted. *Ventura Tips and Tricks: The Experts' Guide to Desktop Publishing with Xerox Ventura Publisher.* 1987. Berkeley, Calif.: Peachpit Press.

Neff, Glenda Tennant. *1988 Writer's Market.* 1987. Cincinnati, Ohio: Writer's Digest Books.

Nelson, Roy Paul. *Publication Design.* 4th ed. 1987. Dubuque, Iowa: Wm. C. Brown Publishers.

Parker, George L. *The Beginnings of the Book Trade in Canada.* 1985. Toronto, Ontario: University of Toronto Press.

Parker, Roger C. *Looking Good In Print: A Guide to Basic Design for Desktop Publishing.* 1988. Chapel Hill, N.C.: Ventana Press.

Peters, Jean, editor. *The Bookman's Glossary.* 5th ed. 1975. New York, N.Y.: R.R. Bowker Company.

Poynter, Daniel F. *The Self-Publishing Manual: How to Write, Print and Sell Your Own Book.* 4th ed. 1986. Santa Barbara, Calif.: Para Publishing.

Poynter, Daniel F. *Word Processors and Information Processing.* 1982. Santa Barbara, Calif.: Para Publishing.

Rice, Stanley. *Book Design: Text Format Models.* 1978. New York, N.Y.: R.R. Bowker Company.

Rivers, William L. *Free-Lancer and Staff Writer Writing Magazine Articles.* 1972. Belmont, Calif.: Wadsworth Publishing Co.

Rogers, Geoffrey. *Editing for Print.* 1985. Cincinnati, Ohio: Writer's Digest Books.

Rogers, Jim; and Guzaitis, Joe. *Gem Desktop.* 1985. Monterey, Calif.: Digital Research Inc.

Rosen, Arnold; and Fielden, Rosemary. *Word Processing.* 2nd ed. 1982. Englewood Cliffs, N.J.: Prentice-Hall.

Rosenberg, Jerry M. *Dictionary of Data Processing and Telecommunications.* 1984. New York, N.Y.: John Wiley and Sons.

Ross, Tom; and Ross, Marilyn. *The Complete Guide to Self-Publishing: Everything You Need to Know to Write, Publish, Promote, and Sell Your Own Book.* 1986. Cincinnati, Ohio: Writer's Digest Books.

Sans, John C. *Handbook of Desktop Publishing: A Guide for Business and Professional People.* 1988. Plano, Tex.: Wordware Publishing, Inc.

Shaw, Harry. *Punctuate It Right!.* 1983. New York, N.Y.: Harper & Row.

Sheldon, George. *Advanced Ventura.* 1988 Portland, Ore.: MIS: Press.

Simon, Herbert. *Introduction to Printing: The Craft of Letterpress.* 1968. London, England: Faber and Faber.

Spencer, Donald D. *Spencer's Computer Dictionary for Everyone.* (Originally published as *Computer Dictionary.* 3rd ed. 1985. New York, N.Y.: Charles Scribner's Sons.

Stevenson, George A. *Graphic Arts Encyclopedia.* 1968. New York, N.Y.: McGraw-Hill.

Strehlo, Kevin. *PageMaker: Desktop Publishing on the IBM PC and Compatibles.* 1987. Glenview, Ill.: Scott, Foresman & Company.

Strunk, Jr., William; and White, E.B. *The Elements of Style.* 3rd ed. 1979. New York, N.Y.: Macmillan Publishing Company.

Stultz, Russell A. *Illustrated MS/PC-DOS.* 1988. Plano, Tex.: Wordware Publishing.

Taylor, Barbara M. *Introduction to Computer Graphics*. 1987. Dallas, Tex.: Barbara M. Taylor.

Webster's Standard American Style Manual. 1985. Springfield, Mass.: Merriam-Wesbster.

Will-Harris, Daniel. *Desktop Publishing With Style: A Complete Guide to Design Techniques and New Technology for the IBM-PC and Compatibles*. 1987. South Bend, Ind.: And Books.

Wolenik, Robert. *Ventura Desktop Publishing: Tips and Techniques*. 1988. Glenview, Ill.: Scott, Foresman & Company.

Xerox Corporation. *Xerox Desktop Publishing Series: Ventura Publisher Edition Quick Reference*. 1987. Lewisville, Tex.: Xerox Corporation.

Xerox Corporation. *Xerox Ventura Publisher Training Guide*. 1987. Lewisville, Tex.: Xerox Corporation.

Appendix 6

Trademark Notices

Apple LaserWriter is a trademark of Apple Computer Inc.
Apple LaserWriter Plus is a trademark of Apple Computer Inc.
Arts and Letters is a trademark of Computer Support Corporation
AST Premium/286 is a trademark of AST Research
AutoCAD is a trademark of Autodesk, Inc.
Bitstream is a registered trademark of Bitstream Inc.
CONVEX is a registered trademark of CONVEX Computer Corporation
CONVEX logo ("C") is a registered trademark of CONVEX Computer Corporation
DisplayWrite is a registered trademark of International Business Machines Corporation
DocuPro is a trademark of DocuPro Inc.
Driography is a trademark of 3M Company
Epson is a registered trademark of Epson America, Inc.
FrameMaker is a trademark of Frame Technology
GEM and GEM Draw are trademarks of Digital Research, Inc.
Helvetica is a registered trademark of Allied Corporation
Hercules is a trademark of Hercules Computer Technology
Hewlett-Packard LaserJet and LaserJet Plus are trademarks of Hewlett-Packard Corporation
HPGL is a trademark of Hewlett-Packard Corporation
IBM is a registered trademark of International Business Machines Corporation
IBM-AT is a trademark of International Business Machines Corporation
IBM-PC is a trademark of International Business Machines Corporation
IBM-XT is a trademark of International Business Machines Corporation
The Idea Factory is a trademark of The Idea Factory
Interleaf is a trademark of Interleaf, Inc.
Interpress is a trademark of Xerox Corporation
ITC Bookman is a registered trademark of International Typeface Corporation
ITC Zapf Chancery is a registered trademark of International Typeface Corporation
ITC Zapf Dingbats is a registered trademark of International Typeface Corporation
Linotronic is a trademark of Allied Linotype
Linotype is a trademark of Allied Linotype
Macintosh is a registered trademark of Apple Computer Inc.
Microsoft is a registered trademark of Microsoft Corporation
MS-DOS is a trademark of Microsoft Corporation
Multimate Advantage is a trademark of Multimate International
National Association of Desktop Publishers is a trademark of NADTP
PageMaker is a trademark of Aldus Corporation
Palatino is a registered trademark of Allied Corporation
PC-DOS is a trademark of International Business Machines Corporation
Personal Computer/2 is a trademark of International Business Machines Corporation
PostScript is a trademark of Adobe Systems Inc.
The Print Shop is a trademark of Brøderbund Software, Inc.
Publish! is a trademark of PCW Communications Inc.
Publish It! is a trademark of Timeworks, Inc.
Publisher's Paintbrush is a registered trademark of ZSoft Corporation
Publisher's PicturePak is a trademark of Marketing Graphics Inc.
Ready-Set-Go is a trademark of Manhattan Graphics Corporation
RightWriter is a registered trademark of RightSoft Inc.
Silentwriter is a trademark of NEC Corporation
Time is a trademark of Time, Inc.
Times is a trademark of Allied Corporation
Ventura Publisher is a trademark of Ventura Software Inc.
Word Workers is a trademark of Word Workers
Wordstar is a registered trademark of MicroPro International Corporation
Xenix is a registered trademark of Microsoft Corporation
Xerox is a trademark of Xerox Corporation

Appendix 7

Colophon

The text for this book was written in *MultiMate Advantage*. *Right-Writer* was used to check style, grammar, punctuation, etc. The final product was proofread and edited by human eyes.

The 6-in x 9-in pages were designed and typeset using *Ventura Publisher*. The body is 9-point *International Typeface Corporation Bookman* on 10-point leading.

Most illustrations were done in the graphics mode in *Ventura Publisher*. Some were produced on *AutoCAD*, and some were scanned in using a *Hewlett-Packard Scan Jet*. Others came from clip art from *Arts and Letters*, *GEM Draw*, and *Desktop Publishing With Style*. Others were drawn using *Publisher's Paintbrush*.

The proof pages were printed on an *NEC Silentwriter LC-890*. The final copy was set on an *Apple LaserWriter*.

The entire document was produced on an *AST Premium/286* with an *MTR* monochrome display.

DESKTOP PUBLISHING BOOKS

Desktop Publisher's Dictionary $19.95
Larry S. Bonura   1-55622-106-1

Discover the language of desktop publishing with this comprehensive, one-stop reference to the terms used in this exploding industry. More than 4000 terms, words, and abbreviations, from typography to binding and finishing, are cleaarly defined and frequently clarified by illustrations. Related terms and concepts are identified for easy cross-reference. Perfect for office, home, or school, this is an indispensable tool for today's contemporary professional.

The Handbook of Desktop Publishing $19.95
John C. Sans, Jr.   0-915381-95-8

Use this excellent source for information on the Macintosh and the IBM microcomputers. Maximize desktop publishing by utilizing the power of the laser printer. Design and produce timely, attractive, and cost- effective business communications. Investment tips on acquiring, operating, and maintaining an in-house desktop publishing system are included.

Illustrated PageMaker 3.0 $21.95
For the PC   1-55622-073-1
Phyllis Moore and Bennie R. Lowery, Ed.D.

From basic setup to final printout, examples and illustrations clarify every stage of page composition. The authors step through all the procedures required to create professional publications by utilizing style sheets and templates. Learn to flow text around graphics and modify graphics through enhanced image control. This excellent tutorial is also an alphabetical reference to the features found in PageMaker 3.0 for the PC.

Illustrated Ventura 2.0 $21.95
For the PC   1-55622-104-5
George Sheldon

All the skills, techniques, and tips needed to master this top-selling desktop publishing program can be found in this comprehensive tutorial reference. Fully illustrated throughout, working examples demonstrate the enhanced user interface and technical publishing features designed to make desktop publishing more functional and easier to use. Step-by-step learning begins with a blank file which you develop into an impressive prfessional-quality document. New and experienced users will find the reference value of this book indispensable.

WORD PROCESSING BOOKS

Illustrated DisplayWrite 4 $19.95
For the PC   1-55622-060-X
George Sheldon

This detailed, thorough resource contains the information necessary to effectively create, revise, edit, and print a wide range of documents. Single-page letters and multi-page reports with footnotes can easily be produced. Beginning, intermediate, and advanced users learn to use pop-up and pull-down menus to select a variety of functions.

Illustrated Sprint $21.95
For the PC   1-55622-101-0
Arnold and Edith Shulman

Regardless of your experience level, this complete tutorial-reference is designed to make you a skilled Sprint professional. Progress from a basic introduction of the program to a thorough working knowledge of Sprint's significant word processing features and shortcuts. Step-by-step instructions and exercises detail every Sprint menu command. This book also describes how to customize keys to conform to a variety of user interfaces.

Illustrated WordPerfect 1.01 $21.95
For the Macintosh   1-55622-105-3
Jordan Gold

Step-by-step instructions, real-world applications, and hands-on exercises are the keys this book provides for learning this graphics-oriented word processor for the Macintosh. All commands, functions, and features are clearly defined and easily referenced. Learn the desktop publishing features that make WordPerfect for the Macintosh an ideal writer's tool.

WORD PROCESSING BOOKS

WordPerfect: Advanced Applications Handbook $19.95
Dr. Forest Lin   1-55622-023-5

Enhance office automation and productivity by applying these advanced techniques and functions. Ready-to-use application programs using WordPerfect's advanced Macro, Math, Sort, and Merge features are included. Numerous macros aimed at various office and business situations serve as models to simplify office tasks. Clear, concise explanations, along with tips and tricks, optimize the use of basic word processing features.

Illustrated WordStar Professional (Release 5) $21.95
For the PC   1-55622-074-X
Russell A. and Dianne Stultz

Master a host of new WordStar features including advanced page preview, footnotes/endnotes, windowing, TelMerge, ListMerge, and many more. Practical hands-on activities demonstrate the new user interface and the pull-down menus used to initiate the latest functions. This step-by-step learning guide is also a complete reference to the all-new advanced document features now available in WordStar 5.0.

Call Wordware Publishing, Inc. for names of the bookstores in your area.
(214) 423-0090

BUSINESS — PROFESSIONAL BOOKS

Occupying the Summit $15.95
The Guide to Successful Retirement Planning   1-55622-102-9
Robert W. Shaffer

With retirement now encompassing as much as 25 percent of our lifespan, this book offers sound advice for making that time the best phase of life. Practical guidance and hands-on worksheets help evaluate current status, determine goals, and develop a positive retirement strategy. Regardless of income and age level, this book provides the essential principles and foresight necessary to successfully anticipate and prepare for a financially independent, healthy, and fulfilling retirement.

How to Win Pageants $24.95
Ginie Polo Sayles   1-55622-112-6

Pageants are the number one television draw in the world today. With over 5 million participants each year, pageants now attract children, teenagers, married women, and men. *How to Win Pageants* contains inside information for a competitive edge in this exploding industry. Detailed interviews provide invaluable insights from Miss America, Miss Universe, Mr. Male America, Miss National Teenager, children's international Diamond Miss, and many others. Inside information from numerous winners and "powers behind the throne" identify what the judges look for, who the top trainers are, and where to find them. This book provides keys to people-awareness skills, positive personality projection, and physical fitness habits that can be stepping stones to success as they were for pageant winners Sophia Loren and Diane Sawyer.

MegaTraits $17.95
Dr. Doris Lee McCoy   1-55622-056-1

Dr. McCoy traveled extensively to interview over 1,000 "successful" people. Interviews with such people as Charlton Heston, Malcolm Forbes, and Ronald Reagan led Dr. McCoy to discover 12 traits of success. She sought consistencies and success patterns from which you can benefit. Are there specific points to help all of us become more successful? The answer is a resounding YES! There are traits consistently found in the lives of successful people. Read *MegaTraits* to discover how you too can develop and utilize these unique attributes.

BUSINESS — PROFESSIONAL BOOKS

Business Emotions
Richard Contino

$14.95
1-55622-058-8

Revolutionize your thinking, conditioning, and approach. Learn why emotions are a controlling factor in every success and failure situation. This practical book will guide you through the maze of hidden psychological issues in a simple and straightforward manner. Achieve predictable, positive, and immediate results.

Innovation, Inc.
Stephen Grossman, Bruce Rodgers,
Beverly Moore

$14.95
1-55622-054-5

Unlock your hidden potential to reach a new plane of creative thinking. Seek new avenues of problem-solving by elevating your ability to conceive ideas. Techniques and exercises in this book expand your creativity. The authors take you on a journey designed to spark confidence by reorganizing your thinking processes and patterns. Learn to use innovative thinking to inspire fresh ideas and formulate imaginative concepts.

Investor Beware
Henry Rothenberg

$14.95
1-55622-055-3

Create your own luck with this book detailing the essentials for safe investments. Avoid shady, risky, and unsuccessful investments. Learn how to anticipate and interpret various investment climates and analyze a business from financial statements. The average investor will find what he needs to know about economics, financing, taxes, operating entities, and types of investments. Discover the ramifications of diversified investments such as real estate, franchises, oil and gas, gold, tax shelters, and syndications.

Steps to Strategic Management
Rick Molz

$13.95
1-55622-050-2

This book is the story of one individual. . .YOU. Put yourself in the shoes of Joe Clancy, the imaginary entrepreneur in this book. By following the clear, ongoing example of Joe, you will discover how strategic management works. A series of nine steps will help you develop a systematic approach to strategic management. With honesty and hard work, you can use this book to help shape your future.

Call Wordware Publishing, Inc. for names of the bookstores in your area.
(214) 423-0090

Computer Books from Wordware Publishing, Inc.

Artificial Intelligence
Artificial Ingelligence Programming
    Techniques in BASIC
Illustrated Turbo Prolog 2.0
Illustrated VP-Expert

Computer-Aided Drafting
Illustrated AutoCAD (Release 9)
Illustrated AutoCAD (Release 10)
Illustrated AutoSketch 1.04
Illustrated GenericCAD

Database Management
The DataFlex Developer's Handbook
Illustrated dBASE II (2nd Ed.)
Illustrated dBASE III Plus
Illustrated dBASE IV
Illustrated Paradox Volume I 1.2
Illustrated Paradox Volume II 1.2
Illustrated Paradox Volume II 2.0
Illustrated VP-Info 1.2
Illustrated VP-Info 1.4

Desktop Publishing
Desktop Publisher's Dictionary
Handbook of Desktop Publishing
Illustrated PageMaker 3.0
Illustrated Ready, Set, Go! 4.5
    (Macintosh)
Illustrated Ventura 1.1
Illustrated Ventura 2.0

General Advanced Topics
The Complete Communications
    Handbook
Consulting Handbook for the
    High-Tech Professional
Illustrated Dac Easy Accounting 2.0
Illustrated Dac Easy Accounting 3.0
Illustrated Novell NetWare
Managing Your Megabytes

Programming Languages
Advanced Programming Techniques
    in Turbo Pascal
Illustrated C Programming (ANSI)

Programming Languages cont.
The FOCUS Developer's Handbook
From BASIC to 8086/8088 Assembly
    Language
Library of Turbo Pascal Programs
Illustrated PC/FOCUS
Illustrated QuickBASIC 4.0
Illustrated RM/COBOL
Illustrated Turbo Pascal 3.01
Illustrated Turbo Pascal 4.0
Illustrated Turbo Pascal 5.0

Spreadsheet/Integrated
Illustrated Framework II
Illustrated Framework III
Illustrated Lotus 1-2-3 2.01
Illustrated Microsoft Excel 2.01 (IBM)
Illustrated Microsoft Excel 1.5
    (Macintosh)
Illustrated Multiplan 2.0
Illustrated Q & A
Illustrated Quattro
Illustrated Symphony 1.2

Systems and Operating Guides
Illustrated Microsoft Windows 2.0
Illustrated MS/PC-DOS 3.3
Illustrated MS/PC-DOS 4.0
Illustrated OS/2

Word Processing
Illustrated DisplayWrite 4
Illustrated Microsoft Word 5.0
Illustrated Sprint
Illustrated WordPerfect 1.01
    (Macintosh)
Illustrated WordPerfect 4.2
Illustrated WordPerfect 5.0
Illustrated WordStar 3.3
Illustrated WordStar Professional (Rel. 4)
Illustrated WordStar Professional (Rel. 5)
The New WordStar Customizing Guide 4.0
WordPerfect: Advanced Applications
    Handbook
The WordStar Customizing Guide 3.3

Call Wordware Publishing, Inc. for names of the bookstores in your area.
(214) 423-0090